The Complete Barry Manilow Illustrated Discography

Daniel Selby

<u>Note:</u> Many foreign 45 releases were issued with the same catalog # and picture sleeves for different countries, especially neighboring. Also some were re–issued with a different design, number or other type of variation at a later time. Not all such releases are presented here. Nor are all Greatest Hits, Best Of or similar compilation albums documented. Album release dates, recording dates and other information researched through Billboard and Cashbox magazines websites, press releases, Barry Manilow official web page and ARISTA / RCA Records archives. I have not listed all chart statistics for every release, mainly US. Catalog numbers will mainly be US. In addition release dates will tend to be U.S. dates and foreign dates may differ, unless it is a foreign only release of course. Not all re-issues (single or LP) are listed, nor are all album graphics. I have strived to be as complete and accurate as possible, but occasionally mistakes make it through. If found, please send corrections (with sources) to me through: bookwriter@gmail.com.

Published in the USA and abroad by:

BEARMANOR MEDIA
New books on classic stars.
www.bearmanor–digital.myshopify.com/

Cover Layout & Interior Design:
From Design to Done Graphics / Daniel Selby

ISBN: 978-1-62933-909-2

Other book titles available by Daniel Selby from BearManor Media Publications

<u>Special Thanks To:</u>

Barry Manilow for recording all this material and making this book possible. Manilow = Magic.

Ron Dante, record producer to Barry's first nine albums, for sending encouraging messages to me for taking the time to compile Barry's recorded work. Ron feels very proud of the material he created with Barry in the recording studio, as he should! I feel proud to have it all in my record collection!

Ben at *BearManor Media* for constantly supporting my books, giving helpful suggestions for improvement and publishing my books.

Allan for the love these last 35 years. For always believing I could do anything I set out to do. Also for the book template that helped keep information on correct pages and keeping photos from jumping around.

Introduction

What is a discography? I was curious about this after my Dolly Parton Discography book received a mixed review from a gentleman named Allen in Stafford Springs, CT. He said the book was not essential reading or even near complete since I had not included the back jacket of every LP, all the LP and 45 Labels (Sides A & B!), the hundreds of Dolly compilation LP's, all the compilation labels and covers, the printed inner LP sleeves and a particular Dolly solo box set. All that alone would have put the book over the thousand page count mark.

So what exactly is a discography? One online dictionary reads: _A descriptive catalog of musical recordings, particularly those of a particular performer or composer._ Webster's Dictionary says: _A descriptive list of recordings by category, composer, performer, or date of release._

So for me it is what I thought it was— a _list_ of the recordings by a performer or composer and not all the graphic contents of an album. I wrote a little article about this in my music blog (that I have had for 20+ years) and asked readers what came to mind when they thought of a discography and 98% said a "listing of recordings / material." Some people said I could have added those things the one reviewer said I left out, but they were not necessary and others said to make myself happy and not try to please everyone or whine about a bad review since _every_ book gets those! OK, I won't whine. Thank you Allen for sparking a very interesting debate! But I will say if you bought this book looking for _all_ the album graphics you will be disappointed. I compile my books with only the front and sometimes back album cover and the important production information on each album as I see fit. I want to concentrate on the song material (recordings) of each album, not the graphics. It is just a fact of life, some are going to like the book and what its intentions are and some will not like the book.

You may have also read some of what is in this book or seen photos here elsewhere. That is due to the fact that I have added content to _many_ on-line sources for dozens of artists, including Barry, over the years and others copied what I uploaded. I am fine with people sharing this information since it is not mine, but meant for the public. Much of this information can be found on albums, in magazines or fan newsletters and on the internet. My books are meant to be fun and informative. Long before the internet I would compile information on hundreds of artists using an electric typewriter, re-doing each page as new information came in for or about a particular artist, album, recording studio, record label, tour date, etc. Everything was listed in chronological order. I read Billboard, Cash Box, "Country Music" and many foreign music magazines. My work has been used by MTV, ABC, CBS, NBC, CBC, BBC, People Magazine and various other sources.

And finally the letters I have received, even from the artists I have complied, who enjoy my books have certainly far out numbered the negative reviews, for that I am thankful. You have to take the good with the bad in life... it is inevitable, but I try to concentrate on the good!

I hope you are able to find _some_ joy in this book, maybe learn something about Barry's music you may not have known. It was certainly a labor of love the time put into the book. All proceeds go to the _American Heart Association_ since Barry himself has dealt with heart issues.

Musically Yours,
~Daniel

Bio

Barry Manilow was born Barry Alan Pincus on Thursday, June 17, 1943, in Brooklyn, New York, the son of Edna Manilow and Harold Pincus. His father was born to a Jewish father and an Irish-American Catholic mother. His maternal grandparents were both of Russian - Jewish background. Just before his bar mitzvah Barry adopted his mother's maiden name, Manilow.

Barry grew up in the Williamsburg section of Brooklyn and attended Eastern District High School, graduating in 1961. That same year, he enrolled in the City College of New York where he briefly studied before leaving for New York College of Music. While he was a student Barry also worked at CBS in order to pay his expenses. He would later study Musical Theater at the prestigious Juilliard performing arts school.

Barry married Susan Deixler, his high school sweetheart, in 1964. Unfortunately the marriage was a short-lived one. Barry's passion for music got in the way. He left after a year. Susan did not take the news well. She told him he could only take his clothes, but he insisted on having his piano too and she relented.

In 1964, Barry met Bro Herrod, a CBS director, who asked him to arrange some songs for a musical adaptation of the melodrama The Drunkard. Instead, Barry wrote an entire original score, which Herrod used in the Off Broadway musical, which enjoyed an eight-year run at New York's 13th Street Theatre. Barry then earned money by working as a pianist, producer and arranger for others in New York.

During this time in the mid-1960s he began to work as a commercial jingle writer, continuing this job well into the 1970s. A 1965 Polaroid Swinger commercial featuring Barry's "Meet The Swinger" jingle starred a young Ali MacGraw.

Aside from Barry being a pianist, producer and arranger for singers auditioning in New York he also played a number of seedy and not so seedy places in the city. One such place was the Continental Baths. While there Bette Midler, who also performed at the baths, happened to catch his set in 1971. Later Bette asked him to be her accompanist and, once she signed her first recording contract with Atlantic Records, to assist her with the production of both her first and second albums: *The Divine Miss M* (1972) and *Bette Midler* (1973). Barry would act as Bette's musical director 1971 to early 1975.

Just before Barry's association with Bette Midler began at the Continental Baths in New York City in 1971, he had recorded four songs under the name "Featherbed." The group was actually session musicians produced by Tony Orlando. Three of the tracks: "Morning," "Amy," and an early version of his own composition "Could It Be Magic" did little to the charts. But this was common for most artists with their first release. Later it was said that Barry was grateful the songs were not big hits, especially "Could It Be Magic." That was because the arrangement, that he was not happy with, was too uptempo. Barry had envisioned the tune as a classical piece that would slowly build in intensity. Also this early failure on the charts allowed Barry to branch out and use his own name as a solo artist, which was actually not something Barry had ever envisioned.

After the Featherbed singles went nowhere Bell Records released his debut album, *Barry Manilow* (BELL-1129), on July 7, 1973, which offered a broad and diverse mix of piano-driven pop and guitar-driven rock music, including a song called *I Am Your Child*, which Barry had composed for the July 24, 1972 Vietnam War drama film "Parades." The song had been written by Barry with Marty Panzer. Initially the album did not sell well. Only about 30,000 copies all told, but that later changed.

When Bell Records was taken over and dissolved by Clive Davis, the former head of Columbia Records, created Arista Records out of all the labels under the Columbia Pictures umbrella including; Colgems, Colpix and Bell. Under his guidance many artists were dropped; however Clive Davis was reassured that Barry Manilow was a sound acquisition after seeing him perform as the opening act at a Dionne Warwick concert, on Wednesday, June 26, 1974.

The Arista-Barry partnership began to gain momentum in 1974 with the release of his second album, *Barry Manilow II* first on Bell Records (BELL-1314) October 1, 1974 and reissued on Arista (AL-4016), which contained the breakthrough number-one hit, *Mandy*. Barry had at first not wanted to record the song, which had originally been titled *Brandy*, and recorded by its co-writer Scott English, but the song was recorded at the insistence of Barry's new label chief. The name was changed to Mandy during the actual recording session on August 20, 1974, due to the fact that there had already been a song called *Brandy (You're a Fine Girl)* performed by Looking Glass and released in 1972 on Clive Davis' Epic Label.

By 1975 Barry was on a roll. Arista had Barry go back into the studio and revamp his 1973 album. Four songs of the album were re-recorded for the re-release, including "Could It Be Magic," which served as the only single off the newly packaged album. The re-released album was certified gold by the RIAA in 1976 for over half a million copies sold.

His next album *Tryin' To Get The Feeling Again* (Arista-4060) released one year to the day as his second album, October 1, 1975 was a solid hit which would see sales of over 2 million copies. The album debuted on Billboard's Top 200 Album Chart on November 8, 1975, reaching number five in early 1976. The album had several best selling singles, however the chart topping "I Write the Songs" went all the way to # 1 in the US, # 3 Canada. It reached # 5 in Australia and South Africa.

His fourth studio album, *This One's For You* (AL-4090) released July 30, 1976 is one of his best of the 1970's. The album debuted on the Billboard Top 200 chart on August 21, 1976, reaching number six in early 1977. The title song, which was also the lead single from the album, begins with the line: "This one will never sell, they'll never understand," which was somewhat foreshadowing, since this was his smallest hit in the 70s (US #29, Canada #28.) However his next release, *Weekend in New England*, returned him to the Top 10 and the third single off this album, *Looks Like We Made It*, returned him to #1, for the third time in less than three years.

For his next album, *Even Now* (AB-4164) released January 13, 1978, Barry managed to finally breakthrough in Britain. The album had some of his strongest material to date and biggest hits, one was *Can't Smile Without You*, a Top 3 hit and gold record winner for sales of 1 million copies. The title track hit the Top 20 charts and was his ninth #1 on the US Adult Contemporary chart, out of thirteen in total. One of his best loved songs, perhaps his most popular international hit, was from this album: *Copacabana (At the Copa)* was certified gold and made it into the top ten reaching #8 in the US, this tropical melodrama is still being played today. It's beautifully camp, and, naturally, has always been a gay favorite. He is ranked as the top Adult Contemporary chart artist of all time and for good reason.

His follow-up single, *Ready To Take A Chance Again*, appeared in the summer 1978 film *Foul Play*, starring Goldie Hawn and Chevy Chase was a big hit reaching #11 in the US and #4 in Canada. The song was also nominated for the Best Song Oscar in 1978.

Barry's final hit from his *Even Now* album was *Somewhere in the Night*, a Top 10 in the US and Canada. This song had also been recorded by Helen Reddy three years prior who took the song to # 2 on the US Easy Listening Chart in November 1975.

Barry's next album *One Voice* (AL-9505) was released on September 25, 1979. The first single culled from it was *Ships*, an Ian Hunter composition. This reflection on father-son relationships was yet another Top 10 hit for Barry. The second single off this album was *When I Wanted You* reached # 20 on Billboard's Top 100 Chart and # 1 on Billboard's Adult Contemporary Chart. *I Don't Wanna Walk With You"* was the last single released from the *One Voice* album. It reached # 36 in the US, yet # 1 in Canada.

1980 saw the LP *Barry* released on November 19 (AL-9537). The first US single release *I Made It Through the Rain* made it up to # 10 on Billboards Top 100 Chart. However, the next single, the beautiful *Lonely Together* only managed to get to # 45. Another album track *Bermuda Triangle* was a UK only release.

The *If I Should Love Again*, album released on September 1, 1981, contained two hit singles in the US. The first *The Old Songs* made it to # 15 on Billboard's Top 100 Chart. The next release *Somewhere Down the Road* reached the top 30 at # 21 in Billboard's Top 100 Chart and all the way to #1 on the Billboard Adult Contemporary chart. In the UK *If I Should Love Again* made it to # 66 on the UK Singles Chart. The final single release from the album was *Let's Hang On* in September 1982, the song peaked at #32 on Billboard's Top 100 and # 6 on the Adult Contemporary Chart. It had originally been a hit for The Four Seasons in September 1965.

On November 1, 1982 Barry's album *Here Comes the Night* was released. Singles from the album were *I Wanna Do It With You* which oddly did not chart in the US even though it was a catchy song and a favorite of the author. It did however reach the top ten in the UK at # 8. Next up was *Memory* which made it to # 8 followed by singles *I'm Gonna Sit Right Down And Write Myself a Letter* and *Some Kind Of Friend.* The later also being a favorite of the author.

Jim Steinman was the songwriter/producer with Wagnerian tendencies that made a superstar out of Meat Loaf and briefly resurrected the careers of Bonnie Tyler and Air Supply. He would do the same for Barry in 1983 with *Read 'Em and Weep* which made it up to # 18 on Billboard's Hot 100 and # 1 on Billboard's Adult Contemporary. It also reached # 22 in Canada and # 17 in the UK. It can be found as a new song on Barry Manilow's Greatest Hits Vol. II (AL8-8102 / December 13, 1983)

As with every performer in the history of performers Barry's chart action ebbed and flowed. However his concerts never faltered. In the UK, he had five sold-out performances at Royal Albert Hall. In the United States, at Radio City Music Hall in 1984 his 10-night run set a box-office sales record of nearly $2 million, making him the top draw in the then 52-year history of the venue. Selling records was nice as was having top hits, but I always felt Barry was in the business to make music first.

Barry's last US Top 30 album for the 20th century was *2:00 AM Paradise Cafe*, released on November 15, 1984. It contains two duets with two legendary jazz artists. *Blue* with Sarah Vaughan and *Big City Blues* with Mel Tormé.

Barry Manilow spent the 90s and the 00s touring and releasing albums. In early 2006 with the release of *The Greatest Songs of the Fifties* Barry had returned to his former label, Arista. He had decided to made an album of 1950s classics. The album was an amazing hit in the United States. It entered the Billboard Top 200 Chart at #1 giving Barry the second chart-topping album of his career. The strategy was successful, so plans were laid to continue. This was a good business and career move. Next *The Greatest Songs of the Sixties* came out that October, and peaked at #2 US.

In 2007, *The Greatest Songs of the Seventies* peaked at #4 in the US. In 2008, *The Greatest Songs of the Eighties* peaked at #14 in the US. In 2010 the concept was *The Greatest Love Songs of All Time*; it peaked at #5 in the US. Barry left Arista again, and in 2011 released his album *15 Minutes*. This was the first independent release of his career, through his own Stiletto Entertainment label. It was his first album of original material in many years. The album was a concept album and told the story of a fictional singer-musician who dreams of fame. It did well; peaking at #7 in the US and at #20 in the UK. *15 Minutes* won Barry a Best Traditional Pop Vocal Album Grammy nomination in 2012.

In 2014 came *Night Songs*, an album of covers which was released to critical acclaim. A few months later *My Dream Duets*, which consisted of duets with artists who had passed away, some decades before, it too was hugely popular.. Both 2014 albums made the Top 10 in the US.

On April 17 2017 Barry released *This Is My Town: Songs of New York*. The album, again on his own label and reaching # 12 on Billboard's Top 200. The album consists or material written by Barry and other well known writers.

Barry's final album, so far, *Night Songs II*, was released on February 14, 2020. This is one of Barry's most romantic albums. Songs include My Funny Valentine, Little Girl Blue, We'll Be Together Again.

Barry Manilow has been ranked as the top Adult Contemporary chart artist of all time, according to R&R (Radio & Records), with no less than 25 consecutive Top 40 hits on the Billboard Hot 100 between 1975 and 1983. The list includes all-time favorites that Manilow still sings today:

"Mandy," "It's A Miracle," "Could It Be Magic," "I Write the Songs," "Tryin' To Get the Feeling Again," "This One's For You," "Weekend In New England," "Looks Like We Made It," "Can't Smile Without You" and "Even Now."

Getting a bit personal:

Though it was often speculated through the years, Barry had never spoken publicly about his sexuality nor his private life in general. Until recently he had never really confirmed anything about his being gay. Part likely fear and part it was just no one's business, it was not a part of his music after all. However in 2017 Barry finally admitted he was indeed gay and married, since April 2014, to a wonderful man who is also his manager Garry Kief, his partner since 1978. So then why didn't Barry come out during all these years? "I'm so private," he said. "I always have been. I thought I would be disappointing them [fans] if they knew I was gay. So I never did anything."

He said he had been shocked by the positive reaction after fans discovered he was in a relationship with Garry: "They were so happy. The reaction was beautiful – strangers commenting: 'Great for you!' I'm just so grateful for it." His former wife was even among the well-wishers: "I wish him well. I'm happy for him. I'm glad that he's found love and happiness."

Through his career Barry was never a critics' favorite. The audience was divided; many loved him and just as many didn't. That is true for any artist. During the last few decades, however, the way that the public perceives pop music has changed. Genre hard divisions are a thing of the past, and it seems everybody listens to everything now. That's one of the reasons that the careers of legacy artists like Barry Manilow as well as Rod Stewart, Neil Diamond, and so many others have experienced a commercial rebirth. Whatever happens in the near future, Barry is a very important and influential part of the pop history of the 20th century. As testament to his musical significance, Barry Manilow was inducted into the Songwriters Hall of Fame in June 2002, alongside Sting.

The
Albums

Barry Manilow
Bell-1129

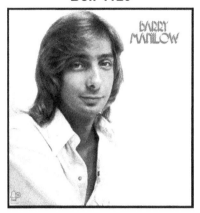

Track Listing:
Sing It (Barry with his grandfather, Joseph Manilow, in a Times Square Self-Recording Booth, 1948) / *Sweet Water Jones / Cloudburst / One Of These Days / Oh My Lady / *I Am Your Child / Could It Be Magic (Inspired By Prelude In C Minor, F. Chopin) / Seven More Years / Flashy Lady / Friends / *Sweet Life

Production Information:
Produced by: Barry Manilow & Ron Dante
Arranged and Conducted by: Barry Manilow
Recorded and Mixed at: A&R Sound Studios, Inc, New York City, New York
Engineered by: Elliot Scheiner / Jerome Gasper
*Except recorded at: Associated Sound Studios, New York City, New York
Engineer: Artie Friedman
"Sweetwater Jones" re-mixed at: Associated Sound Studios, New York City, New York
Remix engineer: Artie Friedman
Cover Photography: Kenn Duncan
Liner Photograph of Barry in studio: Linda Allen
Album Design: The Music Agency
Art Direction: Beverly Weinstein
Special Thanks: Miles Lourie, My Lady Linda, Steve and Lexy, Ron and Penny, Melissa, Mother Murphy, Bette, Adrienne, Marty and Bagel
With Love To: Esther and Joe

Musicians:
Piano: Barry Manilow
Electric Guitar: Dick Frank
Acoustic Guitar: Stuart Scharff
Guitars: Bob Mann / Ron Dante on "Flashy Lady."
Bass: Stu Woods / except: Russell George on "Sweetwater Jones," "I am Your Child" and "Sweet Life" / Bob Babbitt on "Flashy Lady."
Drums: Steve Gadd / except: Andrew Smith on "Flashy Lady."
Congas and Tambourines: Norman Pride
Percussion: Jimmy Maelen on "Flashy Lady."'
Joseph "Grandpa Joe" Manilow, vocals on "Sing It"
Background Vocals: Gail Kantor / Melissa Manchester / Merle Miller / Ron Dante / Adrienne Anderson / Jane Scheckter / Jane Stuart / Kathe Green / Laurel Massé / Pamela Pentony / Robert Danz / Sheilah Rae

Singles Released From This Album:

"Sweet Water Jones" b/w "One of these Days" (Bell – 45,357) – May 9, 1973
"Cloudburst" b/w "Could It Be Magic" (Bell – 45,422) – December 4, 1973
"Could it Be Magic" b/w "I Am Your Child" (ARISTA – 0126) – June 4, 1975 (Peaked at # 6 on the Billboard Hot 100 Chart in August 1975)

Album Data (1975 reissue):

Highest Chart Position: # 28 on October 24, 1975
Billboard Chart: Billboard Top 200
Number of Weeks on Chart: 51

Notes & Trivia:

- This album was released on July 7, 1973 on LP, 8-Track and Cassette.
- This album was remixed and re-released in 1975 on ARISTA (AL-4007) with different graphics and titled Barry Manilow I. "Sweet Life" / "Could It Be Magic" / "One of These Days" / "Oh My Lady" were re-recorded at Media Sound Studios, New York City, NY in April 1975 for the re-release.
- The 1975 re-release was certified Gold on October 22, 1976 for sales of 500,000 copies.
- This album was re-issued on LP again in 1982 by Mobile Fidelity Sound Lab (#: MFSL 1-097) in the Half-Speed mastered format. Cover graphics used were 1975 re-issue.
- This album was re-issued in CD format first in 1989 with the 1975 graphics (ARCD-8559).
- On October 10, 2006 this album was re-released on CD by ARISTA / Legacy with the original graphics and four previously unreleased tracks; "Caroline" / "Rosalie Rosie" / "Star Children" / "Let's Take Some Time to Say Goodbye." (Arista 82876 867172)
- A songbook was released to tie in with the album. coupled with Barry's second album.
- Of this album Barry said while it was a joy to make, the first pressing in 1973 did not sell.
- A full page ad was taken out in Billboard in the September 15, 1973 issue pushing this album and giving tour dates that Barry appeared with Bette Midler on her tour.

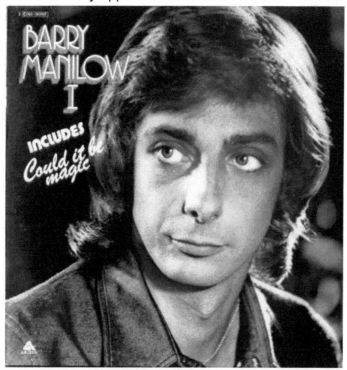

The 1975 reissue graphics of Barry's debut 1973 album.

Barry Manilow II
Bell-1314 (ARISTA-4016)

Track Listing:
I Want To Be Somebody's Baby / Early Morning Strangers / Mandy / The Two Of Us / Something's Comin' Up / It's A Miracle* / Avenue C / My Baby Loves Me / Sandra / Home Again

Production Information:
Produced by: Barry Manilow & Ron Dante
Recorded at: The Hit Factory and Media Sound Studios, New York City, NY
Engineered by: Bruce Tergesen / Harry Maslin / Michael DeLugg
Arrangements: Barry Manilow
Horn and string arrangements: Jack Cortner
Cover Photography: Joel Brodsky
Liner Photography: Linda Allen
Cover Design: The Music Agency

Musicians:
Piano: Barry Manilow / Don Grolnick / Ellen Starr
Electric Piano: Jon Stroll
Clavinet: Jon Stroll
Guitar: John Barranco / Dick Frank / Bob Mann / Charlie Brown / Stuart Scharf / Sam T. Brown
Bass Guitar: Will Lee / Russell George / Bob Cranshaw
Drums: Chris Parker / Jimmy Young / Bill Lavorgna / Allan Schwartzberg
Percussion: Lee Gurst
Congas: Norman Pride
Saxophone: George Young / Artie Kaplan / Stanley Schwartz
Background Vocals: Ron Dante / Barry Manilow
*Background Vocals: Melvin Kent / Ken Williams / Charlotte Crossley / Robin Grean / Sharon Red / James R. Bailey

Singles Released From This Album:
"Mandy" b/w "Something's Comin'" Up (BELL – 45,613) October 7, 1974 (Peaked at # 1 in the US on the Billboard Hot 100 Chart on January 18, 1975 and #1 on the Billboard Adult Contemporary Chart) Certified gold on January 31, 1975 for 1 million copies sold. It was nominated for a Grammy for Record Of The Year in 1976.
"It's A Miracle" b/w "One Of These Days" (ARISTA – 0108) February 12,1975 (Peaked at # 12 in the US on the Billboard Hot 100 Chart and # 1 on the US Adult Contemporary Chart)

Album Data:
Highest Chart Position: # 9 on February 22, 1975
Billboard Chart: Billboard Top 200

Number of Weeks on Chart: 58

Notes & Trivia:

- This album was released on LP, 8-Track and Cassette on October 3, 1974.
- This album was released in the Quadraphonic format on LP (AQ-4016). and 8 Track tape cartridge (7301-4016 H).
- This album was certified Platinum for sales of over one million copies on September 2, 1987.
- In Germany, UK and Italy this album was simply titled "Barry Manilow."
- This album was reissued in 1996 on CD and Cassette with a bonus track; "Halfway Over The Hill" (Arista – 07822-18944-2) and reissued again on May 9, 2006 as an "expanded edition" with two bonus tracks; "Good News" and "Halfway Over The Hill." (Arista – 82876 812372) The 1996 re-issue was mastered by Wally Traugott at Capitol Recording Studios, Hollywood, CA
- A songbook was released to tie in with the album, coupled with Barry's first album *Barry Manilow I* using the cover artwork of this 2nd album.
- Custom printed inner lyric / credit page.
- Cher recorded a version of the Barry Manilow – David composition "Early Morning Strangers" for her Warner Brothers album *I'd Rather Believe In You* (October 12, 1976 - BS-2898).
- Copies of both the LP and single releases can be found on both Bell and ARISTA Records.
- 'Mandy' is actually a cover version of this hit Scott English song "Brandy" with altered lyrics.
- "Mandy" was Barry's first hit single and the first song on Clive Davis' Arista Records label (formerly Bell) to hit the Billboard Hot 100. It was also Barry's first Gold Record Award

The Japanese 45 release of "It's A Miracle" b/w "One Of These Days"
(BLPB-242-AR)

Tryin' to Get The Feeling
AL-4060

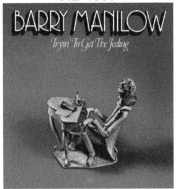

Track Listing:
New York City Rhythm / Tryin' To Get The Feeling Again / Why Don't We Live Together / Bandstand Boogie / You're Leaving Too Soon / She's A Star / I Write The Songs / As Sure As I'm Standing Here / A Nice Boy Like Me / Lay Me Down / Beautiful Music

Production Information:
Produced by: Barry Manilow & Ron Dante
Recorded at: Media Sound Studios, New York City / Sigma Sound Studios, Philadelphia, Pa
Engineered by: Michael DeLugg
Rhythm tracks arranged By: Barry Manilow
Arranged By: T.G. Conway
Horns arranged by: Arif Mardin / Gerald Alters / Norman Harris
Strings arranged by: Arif Mardin / Barry Manilow / Gerald Alters / Joe Renzetti / Norman Harris
Photography by: Lee Gurst
Design: Bob Heimall

Musicians:
Piano: Barry Manilow
Bass: Steve Donaghey
Congas / Bongos / Shaker: Jimmy Maeulen
Drums / Percussion: Lee Gurst
Guitar: Charlie Brown / Sid McGinnis
Keyboards: Alan Axelrod
Pedal Steel Guitar: Sid McGinnis
Background Vocals: Barry Manilow / Ron Dante / Debra Byrd / The Flashy Ladies / Reparata (Lorraine Mazzola) / Ramona Brooks
Barry Manilow: all 32 voices on track "Bandstand Boogie"

Singles Released From This Album:
"I Write The Songs" b/w "A Nice Boy Like Me" (ARISTA – 0157) October 24, 1975 (Peaked at # 1 in the US on the Billboard Hot 100 Chart on January 17, 1976 and # 1 on the Billboard Adult Contemporary Chart and reached # 2 on the Canadian RPM Chart). Single certified Gold on January 6, 1976 for 1 million copies sold. It was nominated for a Grammy for Record Of The Year in 1977. Billboard ranked it as the 13th song of the year in 1976. The original version of the song, written by Bruce Johnston of the Beach Boys, had been recorded by Captain & Tennille, who worked with Bruce in the early '70s with the Beach Boys. It appears on their May 23, 1975 A&M album *Love Will Keep Us Together*.

"Tryin' To Get The Feeling Again" b/w "Beautiful Music" (ARISTA – 0172) March 3, 1976 (Peaked at # 10 in the US on the Billboard Hot 100 Chart in May 1976 and # 1 on the Billboard Adult Contemporary Chart)

Album Data:
Highest Chart Position: # 5 February 6, 1976
Billboard Chart: Billboard Top 200
Number of Weeks on Chart: 87

Notes & Trivia:
- This album was released on LP, Open Reel, 8-Track and Cassette on October 15, 1975. This album was also released in the Quadraphonic format on LP (AQ-4060).
- This album was reissued in Japan on CD on August 2, 2017 with two bonus tracks; "I'll Make You Music" and "Marry Me a Little." (SICP-5448).
- This album was certified gold on December 30, 1975 for sales of over 500,000 copies and double platinum on September 2, 1987 for sales of over 2,000,000 copies.
- A songbook was released to tie in with the album.
- This album was reissued in 1998 with a bonus track; "Marry Me A Little." (Arista – 07822-19040-2) The album was again reissued on May 9, 2006 with two bonus tracks; "I'll Make You Music" and "Marry Me a Little." (Arista – 82876 81235 2)
  The 1998 re-release was remastered by Robert Vosgien at Capitol Recording Studios, Hollywood, CA. Of the bonus track "Marry Me A Little," Barry says: *The bonus cut on this reissue is a real odd choice. It's called "Marry Me A Little." It's a song that was cut from the Broadway production of Stephen Sondheim's groundbreaking musical, Company (which I saw 17 times from the standing room only section at the Alvin Theatre in New York!). We cut it from this album, too, but I always regretted it because it's such a fantastic song.*
- Karen Carpenter had recorded "Trying' To Get The Feeling Again" in January 1975, but the master was misplaced for a number of years before being found and released finally in 1994.
- Custom printed inner lyric / credit sleeve.

The Japanese 45 release of "I Write The Songs" b/w "A Nice Boy Like Me"
(IER-10892)

This One's For You
AL-4090

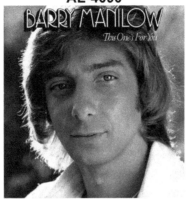

Track Listing:
This One's For You / Daybreak / You Ought To Be Home With Me / Jump Shout Boogie / Weekend In New England / Riders To The Stars / Let Me Go / Looks Like We Made It / Say The Words / All The Time / See The Show Again

Production Information:
Produced by: Ron Dante & Barry Manilow
Recorded and Mixed at: Mediasound Studios, New York City
Engineered by: Michael DeLugg
Photography and Cover Design: Lee Gurst
Arranged by: Barry Manilow

Musicians:
Piano: Barry Manilow
Keyboards: Alex Axelrod / Paul Shaffer
Bass: Will Lee / Steven Donaghey
Guitar: Dennis Farac / Richard Resnicoff / David Spinoza / Gerry Friedman / Ron Dante
Drums: Lee Gurst / Ron Zito
Congas: Carlos Martin
Background Vocals: Barry Manilow / Ron Dante / Debra Byrd / Lady Flash / Monica Burruss
Grunts on *Jump Shout Boogie*: Carlos Martin

Singles Released From This Album:
"This One's For You" b/w "Riders To The Stars" (ARISTA – 0206) September 1, 1976 (Peaked at # 29 in the US on the Billboard Hot 100 Chart in October 1976 and # 1 on the Billboard Adult Contemporary Chart)
"Weekend In New England" b/w "Say The Words" (ARISTA – 0212) November 3, 1976 (Peaked at # 10 in the US on the Billboard Hot 100 Chart in February 1977 and # 1 on the Billboard Adult Contemporary Chart)
"Looks Like We Made It" b/w "New York City Rhythm" (Live) (ARISTA – 0244) April 20, 1977 (Peaked at # 1 in the US on the Billboard Hot 100 Chart on July 23, 1977 and # 1 on the Billboard Adult Contemporary Chart) Certified gold on September 7, 1977 for 1 million copies sold.

Album Data:
Highest Chart Position: # 6 on April 15, 1977
Billboard Chart: Billboard Top 200
Number of Weeks on Chart: 60

Notes & Trivia:

- This album was released on LP, Open Reel, 8-Track and Cassette on July 30, 1976.
- This album was released in the quadraphonic format on LP (AQ-4090) and was the last Barry Manilow quad album and the final quad LP ARISTA issued of pop music. There was no quad 8 track tape release of this album.
- This album was certified Gold on August 17, 1976 for sales of over 500,000 copies, Platinum on January 6, 1977 and double Platinum on September 2, 1987 for sales of over 2,000,000 copies.
- This album was re-issued on October 10, 2006 as an Expanded Edition CD (Arista/Legacy 82876 86719 2) and included the bonus tracks: "Don't Throw It All Away" / "Can't Go Back Anymore" / "This Is Fine" and "I Really Do Write The Songs."
- A songbook was released to tie in with the album.
- This album had a tour book tie-in.
- Custom printed inner lyric / credit sleeve.

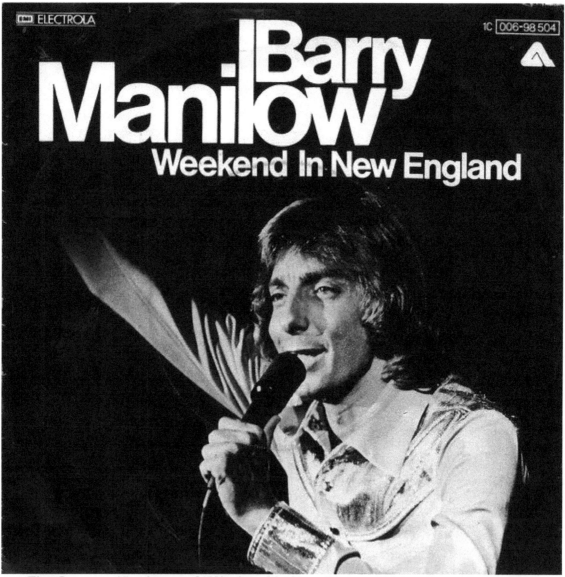

The German 45 release of "Weekend in New England" b/w "Say The Words"
(1C 006-98 504)

Even Now
AB-4164

Track Listing:
Copacabana (At The Copa)+ / Somewhere In The Night* / Can't Smile Without You / Leavin' In The Morning / Where Do I Go From Here / Even Now / I Was A Fool (To Let You Go) / Losing Touch / I Just Want To Be The One In Your Life / Starting Again / Sunrise

Production Information:
Produced by: Ron Dante & Barry Manilow
Recorded at: A&M Recording Studios, Hollywood, Ca
*Recorded at: Media Sound Studios, New York, NY
Engineer: Michael DeLugg
Assistant Engineer at A&M: Derek Dunan
Album recorded July - November 1977
Front & Back Cover photography: Lee Gurst
Cover Design: Barry Manilow & Lee Gurst

Musicians In Hollywood:
Piano: Barry Manilow
Drums: Ronnie Lito
Bass: Will Lee
Keyboards: Bill Mays
Guitar: Mitch Holder / Jay Graydon / Lee Ritenour
Percussion: Allan Estes
String Arp: Barry Manilow
Background Vocals: Ginger Blake+ / Linda Dillard+ / Laura Creamer+ / Ron Dante / Barry Manilow

Musicians In New York:
Piano: Barry Manilow
Drums: Jimmy Young
Bass: Bob Babbit
Electric Piano: Paul Shaffer
Guitar: Jeff Mirinoff
Percussion: Jimmy Maelen

Singles Released From This Album:
"Can't Smile Without You" b/w "Sunrise" (ARISTA – 0305) January 20, 1978 (Peaked at # 3 in the US on the Billboard Hot 100 Chart in April 1978 and # 1 on the Billboard Adult Contemporary Chart in

March 1978) Certified gold on April 6, 1978 for 1 million copies sold.

"Even Now" b/w "I Was A Fool (To Let You Go)" (ARISTA – 0330) April 14, 1978 (Peaked at # 19 in the US on the Billboard Hot 100 Chart in June 1978 and # 1 on the Billboard Adult Contemporary Chart)

"Copacabana (At The Copa)" (Short Version) b/w Copacabana (At The Copa) (Long Version) (ARISTA – 0339) May 24, 1978 (Peaked at # 8 in the US on the Billboard Hot 100 Chart in July 1978) Certified gold on September 7, 1978 for 1 million copies sold.

"Somewhere In The Night" b/w "Leavin' In The Mornin'" (ARISTA – 0382) November 29, 1978 (Peaked at # 9 in the US on the Billboard Hot 100 Chart in February 1979)

Album Data:
Highest Chart Position: # 3 on April 7, 1978
Billboard Chart: Billboard Top 200
Number of Weeks on Chart: 58

Notes & Trivia:
- This album was released on LP, Open Reel, 8-Track and Cassette on January 13, 1978.
- Two different pressings can be found with different lengths of the track Copacabana. One pressing has a 4:08 version and another has a 5:46.
- This album was certified platinum 3x on September 2, 1987 for sales in excess of 3 million copies sold.
- This album was nominated for a Grammy for Album Of The Year in 1979.
- Barry won a Grammy for Best Pop Vocal Performance, Male For "Copacabana (At The Copa)"
- This album was a Billboard Top Album Pick for February 18, 1978.
- A songbook was released to tie in with the album.
- The 1996 CD re-release (# 07822-18946-2) features a bonus unreleased track from the album recording sessions titled: "No Love For Jenny." The 2006 CD reissued (# 82876 81236 2) had the track "I'm Comin' Home Again." in addition to "No Love For Jenny."
- Barry noted on the 1996 CD re-issue: "...I remember beautiful Karen Carpenter stopping by the A&M control room to say hello. We played her "Can't Smile Without You" and she nodded and said, "That's going to be a number one record, I wish it were mine!" The Carpenters had recorded the song two years prior for their 1976 "A Kind of Hush" LP and released it as the flip side to the 2nd single from their album "Passage" on September 9, 1977.
- Custom printed inner lyric / credit sleeve.

The 45 picture sleeve and label for the US release of "Even Now" (AS-0330)

One Voice
AL-9505

Track Listing:
One Voice / (Why Don't We Try) A Slow Dance / Rain / Ships / You Could Show Me / I Don't Want To Walk Without You / Who's Been Sleeping In My Bed / Where Are They Now / Bobbie Lee (What's The Difference, I Gotta Live) / When I Wanted You / Sunday Father

Production Information:
Produced by: Ron Dante & Barry Manilow
Recorded at: United Western Studios, Hollywood, CA / Allen Zentz Recording, Hollywood, CA
Engineered by: Michael DeLugg
Photography: Victor Skrebneski
Art Direction: Donn Davenport

Musicians:
Piano: Barry Manilow
Keyboards: Bill Mays / Jai Winding
Drums: Ed Greene / Jim Gordon
Bass: Will Lee / David Hungate / Dennis Belfield
Guitar: Mitch Holder
Percussion: Alan Estes
Saxophone: Jim Horn
Synthesizer: Michael Boddicker / Ian Underwood
Background Vocals: Ron Dante / Barry Manilow / Monica Burruss / Reparata / Muffy Hendricks
Musician Contractor: Shaun Harris
Concertmaster: Sid Sharp
Orchestration: Artie Butler

Singles Released From This Album:
"Ships" b/w "They Gave in to the Blues" (ARISTA – 0464) October 1979 (Peaked at # 9 in the US on the Billboard Hot 100 Chart in Winter 1979 and # 28 in Canada on the RPM Chart)
"When I Wanted You" / "Bobbie Lee (What's the Difference, I Gotta Live)" December 1979 (ARISTA – 0481) (Peaked at # 20 in the US on the Billboard Hot 100 Chart in Winter 1980 and # 24 in Canada on the RPM Chart)
"I Don't Want to Walk Without You" / "One Voice" (ARISTA – 0501) (Peaked at # 36 in the US on the Billboard Hot 100 Chart in Winter 1980 and # 1 in Canada on the RPM Chart)

Album Data:
Highest Chart Position: # 9 on November 16, 1979

Billboard Chart: Billboard Top 200
Number of Weeks on Chart: 25

Notes & Trivia:

- This album was released on LP, Open Reel, 8-Track and Cassette on September 25, 1979.
- A songbook was released to tie in with the album.
- This album was certified Platinum for sales of over 1,000,000 copies on January 28, 1980.
- The album was re-issued in 1998 (#Arista 07822-19042-2/4) on CD and Cassette with the bonus track "They Gave In to the Blues" (non-LP B-side of "Ships" single.) and again on October 10, 2006 (Arista/Legacy 82876 86718-2) and contained 4 bonus tracks: "They Gave Into The Blues" / "Learning to Live Without You" / "Where I Want to Be" / "I Let Myself Believe"
- Barry's take on this album: "Great songs on this album. Bad hair -- great songs."
- The song "Who's Been Sleeping in My Bed?" was sampled in the song "Superheroes" by Daft Punk on their 2001 album *Discovery*.
- Custom printed inner lyric / credit sleeve.

The French 45 picture sleeve for the release of "Who's Been Sleeping In My Bed"
(ARISTA– 101197)

Barry
AL-9537

Track Listing:
Lonely Together / Bermuda Triangle / I Made It Through The Rain / Twenty-Four Hours A Day / Dance Away / Life Will Go On / Only In Chicago / The Last Duet (with Lily Tomlin) / London / We Still Have Time (Theme from the motion picture "Tribute.")

Production Information:
Produced by: Barry Manilow & Ron Dante
Recorded and Mixed at: Evergreen Recording Studios, Burbank, CA / Media Sound Studios, New York, NY / Wally Heider Recording, Hollywood, CA / A & M Studios, Hollywood, CA / Dirk Dalton Recorders, Santa Monica, CA / Criteria Recording Studios, Miami, FL.
Engineered by: Michael DeLugg / Murray McFadden / Dirk Dalton
Mastered at: Criteria Recording Studios, Miami, FL.
Cover photography: Paul Jasmin
Back Cover Photography: Jay Thompson
Art Direction: Donn Davenport

Musicians:
Piano: Barry Manilow
Keyboards: Paul Shaffer / Victor Vanacore / Bill Mays / Barry Manilow
Fender Rhodes: David Wheatley
Drums: Carlos Vega / Ron Zito / Bud Harner / Ed Greene / Ron Krasinski
Bass: Will Lee / Lou Shoch / Dennis Belfield / Abraham Laboriel
Guitar: Dennis Belfield / Dean Parks / Jeff Mironov John Pondel / Mitch Holder / Thom Rotella
Petal Steel Guitar: Jay Dee Maness
Percussion: Jimmy Maelen / Ken Park / Alan Estes
Synthesizer: Robert Marullo / Barry Manilow / Michael Boddicker
Calliope: Artie Butler
Harmonica: Tommy Morgan
Background Vocals: Keith DiSimone / James Jolis / Jon Joyce / Ron Dante / Stephanie Spruill / Barry Manilow / Maxine Waters / Pat Henderson / Robin Green / Loren Farber / Jimmy Haas
Musician Contractor: Shaun Harris
Concertmaster: Sid Sharp

Singles Released From This Album:
"I Made It Through The Rain" b/w "Only In Chicago" (ARISTA – 0566) November 1980 (Peaked at # 10 in the US on the Billboard Hot 100 Chart in early 1981)
"Lonely Together" b/w "The Last Duet" (With Lily Tomlin) (ARISTA – 0596) March 1981 (Peaked at # 45 in the US on the Billboard Hot 100 Chart in 1981 / # 7 on the Billboard Adult Contemporary Chart)

"Bermuda Triangle" b/w "One Voice" (ARIST – 406) (Peaked at # 15 on the UK Singles Chart, # 16 in Germany on the GfK Entertainment Chart and # 23 in Ireland on the Irish Singles Chart.) This was a European only release.

Album Data:
Highest Chart Position: # 15 on January 23, 1981
Billboard Chart: Billboard Top 200
Number of Weeks on Chart: 20

Notes & Trivia:
- This album was released on LP, Open Reel, 8-Track and Cassette on November 19, 1980.
- A songbook was released to tie in with the album.
- This album was certified Platinum on February 4, 1981 for sales of over 1,000,000 copies
- This album has not been released on CD as of this writing in the US, but is available via digital download. It has, however, had a CD release in Japan.
- Custom printed inner lyric / credit sleeve.

**The 45 picture sleeve for the Australian release of "Lonely Together" b/w "London."
(ARISTA– K8146)**

If I Should Love Again
AL-9573

Track Listing:
The Old Songs / Let's Hang On* / If I Should Love Again / Don't Fall In Love With Me / Break Down The Door / Somewhere Down The Road / No Other Love / Fools Get Lucky / I Haven't Changed The Room / Let's Take All Night (To Say Goodbye)

Production Information:
Produced by: Barry Manilow
Associate Producer: Michael DeLugg
Recorded, Overdubbed and Mixed at: United Western Recording Studios, Hollywood, CA
Engineered by: Michael DeLugg
Assistant Engineers: Gary Boatner and Ira Seigal
Mastered at: Capitol Recording Studios, Hollywood, CA
Mastering Engineer: Ken Perry
Cover and insert Illustrations: Linda Fennimore
Design: Neal Pozner
Art Direction: Donn Davenport

Musicians:
Piano: Barry Manilow / Victor Vanacore
Keyboards: Victor Vanacore / Bill Mays / Robert Marullo
Fender Rhodes: Robert Marullo
Drums: Bud Harner / Ed Greene
Bass: Carl Sealove / Will Lee
Guitar: John Pondel / Dean Parks / Paul Jackson Jr. / Mitch Holder
Percussion: Robert Forte / Alan Estes
Synthesizer: Robert Marullo
English Horn: Bill Page
Saxophone: Tom Scott
Background Vocals: Bill Champlin / Richard Page / Tom Kelly / Barry Manilow*
Concertmaster: Sid Sharp
Musician Contractor: Shaun Harris
Rhythm Arranged by: Barry Manilow / Victor Vanacore
String and Horn Orchestrated by: Artie Butler / Victor Vanacore / Jimmy Haskell

Singles Released From This Album:
"The Old Songs" b/w "Don't Fall In Love With Me" (ARISTA – 0633) October 6, 1981 (Peaked at # 15 in the US on the Billboard Hot 100 Chart and # 1 on the Billboard Adult Contemporary Chart)

"Somewhere Down The Road" b/w "Let's Take All Night (To Say Goodbye)" (ARISTA – 0658) December 1981 (Peaked at # 21 in the US on the Billboard Hot 100 Chart and # 1 on the Billboard Adult Contemporary Chart in February 1982).

Album Data:
Highest Chart Position: # 14 on November 11, 1981
Billboard Chart: Billboard Top 200
Number of Weeks on Chart: 25

Notes & Trivia:
- This album was released on LP, Open Reel, 8-Track and Cassette on September 1, 1981
- A songbook was released to tie in with the album.
- This album was certified Gold for sells of over 500,000+ copies on November 24, 1981.
- Re-released on November 24, 1998 (Arista 07822-19041-2/4) on CD and Cassette with a bonus track: "You're Runnin' Too Hard."
- The song "Somewhere Down The Road" was introduced to new audiences when it was prominently featured in an episode of the popular TV show *Ally McBeal* in 2001. In the episode "Reach Out and Touch" (which guest-starred Barry Manilow as the subject of the title character's hallucinations), the song was performed by Barry and singer/series regular Vonda Shepard.
- Barry refers to it as "The most romantic album that I ever made", and remarks "I was so caught up in romance that I actually wrote music and lyrics to the title song while playing the piano facing the ocean, in a rented house on the beach in Atlantic City, New Jersey."
- Custom printed inner lyric / credit sleeve.

The 45 picture sleeve for the Japanese release of "The Old Songs."
(ARISTA– 7RS-31)

Here Comes The Night
AL-9610

Track Listing:
I Wanna Do It With You / Here Comes The Night / Memory / Let's Get On With It / Some Girls / Some Kind Of Friend* / I'm Gonna Sit Right Down And Write Myself A Letter* / Getting Over Losing You / Heart Of Steel / Stay

Production Information:
Produced by: Barry Manilow
Associate Producer: Bill Drescher
Recorded and Mixed at: Sound City Recording Studios, Van Nuys, CA
*Recorded at Allen Zentz Recording, Los Angeles, CA
Engineered by: Bill Drescher
Assistant Engineers: Rick Polakow
Mastered at: Artisan Sound Recorders, Hollywood, CA by Greg Fulginiti
Cover Photography: George Hurrell
Art Direction: Ria Lewerke-Shapiro
Grooming: Richard Bradshaw, Antonio V and Charles Mercuri

Musicians:
Piano: Barry Manilow / Victor Vanacore / Bill Mays
Keyboards: Barry Manilow
Synthesizer: Barry Manilow / Ian Underwood / Gabriel Katona / Robert Marulla
Drums: John Ferraro / Ed Greene / Vinnie Colaiuta / Bud Harner
Percussion: Alan Estes
Bass: Leon Gaer / Dennis Belfield
Guitar: Richie Zito, John Pondel, Robben Ford, Art Phillips, Paul Jackson Jr., John Goux, Mitch Holder, George Doering
Saxophone: Gary Herbig
Background Vocals: Bill Champlin / Steve George / Tom Kelly / Richard Page / James Jolis / Kevin DiSimone / Muffy Hendrix / Pat Henderson
Musician Contractor: Shaun Harris

Singles Released From This Album:
"Memory" b/w "Heart Of Steel" (ARISTA – 1025) (Peaked at # 39 in the US on the Billboard Hot 100 Chart and # 10 on the Billboard Adult Contemporary Chart in January 1983)
"Some Kind Of Friend" b/w "Heaven" (ARISTA –1046) (Peaked at # 26 in the US on the Billboard Hot 100 Chart in 1983)
"I'm Gonna Sit Right Down And Write Myself A Letter" b/w "Heart Of Steel" (ARTIST–503) European Only Release.

<u>**Album Data:**</u>
Highest Chart Position: # 32 on January 21, 1983
Billboard Chart: Billboard Top 200
Number of Weeks on Chart: 27

<u>**Notes & Trivia:**</u>
- This album was released on LP, Open Reel, 8-Track and Cassette on November 1, 1982.
- A songbook was released to tie in with the album.
- This album was certified Gold for sells of over 500,000+ copies on January 17, 1983.
- This album was released with the title "**I Wanna Do It with You**" in some European markets.
- On the UK **cassette** release side one had the song "Oh Julie" added as a bonus track. Side two had "Heaven" as a bonus track. In Japan the album has been re-issued twice on CD: once in 1985 (32RD-22) which included a remix of "Oh Julie" (with overdubbed instrumentation and background vocals), and again in 1994 (BVCA-7312) which contained the original mix of "Oh Julie" as released in the US in 1982 on a 12" EP.
- This was the final Barry Manilow album released in the open reel tape format.
- Custom printed inner lyric / credit sleeve.

The cassette tape from the UK (ARISTA - TCBM2) had two extra songs that had not been released on the LP in the US, nor in other markets. Those were "Oh, Julie" and "Heaven." However "Oh, Julie" and "Heaven" were released on the 1982 ARISTA 4 track EP "Oh, Julie" (AB-2500) in the US.

2:00 A.M. Paradise Cafe
AL-8254

Track Listing:
Paradise Cafe / Where Have You Gone / Say No More / Blue (duet with Sarah Vaughan) / When October Goes / What Am I Doin' Here / Goodbye, My Love / Big City Blues (duet with Mel Tormé) / When Love is Gone / I've Never Been So Low On Love / Night Song

Production Information:
Produced by: Barry Manilow
Recorded and Mixed at: Westlake Audio in Studio C, Los Angeles, CA
Engineered by: Michael Braunstein
Assistant engineers: Deni King / Greg Laney
Mastered at: Future Disc, Hollywood, CA
Cover photography: Leon Lecash
Back jacket photography: Jay Thompson
Art Direction: Ria Lewerke
Logo Design: Sue Reilly & Barry Manilow
Grooming: Charles Mercuri

Musicians:
Piano: Barry Manilow
Baritone Saxophone: Gerry Mulligan
Bass: George Duvivier
Drums: Shelly Manne
Guitar: Mundell Lowe
Rhodes Electric Piano: Bill Mays
Arranged by: Barry Manilow
Musician contractor: Shaun Harris

Singles Released From This Album:
"Paradise Cafe" / "Paradise Cafe" March 1985 (ARISTA – 9318) (Peaked at # 24 in the US on the Billboard Adult Contemporary Chart) Promotional only singles on clear vinyl released. No store stock. "When October Goes" / "Paradise Cafe" (ARIST – 599) (Peaked at # 6 in the US on the Billboard Adult Contemporary Chart) No US pressing can be found of this single. UK release presented here.

Album Data:
Highest Chart Position: # 28 on January 25, 1985
Billboard Chart: Billboard Top 200

Notes & Trivia:

- This album was released on LP, 8-Track, Cassette and CD on November 15, 1984.
- This album was certified platinum for sells in excess of one million copies on January 14, 1985.
- A songbook was released to tie in with the album.
- Tour book printed to tie-in with release.
- A video cassette was released in 1985 by RCA/Columbia on the making of this album. The 55 minute video shows the rehearsal and recording process that went into the making of Barry's first jazz inspired album. The video was produced by Les Joyce with executive producer Garry C. Kief.
- This album was rereleased on October 29, 1996 on CD and Cassette (Arista 07822-18945-2/4)
- The CD version was issued in Japan on December 10, 1984 and again on March 5, 1988.
- Custom printed inner lyric / credit sleeve.

The 45 picture sleeve / label for the UK release of "When October Goes" b/w "Paradise Cafe." (ARIST–599)

Manilow
RCA AFL1-7044

<u>**Track Listing:**</u>
US Release:
I'm Your Man / It's All Behind Us Now / In Search Of Love/ He Doesn't Care (But I Do) / Some Sweet Day / At The Dance / If You Were Here With Me Tonight / Sweet Heaven I'm In Love Again (From The Movie Copacabana) / Ain't Nothing Like The Real Thing (duet with Muffy Hendrix) / It's A Long Way Up

French Release:
I'm Your Man / It's All Behind Us Now / In Search of Love / He Doesn't Care But I Do / Some Sweet Day / At the Dance / If You Were Here With Me Tonight / Sweet Heaven (I'm in Love Again) / Don't Talk to Me of Love (duet with Mireille Mathieu) / It's a Long Way Up

Italian Release:
Amare Chi Si Manchi Tu (Who Needs To Dream) / I'm Your Man / It's All Behind Us Now / In Search of Love / He Doesn't Care But I Do / Con Chi Sei (Some Sweet Day) / At the Dance / If You Were Here With Me Tonight / Sweet Heaven (I'm In Love Again) / It's a Long Way Up

Japanese Release:
I'm Your Man / It's All Behind Us Now / In Search of Love / He Doesn't Care But I Do / Some Sweet Day / Sakura / At the Dance / If You Were Here with Me Tonight / Sweet Heaven (I'm in Love Again) / Ain't Nothing Like the Real Thing (duet with Muffy Hendrix) / It's a Long Way Up / In Search of Love (duet with Hideki Saijo)

<u>**Production Information:**</u>
Producers: Barry Manilow / Howie Rice / Tasuku Okamura / Kevin DiSimone / Michael DeLugg / George Duke / Bob Gaudio / Eric Borenstein
Recorded at: Cherokee Studios, Hollywood, CA / Studio 55, Los Angeles, CA / The Village Recorder, Los Angeles, CA / Media Sound, New York, NY / Lion Share Recording Studios, Hollywood, CA / Ambience Recorders, Farmington Hills, Michigan / Sheffield Studios, Baltimore, MD / Record Plant, Los Angeles / Sigma Sound Studios, New York / Le Gonks West, West Hollywood, CA / Sound Labs, Hollywood
Overdubs recorded at: Capitol Studios, Hollywood, CA
Engineers: John Boghosian / John Arrias / Tommy Vicari / Joe Marciano / Michael DeLugg / Erik Zobler / Tony D'Amico
Assistant Recording / Mix Engineers: John Arrias / Glen Holguin / Bruce Robb / Khaliq Glover / Bruce Smith / Mitch Gibson / Julie Last / Kraig Miller / Daniel Reed / David Eaton / Steve Hirsch / Jimmy Preziosi
Mixed at: Larrabee Sound Studios, Hollywood, CA / Studio 55, Los Angeles, CA / Lion Share

Recording Studios, Hollywood, CA
Mixed by: Michael DeLugg / John Arrias / Tommy Vicari
Mastered at Bernie Grundman Mastering, Los Angeles, CA
Mastered by: Brian Gardner
Art Direction: Ria Lawerke
Design: Sue Reilly
Photography by: Matthew Rolston
Conductor: Victor Vanacore
Arranged by: Kevin DiSimone / Artie Butler / Barry Fasman / Howie Rice / Alan Foust / George Del Barrio / Barry Manilow / Bob Gaudio
Orchestrations by: Artie Butler
Executive in Charge of Production: Eric Borenstein
Assistant to Barry Manilow: Marc Hulett

Musicians:
Piano: Barry Manilow / Raymond Crossley / Randy Kerber / Kevin DiSimone
Drums: Barry Manilow / Howie Rice / Kevin DiSimone / John Robinson, Rick Shlosser, Kerry Ashby / Bud Harner
Electronic drum programming: Bud Harner / Peter Moshay
Percussion: Terral Santiel / Paulinho Da Costa
Keyboards: Barry Manilow / Howie Rice / Ron Pedley / Victor Vanacore / Kevin Jones / Jon Gilutin
Guitar: John Pondel / Michael Landau / Howie Rice
Bass: Howie Rice / Neil Stubenhaus / Marc Levine / Will Lee / "Ready" Freddie Washington / Lequeint "Duke" Jobe
Synthesizer: John Philip Shenale
Synclavier II: George Duke
Yamaha DX-8 synthesizer: Randy Kerber
Yamaha DX-7 synthesizer, Roland Super Jupiter synthesizer, Synclavier: Kevin DiSimone
Saxophone: Joel Peskin
Background Vocals: Billie Hughes / Jason Scheff / Jon Lind / Luther Waters / Oren Waters / Barry Edward Hirschberg / James Jolis / Kevin DiSimone / Tom Kelly / Tommy Funderbunk / Bob Carlisle / Steve George

Singles Released From This Album:
"In Search of Love" b/w "At The Dance" 1985 (PB-14223) (Peaked at # 11 in the US on the Billboard Adult Contemporary Chart and # 80 in the UK on the UK Singles Chart)
"He Doesn't Care (But I Do)" b/w "It's All Behind Us Now" 1986 (PB-14302) (Peaked at # 22 in the US on the Billboard Adult Contemporary Chart)
"I'm Your Man" (Club Mix) b/w "I'm Your Man" (Dub Mix) July 1986 (Peaked at # 86 in the US on the Billboard Hot 100 Chart / at # 69 on the US Cash Box Chart / at # 96 on the UK Singles Chart / at # 98 on the Australian Kent Music Report)

Album Data:
Highest Chart Position: # 42 on December 27, 1985
Billboard Chart: Billboard Top 200
Number of Weeks on Chart: 24

Notes & Trivia:
- This album was released on LP, 8-Track, Cassette and CD in November 5, 1985
- This was Barry's first album with RCA after leaving ARISTA.
- On the Japanese release there is a duet ("In Search Of Love") with the late Japanese singer

Hideki Saijo. Barry sings this track in Japanese.

- On the French release there is a duet ("Don't Talk To Me Of Love") with French singer Mireille Mathieu. The French CD was released on January 15, 1986.
- Reissued as a bonus CD for QVC to help promote "The Greatest Songs Of The Eighties," on November 20, 2008 (RCA/Legacy 88697 42903-2)
- Custom printed inner lyric / credit sleeve.

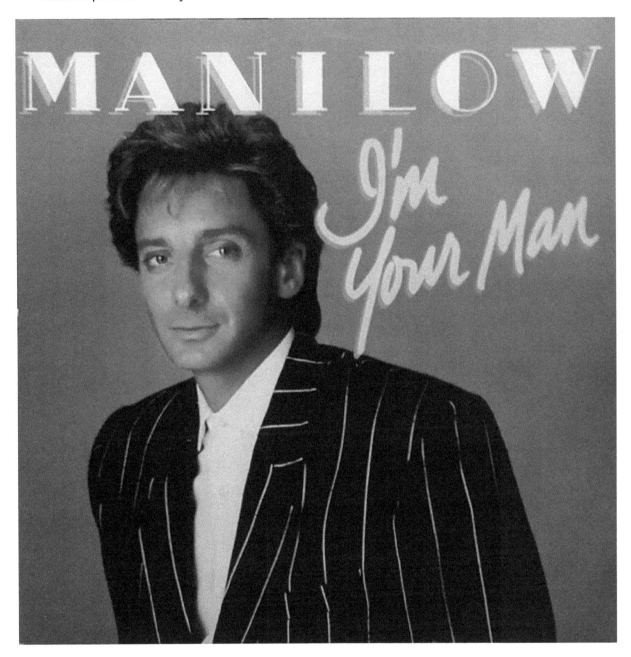

The 45 picture sleeve for the US release of
"I'm Your Man" (Club Mix) b/w "I'm Your Man" (Dub Mix)
RCA PB-14397

Grandes Exitos en Espanol
RCA IL8-7459

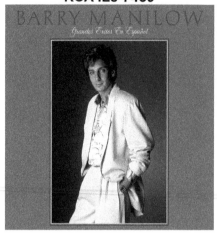

Track Listing:
Mandy / Amanece (Daybreak) / Copacabana (At The Copa) / Ay Caramba! (duet with Lucia Mendez) / Es Para Ti (This One's For You) / Un Dia Feliz (Some Sweet Day) / Hasta Hoy (Even Now) (duet with Valeria Lynch) / Siempre Alli (All The Time) / Sera Esto Magia (Could It Be Magic) / Soy La Cancion, Soy La Cancion (I Write The Songs)

Production Information:
Produced by: Barry Manilow and Ron Dante
Ay Caramba! Produced by: Barry Manilow and Bob Gaudio
"Un Dia Feliz" ("Some Sweet Day") Produced by: Barry Manilow and Michael DeLugg
Recording Coordinators for Spanish Recordings: Buddy and Mary McCluskey
Associate Producer and Sound Engineer: Michael DeLugg
Executive in Charge of Production: Eric Borenstein
Management of Personal Representation: Stiletto, Ltd., Los Angeles, California

Notes & Trivia:
- This album was released on LP and Cassette in October 1985.
- Released in Venezuela on CD (BMG-80492) in 2001.
- Barry singing some of his biggest hits in Spanish, including two duets. Title translates to "Greatest Hits in Spanish."
- All Spanish Translations by Buddy and Mary McCluskey, Except "Soy La Cancion, Soy La Cancion" by Buddy and Mary McCluskey and Leonardo Schultz.
- Barry's vocals were overdubbed using the original master tapes.
- Track 4 ("Ay Caramba!") is from the movie "Copacabana."
- This release is available as a digital download from various digital music providers - (@iTunes / @Spotify / @Amazon music / @AppleMusic / @Google Play)

Swing Street
AL-8527

Track Listing:
Swing Street / Big Fun (featuring "Full Swing") / Stompin' At The Savoy / Black and Blue (duet with Phyllis Hyman – Featuring Tom Scott) / Hey Mambo (duet with Kid Creole and The Coconuts) / Summertime (duet with Diane Schuur – Featuring Stan Getz) / Brooklyn Blues (Featuring Tom Scott) / Stardust (Featuring "Uncle Festive") / Once When You Were Mine / One More Time (Featuring Gerry Mulligan)

Production Information:
Producers: Barry Manilow / Eddie Arkin / Emilio Estefan Jr. / Lawrence Dermer
Executive Producer: Eric Borenstein
Recorded at: Image Recording Studios, Los Angeles, CA / Westlake Audio, Los Angeles, CA / Criteria Recording Studios, Miami, FL / Sigma Sound Studios, Philadelphia, Pennsylvania / Record Plant, Los Angeles, CA / Clinton Recording Studios, New York, NY / Ocean Way Recording. Los Angeles, CA
Vocal overdubs recorded at: The Hit Factory, New York, NY / Clinton Recording Studios, New York, NY
Engineered by: Harry Maslin / John Van Nest / Michael Braunstein / Eric Schilling / Alan Sides
Assistant Engineers: Bruce Wildstein / Mark Germaine / Rebecca Everett / Squeak Stone / Spencer Chrislu / Allen Abrahamson / Jay Healy / Dana Horowitz / Teresa Verplanck / Ron Da Silva
Digital master tapes prepared by: Michael DeLugg
Mastered at: Frankford/Wayne Mastering Labs, New York, NY by: Tom Coyne
Records pressed by: Hauppauge Record Manufacturing Ltd. 15 Gilpin Avenue, Hauppauge, NY 11788
Cover Photographer: Greg Gorman
Design: Dave Brubaker
Art Direction: Mark Larson
Swing Street Set Design and Construction: Ron Oates
Stylist: Martine Leger
Grooming: Alfonso Noe
Assistant to Barry Manilow: Marc Hulett
Artist Management: Stiletto, Ltd.

Musicians:
Piano: Barry Manilow / Artie Butler / Ron Pedley / Randy Kerber
Keyboards: Eddie Arkin
Synth Programming: Greg Karukas
Guitars: Dann Huff / Paul Jackson, Jr / John Pondel
Bass: Dave Stone / Marc Levine
Drums: Vinnie Colaiuta / Bud Harner
Percussion: Alan Estes / Bud Harner

Soprano Saxophone: Tom Scott
Tenor Saxophone: Stan Getz / Tom Scott
Baritone Saxophone: Gerry Mulligan
Horns: Jerry Hey / Larry Hall / Gary Grant / Bill Reichenbach / Charlie Loper
Flugel Horn: Jerry Hey
Flute: Tom Scott
Background Vocals: Joe Galdo / Lawrence Dermer / Eddie Arkin / Kid Creole (August Darnell) / Jon Joyce / Gary Falcone / Joe Pizzulo
Horn Arrangements: Eddie Arkin / Jerry Hey

"Uncle Festive" is: Ron Pedley
"Full Swing" is: Lorraine Feather / Charlotte Crossley / Augie Johnson

Singles Released From This Album:
"Brooklyn Blues" b/w "Brooklyn Blues" 1987 (ADP–9648) (33-⅓ 12" promotional only blue vinyl with picture sleeve)
"Stompin at the Savoy" / "Black and Blue*" / "Summertime+" / "Brooklyn Blues^" 1987 (ADP-9649) (33-⅓ 12" promotional only EP) *(duet with Phyllis Hyman – Featuring Stan Getz / +duet with Diane Schuur – Featuring Stan Getz / ^Featuring Tom Scott)
"Hey Mambo" b/w "When October Goes" February 1988 (AS1–9666) (Peaked at # 90 in the US on the Billboard Hot 100 Chart)
"Black and Blue" b/w "Black and Blue" February 1988 (AS1–9702)This album was nominated for a Grammy for Best Traditional Pop Vocal Album in 2009.

Album Data:
Highest Chart Position: # 70 on January 30, 1988
Billboard Chart: Billboard Top 200
Number of Weeks on Chart: 21

Notes & Trivia:
- This album was released on LP, Cassette and CD on November 12, 1987.
- This album marked Barry's return to long time label ARISTA Records.
- This album was certified Gold for sales in excess of 500,000 copies.
- A songbook was released to tie in with the album.
- A tour book was produced to tie in with this album.
- This album was given a four star rating by Rolling Stone Magazine.
- The album title refers to 52nd Street in Manhattan, New York, between 5th and 6th Avenues, which was the jazz center during the late 1930s and early 1940s.
- This album was re-released on CD and Cassette (Arista 07822-18947-2/4) on October 29, 1996 and again on CD (BMG SP 46922) on May 21, 2002. The 1996 re-release was remastered by Wally Traugott at Capitol Recording Studios, Hollywood, CA using the original mastering tapes.
- Barry has said this about the Swing Street album: *I will always remember this album with joy because it served to introduce me to one of the most talented and beautiful people in my life, my Co-Producer Eddie Arkin. I wanted to record a techno-swing album and Eddie's brilliant and powerful arrangements were exactly what I heard in my head. Getting to work with Diane Schuur, Phyllis Hyman, Stan Getz, Kid Creole, Tom Scott and, once again, the great Gerry Mulligan, made this album incredibly special for me. It was also the album that reunited me with my beloved Arista family. A great experience for me all the way around.*
- Custom printed inner lyric / credit sleeve.

**The 45 picture sleeve for the US release of "Hey Mambo" b/w "When October Goes."
(AS1-9666)**

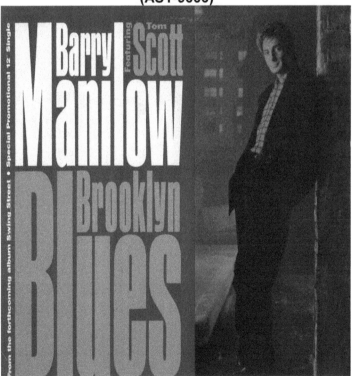

**The 12" promotional only blue vinyl picture sleeve for "Brooklyn Blues."
(ADP-9648)**

Barry Manilow
AL-8570

Track Listing:
Please Don't Be Scared / Keep Each Other Warm / Once and For All / The One That Got Away / When The Good Times Come Again / Some Good Things Never Last / In Another World / You Begin Again / My Moonlight Memories Of You / Anyone Can Do The Heartbreak / A Little Traveling Music, Please

Production Information:
Produced by: Barry Manilow / Eddie Arkin / Michael Lloyd / Paul Staveley O'Duffy / Hammer and Slater / Ric Wake
Executive Producer: Clive Davis
Recorded at: Village Recorders, West Los Angeles, CA / The Manor, Oxfordshire, England / Lillie Yard Studios, London, England / Angel Recording Studios, London, England / The Complex, West Los Angeles, CA / Sarm West Recording Studios, London, England / Image Recording, Hollywood, CA / Cove City Sound, Long Island, New York / Marathon Recording, New York, NY / Shakedown Sound, New York, NY / Ground Control, Los Angeles, CA / Westlake Audio, Los Angeles, CA
Engineered by: Carmine Rubino / Dan Nebenzal / Michael Lloyd / Dennis MacKay / Bob Cadway / Steve Krause
Assistant engineers: Charlie Brocco / John Valentino / Thomas R. Yezzi / Rob Caprio / Squeak Stone
2nd Assistant Engineer: Sam Gladstein
Mixed at: The Village Recorder, West Los Angeles, CA / Conway Studios, Hollywood, CA / Can-Am Recorders, Tarzana, CA
Mixed By:Carmine Rubino / Dan Nebenzal / Michael Lloyd / Steve Krause
Assistant Mix Engineers: Robert Hart / Jeffrey Poe / Richard McKernan
Digitally mastered at: Fullersound, Miami, Florida by Mike Miller
Cover photography: Greg Gorman
Art Direction: Susan Mendola
Stylist: Martine Leger
Grooming: Eric Barnard
Executive in charge of production: Eric Borenstein
Artist Management: Garry C. Kief (Stiletto)
Assistant to Barry Manilow: Marc Hulett

Musicians:
Piano: Barry Manilow / Pat Coil / Reg Powell / Jim Cox / Kevin Bassinson / Michael Lloyd
Guitar: Dean Parks / Robbie McIntosh / Steve Dudas / Dann Huff / Russ Freeman / Laurence Juber
Ukelele: Laurence Juber
Bass: Dennis Belfield / Jeff Slater
Synthesizer: Michael Lloyd / Claude Gaudette

Fairlight Synthesizer: Todd Herreman
Keyboards: Paul "Wix" Wickens / Rich Tancredi / Jeff Slater
Drums: Paul Leim / Vinnie Colaiuta / Ron Krasinski / Joe Franco
Percussion: Michael Fisher / Luís Jardim
Saxophone: Dana Robbins / Gary Herbig
Background Vocals: Dee Lewis / Wayne Hammer / Jeff Slater / Jim Haas / Joe Chemay / Joe Pizzulo
Keyboard and Synthesizer programming: Ed Arkin
Drum Machine and Synthesizer programming: Wayne Hammer / Jeff Slater
F-16 Synthesizer programming: Ben Forat

Singles Released From This Album:

"Keeping Each Other Warm" b/w "A Little Traveling Music, Please" June 1989 (AS1–9838) (Peaked at # 7 in the US on the Billboard Adult Contemporary Chart)

"When The Good Times Come Again" b/w "When The Good Times Come Again" 1989 / June 2020 (AS1–9873) (Peaked at # 12 in the US on the Billboard Adult Contemporary Chart) This track entered the charts in June 2020 due to the COVID-19 pandemic.

"The One That Got Away" b/w "The One That Got Away" 1989 (AS1–9883) (Peaked at # 25 in the US on the Billboard Adult Contemporary Chart)

Album Data:

Highest Chart Position: # 64 on October 6, 1989
Billboard Chart: Billboard Top 200
Number of Weeks on Chart: 16

Notes & Trivia:

- This album was released on LP, Cassette and CD on April 27, 1989.
- Custom printed inner lyric / credit sleeve.
- This album was certified Gold for sales in excess of 500,000 copies.

**The UK 12" picture disc EP for "Please Don't Be Scared" b/w
"A Little Traveling Music, Please" and "Dirt Cheap" (Arista 612 246)**

Because It's Christmas
AL-8644

Track Listing:
The Christmas Song / Jingle Bells (duet with Expose) / Silent Night - I Guess There Ain't No Santa Claus / The First Noel - When The Meadow Was Bloomin' / Excerpt from Handel's Messiah ("For Unto Us A Child Is Born...") - Because It's Christmas (For All The Children) / Baby, It's Cold Outside (duet with K.T. Oslin) / White Christmas / Carol Of The Bells - The Bells Of Christmas / Joy To The World - Have Yourself A Merry Little Christmas / We Wish You A Merry Christmas - It's Just Another New Year's Eve

Production Information:
Produced and Arranged by Eddie Arkin and Barry Manilow
Recorded and Mixed at Sunset Sound, Hollywood, CA / Capitol Studios, Hollywood, CA / Digital Recorders, Nashville, TN / Westlake Audio, Hollywood, CA / Ocean Way, Hollywood, CA
Engineered by: Don Murray / Allen Sides
Assistant Engineer: Mike Kloster
Mixed at: Sunset Sound, Hollywood, CA
Mixed by: Don Murray
Digitally edited by Robert Vosgien at CMS Digital, Pasadena, CA
Mastered by Wally Traugott at Capitol Studios, Hollywood, CA
Art Direction & Design: Carolyn Quan
Photography: Greg Gorman
Set Design: Oates Set Design
Hair & Makeup: Alfonso Noe
Wardrobe Styling: Martine Leger
Artist Management: Garry C. Kief / Stiletto Entertainment
CD's pressed by: Sonopress, Weaverville, North Carolina

Musicians:
Piano and Synthesizers: Randy Kerber
Bass: John Patitucci
Drums: Vinnie Colaiuta
Guitar: Eddie Arkin
Rhythm Guitar: Russ Freeman
Trumpet Solos: Jerry Hey
Vibes: Gene Estes
Brass Arrangements: Jerry Hey
Conducted by: Mark Watters

Orchestra Contractor: Sandy DeCrescent
Copyist: Karen Smith

Singles Released From This Album:
"Jingle Bells" (with Expose) b/w "Because It's Christmas" 1990 (AS–2094) (Peaked at # 38 in the US on the Billboard Adult Contemporary Chart)

Album Data:
Highest Chart Position: # 40 on December 22, 1990
Billboard Chart: Billboard Top 200
Number of Weeks on Chart: 8

Notes & Trivia:
- This album was released on LP, Cassette and CD on September 25, 1990
- This album was certified Gold on December 12, 1990 for sales in excess of 500,000 copies and Platinum for sales in excess of 1 million copies on July 19, 2002.
- A songbook was released to tie in with the album.

The UK 45 promotional single for Jingle Bells. The printing of the perimeter print has been mirrored appearing reversed, a print error. Same track both sides.

Show Stoppers
Arista 07822-18687-2

Track Listing:
Give My Regards To Broadway (a capella) / Overture of Overtures / All I Need Is The Girl / Real Live Girl / Where Or When / Look To The Rainbow (duet with Barbara Cook) / Once In Love With Amy / Dancing In The Dark / You Can Have The TV / I'll Be Seeing You / But The World Goes 'Round / Guys And Dolls Medley: Fugue For Tinhorns (Trio with Michael Crawford & Hinton Battle) / Luck Be A Lady / Old Friends / The Kid Inside / Never Met A Man I Didn't Like / Bring Him Home / If We Only Have Love (Quand On N'a Que L'amour)

Production Information:
Produced by: Barry Manilow and Eddie Arkin
Recorded at: Rumbo Recorders, Canoga Park, CA
Engineered by: Don Murray
Assistant Engineer: Shawn Berman
Mixed at Smoke Tree Ranch, Chatsworth, CA
Mixed by: Don Murray
Assistant Mix Engineer: Squeak Stone
Digitally Edited by: Robert Vosgien at CMS Digital, Pasadena, CA
Mastered by: Wally Traugott at Capitol Studios, Hollywood, CA
Photography: Randee St. Nicholas
Art Direction & Design by: Carolyn Quan
Set Design: Ron Oates / Oates Set Design
Grooming: Alfonso Noe
Wardrobe Stylist: Deborah Waknin/Celistine
Management: Garry C. Kief / Stiletto Management Inc.
Credit Coordination and Assistant to Barry Manilow: Marc Hulett
Copyists: Doug Dana / Janice Hayen / Bill Hughes / Bob Hurrell / Jeff Jones / C. Lake / Diz Mullins / Yvonne Richardson / Jim Surrell / Dick Thurik
Production Coordinator: Les Joyce
Orchestra Contractors: Frank Capp / Bill Hughes

Musicians:
Drums: Sol Gubin / Stephen Houghton / Harvey Mason / Carlos Vega / Dave Weckl
Percussion: Larry Bunker / Judy Chilnick / Alan Estes / Joe Porcaro / Walfredo Reyes
Piano: Randy Kerber
Piano and Synthesizer: Randy Kerber / Tom Ranier
Synthesizer: Pat Coil
Guitar: Dennis Budimir / John Pondel

Bass: John Clayton / Jim De Julio / Arnie Egilsson / Abe Laboriel / John Patitucci
Trumpet: Buddy Childers / Rick Baptist / Oscar Brashear / Bobby Bryant / Stu Blumberg / Chuck Findley / Gary Grant / Walt Johnson / Larry McGuire
Trombone: Bill Booth / Bryant Byers / Alan Kaplan / Charlie Loper / Dick Nash / Jim Self / Kenny Shroyer / Chauncey Welsch
Woodwinds: Don Ashworth / Gene Cipriano / Earle Dumler / Gary Foster / Bill Green / Gary Herbig / Dan Higgins / Ronny Lang / Dick Mitchell / Jack Nimitz / Joe Soldo / Bob Tricarico
Harp: Gail Levant / Joann Turovsky
French Horn: Marni Johnson / Brian O'Connor / Kurt Snyder / Brad Warnaar
Tuba: Tommy Johnson
Violins: Murray Adler / Mari Botnick / Israel Baker / Jackie Brand / Bobby Bruce / Bette Byers / Harold Dicterow / Bonnie Douglas / Assa Drori / Bruce Dukov / Ronald Folsom / Irv Geller / Harris Goldman / Alex Horvath / Ezra Kleger / Bernie Kundell / Razdan Kutumjian / Carl La Magna / Joe Lyle / Michael Markman / Stan Plummer / Sid Sharp / Bob Sanov / Sheldon Sanov / Paul Shure / Alex Treger / Dorothy Wade / Francine Walsh / Tibor Zelig
Violas: Bob Becker / Sam Boghossian / Richard Elegino / Myra Kestenbaum / Linda Lipsett / Dan Neufeld / Carole Mukogawa / Harry Shirinian / Linn Subotnik / Ray Tischer / Herschel Wise
Cellos: Ron Cooper / Christine Ermacoff / Barbara Hunter / Ray Kelley / Ray Kramer / Earl Madison / Nils Oliver / Harry Schultz / Tina Soule

"Give My Regards To Broadway" from the 1904 Musical *LITTLE JOHNNY JONES*, George M. Cohan Music Publishing Company (ASCAP); Arranged by Barry Manilow and Eddie Arkin; Piano - Randy Kerber

"Overture Of Overtures" - Concept by Barry Manilow / Orchestra Arranged by Billy Byers; Conducted by Bruce Broughton; Background Singers - Beth Anderson, Susan Boyd, Jon Joyce and Joe Pizzulo
Great Moments from the Great Broadway Overtures (The album liner notes list individual songwriters and publishers):
"Everything's Coming Up Roses" (From *Gypsy*)
"Best Of All Possible Worlds" (From *Candide*)
"Don't Rain On My Parade" (From *Funny Girl*)
"Company" (From *Company*)
"Sweeney" (From *Sweeney Todd*)
"Evita" (From *Evita*)
"Jesus Christ Superstar" (From *Jesus Christ Superstar*)
"The Most Happy Fella" (From *The Most Happy Fella*)
"The Dance At The Gym" (From *West Side Story*)
"There Is Nothin' Like A Dame" (From *South Pacific*)
"Night Waltz" (From *A Little Night Music*)
"Mazurka" (From *Candide*)
"The Carousel Waltz" (From *Carousel*)
"Somewhere" (From *West Side Story*)
"One" (From *A Chorus Line*)
"Mame" (From *Mame*)
"Hello, Dolly!" (From *Hello, Dolly!*)
"Rose's Tum" (From *Gypsy*)
"Big Spender" (From *Sweet Charity*)

"All I Need Is The Girl" from the 1959 Musical *GYPSY*, Williamson Music, Stratford Music Corp. (Admin. by Chappell and Co.) (ASCAP); Orchestra Arranged and Conducted by Billy Byers

"Real Live Girl" from the 1962 Musical *LITTLE ME*, Notable Music Co., Inc. (Admin. by WB Music Corp.), Junes Tunes (ASCAP); Orchestra Arranged and Conducted by Billy Byers

"Where Or When" from the 1937 Musical *BABES IN ARMS*, Chappell and Co. (ASCAP); Arranged by Eddie Arkin; Piano and Synthesizer - Randy Kerber; Bass - Abe Laboriel; Drums - Carlos Vega; Guitar solo - Mitch Holder

"Look To The Rainbow" from the 1947 Musical *FINIAN'S RAINBOW*, Chappell and Co. (ASCAP); Orchestra Arranged by Billy Byers; Conducted by Bruce Broughton

"Once In Love With Amy" from the 1948 Musical *WHERE'S CHARLEY?*, Frank Music Corp. (ASCAP); Orchestra Arranged and Conducted by Billy Byers; Chorus - Patricia Arkin, Debra Byrd, Kevin Carlisle, Philip Dennis, Susan DuBow, Garry Kief, Paul Levine, Marc Hulett, Dolores Mazolla, Reparata, Steve Wax, Mitzie Welch and Ken Welch

"Dancing In The Dark" from the 1931 Musical *THE BAND WAGON*, Warner Bros. Inc. (ASCAP); Arranged by Eddie Arkin; Piano - Randy Kerber; Bass - Abe Laboriel; Drums - Carlos Vega; Guitar - Mitch Holder

"You Can Have The TV" from the 1977 Revue *NOTES*, Carnelia Music c/o A. Shroeder Int. Ltd. (ASCAP); Arranged by Barry Manilow and Eddie Arkin; Synthesizer - Randy Kerber; Guitar - Eddie Arkin

"I'll Be Seeing You" from the 1938 Musical *RIGHT THIS WAY*, Williamson Music Co. (ASCAP); Arranged by Barry Manilow and Eddie Arkin; Piano and Synthesizer - Randy Kerber; Bass - Chuck Domanico; Drums - Carlos Vega

"But The World Goes 'Round" from the 1991 Revue *AND THE WORLD GOES 'ROUND*, EMI UNART Catalogue Inc. (BMI); Orchestra Arranged and Conducted by Billy Byers; Additional Horn Arrangement by Jerry Hey

"Fugue For Tinhorns" from the 1950 Musical *GUYS AND DOLLS*, Frank Music Corp. (ASCAP); Arranged by Barry Manilow and Eddie Arkin; Horn Arrangement by Jerry Hey; Piano - Randy Kerber; Bass - John Patitucci; Drums - Carlos Vega; Trumpets - Jerry Hey and Gary Grant; Trombone - Bill Reichenbach; Saxophones - Joel Peskin and Dan Higgins

"Luck Be A Lady" from the 1950 Musical *GUYS AND DOLLS*, Frank Music Corp. (ASCAP); Orchestra Arranged and Conducted by Billy Byers

"Old Friends" from the 1982 Musical *MERRILY WE ROLL ALONG*, Revelation Music Publishing Corp., Rilting Music, Inc. (ASCAP); Arranged by Barry Manilow and Eddie Arkin; Piano - Randy Kerber

"The Kid Inside" from the 1982 Musical *IS THERE LIFE AFTER HIGH SCHOOL?*, Carnelia Music c/o A. Shroeder Int. Ltd. (ASCAP); Arranged by Barry Manilow and Eddie Arkin; Piano and Synthesizer - Randy Kerber; Bass - Abe Laboriel; Drums - Carlos Vega; Guitar - Dean Parks

"Never Met A Man I Didn't Like" from the 1991 Musical *THE WILL ROGERS FOLLIES*, Notable Music Co., Inc. (dmin. by WB Music Corp.) (ASCAP); Arranged by Barry Manilow and Eddie Arkin; Piano and Synthesizer - Randy Kerber; Bass - John Patitucci; Drums - Carlos Vega; Guitar - Dean Parks

"Bring Him Home" from the 1985 Musical *LES MISERABLES*, Alain Boublil Music Ltd. (ASCAP);

Orchestra Arranged and Conducted by Artie Butler

"If We Only Have Love" from the 1968 Musical *JACQUES BREL IS ALIVE AND WELL AND LIVING IN PARIS*, Unichappell Music Inc. (BMI); Arranged by Barry Manilow; Piano and Synthesizer - Randy Kerber; Bass - Abe Laboriel; Drums - Carlos Vega; Guitar - Dean Parks and Eddie Arkin

Album Data:
Highest Chart Position: # 68 on October 12, 1991
Billboard Chart: Billboard Top 200
Number of Weeks on Chart: 8

Notes & Trivia:
- This album was released on CD and Cassette on September 24, 1991
- A vinyl LP version was released in Germany in 1991.
- Rumba Recorders, where the album was recorded, was owned at the time by musical duo *The Captain & Tennille* (Daryl Dragon and Toni Tennille).

**Barry celebrated a birthday at Rumbo Recorders while recording the "Showstoppers" album in June 1991 and a cake was presented.
"Happy Birthday Barry" and record label reads: "Showstoppers."
Photo from author's collection.**

Singin' with the Big Bands
Arista 07822-18771-2

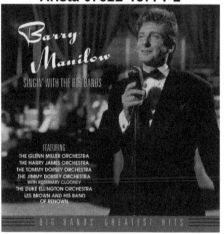

Track Listing:
Singin' With The Big Bands / Sentimental Journey / And The Angels Sing / Green Eyes / I Should Care / Don't Get Around Much Anymore / I Can't Get Started / Chattanooga Choo Choo / Moonlight Serenade / On The Sunny Side Of The Street / All Or Nothing At All / I'll Never Smile Again / I'm Gettin' Sentimental Over You / Don't Sit Under The Apple Tree / (I'll Be With You) In Apple Blossom Time / Where Does The Time Go?

Production Information:
Produced by Phil Ramone and Barry Manilow
Recorded at: Edison Studios New York City, NY / Capitol Studios, Hollywood, CA / Westlake Studios, Los Angeles, CA / Ocean Way Studios, Hollywood. CA / Sunset Sound, Los Angeles, CA
Engineers: Gary Chester / John Richards / Don Hahn / Allen Abrahamson / Bill Molina
Assistant Engineers: Yvonne Yedibalian / Peter Doell / Charlie Paakkari / Bryan Carrigan / Noel Hazen / Al Sanderson / Mike Kloster / Brian Soucy / Mike Piersante
Mixed at: Sunset Sound, Los Angeles, CA
Mixed by: Don Murray
Assistant Mix Engineer: Mike Kloster
Digitally Edited by: Larry Walsh at Capitol Studios, Hollywood, CA
Mastered by: Wally Traugott at Capitol Studios, Hollywood, CA
Photography: Timothy White
Photos shot at the legendary Rainbow Room, Rockefeller Center, New York City, NY
Art Direction: Susan Mendola
Art Coordinator: Amy Finkle
Set Design: William Rohlfing for Bill the Set Builder
Stylist: Wayne Scot Lukas
Grooming: Joe J. Simon for OZ, NY
Project Coordination in New York: Jill Dell'Abate for Dell'Abate Productions / In Los Angeles: Susanne Marie Edgren and Chie Masumoto for Humble Heart Music / Marc Hulett and Roland Baker for Stiletto Entertainment
Assistant to Barry Manilow: Marc Hulett
Special Thanks to: Clive Davis / Garry Kief / Steve Wax / Marc Hulett / Don Ovens / Melanie Baldwin / Roland Baker / Roy Lott / Dick Wingate / Milton Sincoff / Jim Urie / Ken Levy / Tom Ennis / Phil Wild / Bruce Schoen / Mark Rizzo / Russell Sicklick / Susan Mendola / Allen Grubman / Paul Schindler / Joe Brenner
Artist Management: Garry Kief / Steve Wax / Edna Collison for Stiletto Entertainment, Los Angeles, CA

Musicians:
Kirk Bonin / Richard (Dickie) Harris / Nicholas Manville / Robert Wieger / John Schenk / Brad Ross / Bill Wilson / Cord Himelstein / Christopher Stern

Publishers / Other Information:
"Singin' With The Big Bands" (1994) Written by Barry Manilow and Bruce Sussman; Careers-BMG Music Publishing, Inc., Appoggiatura Music (BMI); Arranged and Conducted by Artie Butler

"Sentimental Journey" (1944) Featuring Les Brown and his Band of Renown; Morley Music Co. (ASCAP); Conducted by Les Brown; Based on the original Les Brown arrangement; Re-arranged by Jay Hill

"And The Angels Sing" (1939) Originally recorded by The Benny Goodman Orchestra; WB Music Corp. (ASCAP); Based on the original Benny Goodman arrangement; Re-arranged and Conducted by Dick Hyman; Trumpet solo - Warren Leuning

"Green Eyes" (1941) Featuring The Jimmy Dorsey Orchestra with Rosemary Clooney; Peer International Corp. (BMI); Leader - Jim Miller, Based on the original Jimmy Dorsey arrangement; Re-arranged and Conducted by Mike Melvoin

"I Should Care" (1945) Originally recorded by The Jimmy Dorsey Orchestra; Cahn Music Company, admin. by WB Music Corp., Hanover Music Corp. & Stordahll Music Publishing Co. (ASCAP); Arranged and Conducted by Mike Melvoin

"Don't Get Around Much Anymore" (1940) Featuring The Duke Ellington Orchestra; EMI Robbins Catalogue Inc., Marrison Music Corp. (ASCAP); Leader - Mercer Ellington; Based on the original Duke Ellington arrangement; Re-arranged and Conducted by Mike Melvoin; Alto saxophone solo - Charlie Young

"I Can't Get Started" (1938) Originally recorded by The Bunny Berigan Orchestra; Chappell & Co., Ira Gershwin Music, admin. by WB Music Corp. (ASCAP); Based on the original Bunny Berigan arrangement; Re-arranged and Conducted by Dick Hyman; Trumpet solo - Warren Luening

"Chattanooga Choo Choo" (1941) Featuring The Glenn Miller Orchestra; EMI Feist Catalogue Inc. (ASCAP); Leader - Larry O'Brien; Vocal arrangement by Debra Byrd; Background vocals by Debra Byrd, Kevin DiSimone, Margaret Dorn and James Jolis

"Moonlight Serenade" (1939) Originally recorded by The Glenn Miller Orchestra; EMI Robbins Catalogue Inc. (ASCAP); Arranged and Conducted by Artie Butler

"On The Sunny Side Of The Street" (1945) Featuring The Tommy Dorsey Orchestra; Aldi Music, Ireneadele Publishing Co. (ASCAP); Leader - Buddy Morrow; Original arrangement by Sy Oliver; Background vocals by Jon Joyce, Don Shelton, Donna Davidson and Susan Boyd

"All Or Nothing At All" (1939) Featuring The Harry James Orchestra; MCA Music Publishing, a Division of MCA Inc., MPL Communications Inc. (ASCAP); Leader - Art DePew; Based on the original Harry James arrangement; Re-arranged and Conducted by Artie Butler

"I'll Never Smile Again" (1940) Featuring The Tommy Dorsey Orchestra; MCA Music Publishing, a Division of MCA Inc. (ASCAP); Leader - Buddy Morrow; Based on the original Tommy Dorsey arrangement; Re-arranged and Conducted by Artie Butler; Trombone solo - Buddy Morrow

"I'm Gettin' Sentimental Over You (1936) Originally recorded by The Tommy Dorsey Orchestra; Mills Music, Inc. (ASCAP); Arranged and Conducted by Artie Butler; Trombone solo - Bill Watrous

"Don't Sit Under The Apple Tree (1942) Featuring The Glenn Miller Orchestra with Debra Byrd; EMI Robbins Catalogue Inc., Ched Music Corp. (ASCAP); Leader - Larry O'Brien; Vocal arrangement by Debra Byrd; Background vocals by Debra Byrd, Kevin DiSimone, Margaret Dorn and James Jolis

"(I'll Be With You) In Apple Blossom Time" (1941) Originally Recorded by The Andrews Sisters; Jerry Vogel Music Co., Inc., Broadway Music Corp. (ASCAP); Arranged and Conducted by Artie Butler; Vocal arrangement by Jon Joyce; Background vocals by Jon Joyce, Don Shelton, Donna Davidson and Susan Boyd

"Where Does The Time Go?" (1994) Written by Barry Manilow and Bruce Sussman; Careers-BMG Music Publishing, Inc., Appoggiatura Music (BMI); Arranged and Conducted by Artie Butler

Album Data:
Highest Chart Position: # 59 on December 31, 1994
Billboard Chart: Billboard Top 200
Number of Weeks on Chart: 21

Notes & Trivia:
- This album was released on CD and Cassette on October 11, 1994.
- This album was certified Gold on December 13, 1994.

4 track promotional EP CD of the album

Summer of '78
Arista 07822-18809-2

Track Listing:
Summer Of '78 / Interlude: Love's Theme / Reminiscing / I Go Crazy / When I Need You / The Air That I Breathe / Bluer Than Blue / We've Got Tonight / I'd Really Love To See You Tonight / Sometimes When We Touch / Never My Love / Just Remember I Love You

Production Information:
Produced by: Michael Omartian and Barry Manilow
Recorded at: Starstruck Studios, Nashville, TN / The SoundShop, Nashville, TN / The Sound Kitchen, Nashville, TN
Engineered by: Terry Christian
Assistant Engineers: Scott Ahaus / Mark Capps / John Dickson / Greg Parker / John Thomas II / David Benson
Mixed at: The Sound Kitchen, Nashville, TN
Mixed by: Terry Christian
Assistant Mix Engineer: John Thomas II
Mastered at: Georgetown Masters, Nashville, TN using the HDCD process
Mastered by: Denny Purcell
Cover Photography: Firooz Zahedi
Back Cover Photography - Albert Sanchez
Art Direction: Sheri G. Lee
Styling: Phillip Bloch
Grooming: Eric Barnard
Artist Management: Garry Kief, Steve Wax (Stiletto Entertainment)
Assistant to Barry Manilow: Marc Hulett
Production Coordination: Suzy Martinez in Nashville, TN / Marc Hulett in Los Angeles, CA

Musicians:
Electric Guitar: Jerry McPherson
Acoustic Guitar: Biff Watson
Keyboards and Synthesizers: Barry Manilow / Michael Omartian / Tim Akers / Blair Masters
Piano / Electric Piano / Synth Bass: Michael Omartian
Bass: Jimmie Lee Sloas / Tom Hemby / Mike Brignardello
Guitar: Tom Hemby / Mike Brignardello
Drums: John Hammond / Paul Leim
Percussion: Eric Darken
Electric Guitar: Dann Huff

Background Vocals: Bonnie Keen / Marty McCall / Michael Mellett / Chris Rodriguez

Singles Released From This Album:
"Bluer than Blue" (ASCD–3275) Released as a promotional CD single-only
"I'd Really Love To See You Tonight" (Up-Tempo Mix) / "Could It Be Magic" (Dance Mix)
(07822–13378-2 - CD single) (07822–13378-4 - Cassette single) (Peaked at # 26 in the US on the Billboard Adult Contemporary Chart)
"I Go Crazy" (Album Version) / "I Go Crazy" (Radio Mix) (ASCD–3408) Released as a promotional CD single-only (Peaked at # 30 in the US on the Billboard Adult Contemporary Chart / # 13 on the R&R AC Chart)
Sometimes When We Touch (Radio Mix) / Sometimes When We Touch (Album Version) (ASCD–3426)
Released as a promotional CD single-only

Album Data:
Highest Chart Position: # 82 on December 28, 1996
Billboard Chart: Billboard Top 200
Number of Weeks on Chart: 11

Notes & Trivia:
- This album was released on CD and Cassette on November 19, 1996.
- The album was certified Gold for sales in excess of 500,000 copies.
- An inflatable beach ball was used as a marketing tool.

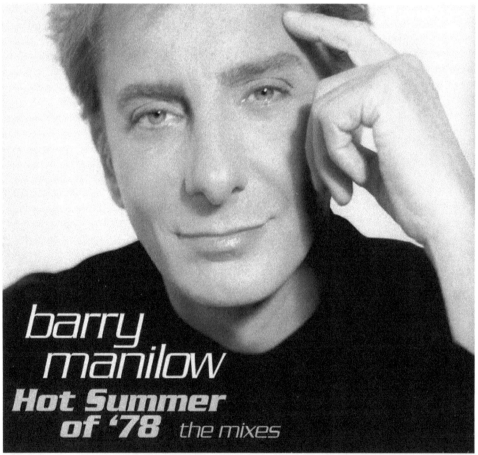

4 track EP UK CD. Contains: I'd Really Love To See You Tonight (Up-Tempo Radio Mix) / I Go Crazy (Radio Mix) / Sometimes When We Touch (Radio Mix) / Copacabana (The 1993 Remix 7")

Manilow Sings Sinatra
Arista 07822-19033-2

Track Listing:
One Man In A Spotlight / I've Got The World On A String / The Second Time Around / Come Dance With Me / Come Fly With Me / All The Way / You Make Me Feel So Young / Strangers In The Night / In The Wee Small Hours Of The Morning / Summer Wind / Saturday Night (Is The Loneliest Night In The Week) / Angel Eyes / My Kind Of Town / Put Your Dreams Away / Here's To The Man

Production Information:
Produced by: Phil Ramone and Barry Manilow
Recorded at: Capitol Studios, Hollywood, CA
Overdubbing completed at: Sublime Music, West Hollywood, CA
Engineered by: Don Murray
Assistant Engineers: Charlie Paakkari / Peter Doell / Stephen Genswick / Eric Cowden
Mixed by: Don Murray / Al Schmitt
Contractors: Jules Chaikin / Frank Capp / Joe Soldo

Musicians:
Piano: Michael Melvin / Pete Jolly / Thomas Rainer
Additional Keyboards & Rhythm Sequencing: Doug Besterman / PierGiorgio Bertucelli / Michael Skloff
Bass: Charles Domanico / Ray Brown / Charles Berghofer / John Pens
Drums: Jeffrey Hamilton / Albie Berk / Gregg Field
Guitar: John Chiodini / Dennis Budimir / John Pisano / Jim Fox / Paul Viapiano
Electric Guitar: James Harrah
Violin: Patricia Aiken / Tamsen Beseke / Eva Butler / Andrea Byers / Russ Cantor / Mark Cargill / Ron Clark / Darius Campo / Joel Derouin / Yvette Devereaux / Maurice Dicterow / Assa Drori / Alan Ellsworth / Kirsten Fife / Ron Folsom / Galina Golovin / Rhonni Hallman / Clinton Haslop / Gwenn Heller / Patricia Johnson / Karen Jones / Igor Kiskatchi / Ezra Kliger / Sarah Knutson / Miran Kojian / Brian Leonard / Dennis Molchan / Ralph Morrison / Jennifer Munday / Yi-Tsui Olivia / Don Palmer / Linda Rose / Anatoly Rosinsky / Rebecca Rutkowski / Robert Sanov / Marc Sazer / Kwihee Shamban / Haim Shtrum / James Stark / David Stenske / Jacqueline Suzuki / Kimiyo Takeya / Mari Tsumura / Elizabeth Wilson / North Wood / Shari Zippert
Viola: Margot Aldcroft / Marilyn Baker / Denyse Buffum / Rollice Dale / Brian Dembow / Jerry Epstein / Suzanna Giordano / Pam Goldsmith / Miriam Granat / Keith Green / Renita Koven / Peter Hatch / Carole Mukogawa / Andrew Picken / James Ross / Jodi Rubin / John Scanion / Julia Staudhammer / Evan Wilson
Cello: Robert Adcock / Jodi Burnett / Antony Cooke / Larry Corbett / Ernie Ehrhardt / Christine Ermacoff / Stefanie Fife / Rowena Hammill / Anne Karam / Suzie Katayama / Raymond Kelley / Earl Madison / Daniel Rothmuller / David Shamban / David Speltz / Nancy Stein-Ross / Sebastian

Toettcher
Bass: Timothy Barr / John Clayton / Constance Deeter / Stephens LaFever / Frances Liu-Wu / Norman Ludwin / John Pena / David Young
Harp: Gayle Levant / Julie Berghofer
Reeds: Lee Callet / Jeffrey Clayton / Pete Chrislieb / Gene Cipriano / Louise Di Tullio / Bob Efford / Terry Harrington / Daniel Higgins / Greg Huckins / Samuel Karam / Stephen Kujala / Sal Lozano / Lanny Morgan / Jack Nimitz / Donald Shelton / Gary Woodward
Trumpet: Frank Baptist / Wayne Bergeron / Conte Candoli / George Graham / Larry Hall / Stephen Huffsteter / Warren Leuning / Larry McGuire / Carl Saunders / Frank Szabo
Trombone: William Elton / Alan Kaplan / Charles Loper / Andrew Martin / Robert McChesney / Richard Nash / Phillip Teele / Donald Waldrop / Chauncey Welsch
French Horn: James Atkinson / Nathan Campbell / Marilyn Johnson / Daniel Kelley / Bradley Kintscher / Paul Klintworth / John Lorge / John Mason / Paul Stevens / Richard Todd / Brad Warnaar / Gregory Williams
Percussion: Larry Bunker / Daniel Greco
Synthesizers: Michael Lang
Concert Master: Assa Drori / Clinton Haslop / Ralph Morrison /
Vocal Arrangements by Barry Manilow

Singles From This Album:
"Strangers in the Night"

Album Data:
Highest Chart Position: # 122 on December 12, 1998
Billboard Chart: Billboard Top 200
Number of Weeks on Chart: 7

Notes & Trivia:
- This album was released on CD and Cassette on November 10, 1998.
- Barry was nominated for a Grammy for Best Traditional Pop Vocal Performance in 2000.
- The album features two new compositions, written by Barry Manilow and Bruce Sussman intended as tributes to Sinatra who had died on May 14, 1998. They are used as bookends on the album.

Strangers in the Night CD Single
ASCD-3589

Here At The Mayflower
(Concord) CCD-2102-2

Track Listing:
US Release:
Do You Know Who's Livin' Next Door? / Come Monday / Border Train / Turn The Radio Up / I Hear Her Playing Music / Talk To Me / Not What You See / Freddie Said / Some Bar By The Harbor / Say Goodbye+ / She Should'a Been Mine / The Night That Tito Played+ / I'm Comin' Back / I Miss You / They Dance! / Welcome Home

Special K-Mart Only Release:
Elevator Operator: Do You Know Who's Livin' Next Door? / Apartments 3B and 5N: Come Monday / Apartment 3E: Border Train / Apartment 2H: Turn The Radio Up / Apartment 2G: I Hear Her Playing Music / Apartment 4J: Talk To Me / Apartment 6C: Not What You See / Elevator Operator: Freddie Said / Apartment 1A: Some Bar By The Harbor / Apartment 2H: Say Goodbye / Elevator Operator: She Should'a Been Mine / Apartment 4G: The Night That Tito Played / Apartment 5F: I'm Comin' Back / Apartment 6C: I Miss You / Elevator Operator: They Dance! / Apartment 3E: Welcome Home / Apartment 1A: Shadow Man

Japanese Release:
Elevator Operator: Do You Know Who's Livin' Next Door? / Apartments 3B and 5N: Come Monday - 3:56 / Apartment 3E: Border Train / Apartment 2H: Turn The Radio Up / Apartment 2G: I Hear Her Playing Music / Apartment 4J: Talk To Me / Apartment 6C: Not What You See / Elevator Operator: Freddie Said / Apartment 1A: Some Bar By The Harbor / Apartment 2H: Say Goodbye / Elevator Operator: She Should'a Been Mine / Apartment 4G: The Night That Tito Played / Apartment 5F: I'm Comin' Back / Apartment 6C: I Miss You / Elevator Operator: They Dance! / Apartment 3E: Welcome Home / Apartment 5F: I Don't Wanna Know / Apartment 1A: Shadow Man

*UK Release:
Elevator Operator: Do You Know Who's Livin' Next Door? / Apartments 3B and 5N: Come Monday / Apartment 3E: Border Train / Apartment 2H: Turn The Radio Up / Apartment 2G: I Hear Her Playing Music / Apartment 4J: Talk To Me / Apartment 6C: Not What You See / Elevator Operator: Freddie Said / Apartment 1A: Some Bar By The Harbor / Apartment 2H: Say Goodbye / Elevator Operator: She Should'a Been Mine / Apartment 4G: The Night That Tito Played / Apartment 5F: I'm Comin' Back / Apartment 6C: I Miss You / Elevator Operator: They Dance! / Apartment 3E: Welcome Home / Elevator Operator: Life Has Its Ups and Downs / Apartment 5F: I Don't Wanna Know

*American Idol vocal coach Debra Byrd, Barry's longtime backup singer, makes an uncredited appearance on "Say Goodbye" and "I Don't Wanna Know" on this release only. Also only on this release, "She Should'a Been Mine" and "The Night That Tito Played" features dialogue by Barry.

Exclusive 2002 Tour Bonus Disc: Apartment 5F: "I Don't Wanna Know" / Elevator Operator: "The Walking Wounded" (Barry Manilow/Enoch Anderson) / Elevator Operator: "They Dance! (Extended Version)"

Production Information:
Produced, Composed and Arranged by: Barry Manilow
Co-Produced and Programming by: David Benson
Executive Producer: Garry Kief
Recorded at: Peppertree Studios, Palm Springs, CA / Ignited Now Studios / Woodland Hills, CA / O'Henry Sound Studios, Hollywood, CA
Recording Engineer and Pro Tools Editing: Greg Bartheld
Assistant Engineers: Bryan Cook / Brian Donovan / Andy Ackland / Bruce Sugar
Mixed at: Henson Recording Studios, Hollywood, CA
Mix Engineer: Andrew Scheps (except "I'm Comin' Back" - Greg Bartheld)
Mastered at: Bernie Grundman Mastering, Hollywood, CA
Additional Programming by Jez Colin and Greg Bartheld
Assistant to Barry Manilow and invaluable musical ears: Marc Hulett
Publishing Administrator: Kirsten Kief
Musician Contractor: Jolie Levine
Photography: Elliott Marks
Additional Photography: Lisa Stein / Judah S. Harris (Yankee Image)
Package Design: Dennis Purcell Design
Art Direction: Dennis Purcell / Abbey Anna
Production Manager: Valerie Whitesell
Stylist: Eric Barnard
Location Assistance: Brian Lovell / Daliah Rogow-Nichols / Cara Coslow / Elizabeth Druyun / Dale Lohrer

Musicians:
Trumpet: Gary Grant, Jerry Hey
Trombone: Andrew Martin
Reeds: Bill Liston, Larry Williams
Violin: Joel Derouin (Concertmaster), Clayton Haslop, Brian Leonard, Michele Reynolds
Viola: Carole Mukogawa, John Hayhurst
Cello: Larry Corbett, Suzie Katayama

Elevator Operator: "Do You Know Who's Livin' Next Door?"
(Music by Barry Manilow/Lyrics by Enoch Anderson)
©2001 Obbligato Music / Catapult Music (BMI)
Lead and Background Vocals: Barry Manilow
All Instruments: Barry Manilow except:
Tenor Sax: Dave Koz
Additional Guitar: Ken Berry
Additional Drums: Vinnie Colaiuta

Apartments 3B and 5N: "Come Monday"
(Music and Lyrics by Barry Manilow)
©2001 Obbligato Music (BMI)

Lead and Background Vocals: Barry Manilow
All Instruments: Barry Manilow except:
Additional Guitar: Ken Berry
Orchestration: Barry Manilow and Steve Welch

Apartment 3E: "Border Train"
(Music by Barry Manilow/Lyrics by Enoch Anderson)
©2001 Obbligato Music / Catapult Music (BMI)
Lead and Background Vocals: Barry Manilow
All Instruments: Barry Manilow except:
Additional Guitar: Ken Berry

Apartment 2H: "Turn The Radio Up"
(Music and Lyrics by Barry Manilow)
©2001 Obbligato Music (BMI)
Lead Vocal: Barry Manilow
All Instruments: Barry Manilow except:
Additional Guitar: Ken Berry
Background Vocals: Ron Dante / Barry Manilow

Apartment 2G: "I Hear Her Playing Music"
(Music by Barry Manilow/Lyrics by Enoch Anderson)
©2001 Obbligato Music / Catapult Music (BMI)
Lead Vocal: Barry Manilow
All Instruments: Barry Manilow except:
Alto Sax: Dave Koz
Additional Guitar: Ken Berry
Additional Drums: Vinnie Colaiuta
Orchestration: Barry Manilow and Steve Welch

Apartment 4J: "Talk To Me"
(Music by Barry Manilow / Lyrics by Marty Panzer)
©2001 Obbligato Music / SwaneeBRAVO! Music (BMI)
Lead and Background Vocals: Barry Manilow
All Instruments: Barry Manilow except:
Additional Guitar: Ken Berry
Additional Drums: Vinnie Colaiuta
Orchestration: Barry Manilow and Doug Walter

Apartment 6C: "Not What You See"
(Music and Lyrics by Barry Manilow)
©2001 Obbligato Music (BMI)
Lead Vocal: Barry Manilow
All Instruments: Barry Manilow except:
Orchestration: Barry Manilow and Doug Walter

Elevator Operator: "Freddie Said"
(Music and Lyrics by Barry Manilow)
©2001 Obbligato Music (BMI)
Lead and Background Vocals: Barry Manilow
All Instruments: Barry Manilow except:

Additional Guitar: Ken Berry
Additional Drums: Vinnie Colaiuta
Orchestration: Barry Manilow and Steve Welch

Apartment 1A: "Some Bar By The Harbor"
(Music by Barry Manilow/Lyrics by Enoch Anderson)
©2001 Obbligato Music / Catapult Music (BMI)
Lead Vocal: Barry Manilow
All Instruments: Barry Manilow except:
Additional Guitar: Ken Berry
Additional Drums: Vinnie Colaiuta
Orchestration: Barry Manilow and Doug Walter

Apartment 2H: "Say Goodbye"
(Music and Lyrics by Barry Manilow)
©2001 Obbligato Music (BMI)
Lead and Background Vocals: Barry Manilow
All Instruments: Barry Manilow except:
Additional Guitar: Ken Berry
Orchestration: Barry Manilow and Steve Welch

Elevator Operator: "She Should'a Been Mine"
(Music by Barry Manilow/Lyrics by Barry Manilow and Bruce Sussman)
©2001 Obbligato Music / Appoggiatura Music (BMI)
Lead Vocal: Barry Manilow
All Instruments: Barry Manilow except:
Additional Guitar: Ken Berry
Orchestration: Barry Manilow and Doug Walter

Apartment 4G: "The Night That Tito Played"
(Music by Barry Manilow/Lyrics by Adrienne Anderson)
©2001 Obbligato Music / VEGAvox Music (BMI)
Lead and Background Vocals: Barry Manilow
All Instruments: Barry Manilow except:
Additional Guitar: Ken Berry
Additional Percussion and Synthesizers: Kenny O'Brien
Orchestration: Barry Manilow and Doug Walter

Apartment 5F: "I'm Comin' Back"
(Music and Lyrics by Barry Manilow)
©2001 Obbligato Music (BMI)
Lead Vocal: Barry Manilow
All Instruments: Barry Manilow except:
Additional Guitar: Ken Berry

Apartment 6C: "I Miss You"
(Music by Barry Manilow/Lyrics by Marty Panzer)
©2001 Obbligato Music / SwaneeBRAVO! Music (BMI)
Lead Vocal: Barry Manilow
All Instruments: Barry Manilow except:
Additional Guitar: Ken Berry

Elevator Operator: "They Dance!"
(Music and Lyrics by Barry Manilow)
©2001 Obbligato Music (BMI)
Lead Vocal: Barry Manilow
All Instruments: Barry Manilow except...
Additional Guitar: Ken Berry
Background Vocals: Barry Manilow, Yvonne Williams, Clydene Jackson, Ron Dante
Orchestration: Barry Manilow and Steve Welch

Apartment 3E: "Welcome Home"
(Music by Barry Manilow and Eddie Arkin/Lyrics by Barry Manilow and Mindy Sterling)
©2001 Obbligato Music / Mama's Girl Music / Somisongs (BMI)
Lead Vocal: Barry Manilow
All Instruments: Barry Manilow except:
Additional Guitar: Ken Berry
Background Vocals: Barry Manilow / Yvonne Williams / Clydene Jackson / Ron Dante
Tenor Sax: Dave Koz

*Apartment 1A: "Shadow Man"
(Music by Barry Manilow/Lyrics by Bruce Sussman and Jack Feldman)
©2001 Obbligato Music / Appoggiatura Music / Camp Songs Music (BMI)
Lead and Background Vocals: Barry Manilow
All Instruments: Barry Manilow except:
Additional Guitar: Ken Berry
Additional Drums: Vinnie Colaiuta

/*Apartment 5F: "I Don't Wanna Know"
(Music and Lyrics by Barry Manilow)
©2001 Obbligato Music (BMI)
Lead and Background Vocals: Barry Manilow
All Instruments: Barry Manilow except:
Additional Guitar: Ken Berry
Orchestration: Barry Manilow and Steve Welch

**Elevator Operator: "The Walking Wounded"
(Music by Barry Manilow/Lyrics by Enoch Anderson)
©2001 Obbligato Music / Catapult Music (BMI)
Lead and Background Vocals: Barry Manilow
All Instruments: Barry Manilow except:
Additional Guitar: Ken Berry
Orchestration: Barry Manilow and Doug Walter

**Elevator Operator: "They Dance! (Extended Version)"
(Music and Lyrics by Barry Manilow)
©2001 Obbligato Music (BMI)
Lead and Background Vocals: Barry Manilow
All Instruments: Barry Manilow except:
Additional Guitar: Ken Berry
Ballroom Piano: John Berkmam
Additional Background Vocals: Barry Manilow / Ron Dante / Yvonne Williams / Clydene Jackson
Orchestration: Barry Manilow and Steve Welch

***Elevator Operator: "Life Has Its Ups And Downs"
(Music and Lyrics by Barry Manilow)
Lead and Background Vocals: Barry Manilow
All Instruments: Barry Manilow except:
Additional Guitar: Ken Berry
Orchestration: Barry Manilow and Steve Welch

Singles Released From This Album:
"Turn The Radio Up" / "They Dance!" (Concord PRO–CJ–0009 / PRO-CJ-0015) (Peaked at # 25 in the US on the Billboard Adult Contemporary Chart on February 9, 2002)

Album Dats:
Highest Chart Position: # 90 on December 1, 2001
Billboard Chart: Billboard Top 200
Number of Weeks on Chart: 3

Notes & Trivia:
- This album was released on CD on November 11, 2001
- UK version was released on Columbia Records on CD on May 13, 2002
- The US and UK versions had different cover art
- *Here At The Mayflower-Limited Edition (2001) (Concord Records CCD-2109-2) includes bonus track: "Shadow Man"
- **Here At The Mayflower-Exclusive 2002 Tour Bonus Disc (2001) (Concord Records CCD-2148-2), includes tracks: "I Don't Wanna Know" / "The Walking Wounded" / "They Dance! (Extended Version)"
- ***Here At The Mayflower-UK Version (2002) (Sony/Columbia/Citrus 507734 2) includes bonus tracks: "Life Has Its Ups And Downs" / "I Don't Wanna Know"
- +Here At The Mayflower-UK Version includes alternate versions of tracks: "Say Goodbye" / "The Night That Tito Played" / "I Don't Wanna Know"
- The Japanese release includes two bonus tracks: "I Don't Wanna Know" / "Shadow Man"

The UK album cover art

A Christmas Gift Of Love
CK 86976

Track Listing:
Winter Wonderland / Happy Holiday / White Christmas / Santa Claus Is Coming To Town / (There's No Place Like) Home For The Holidays / I'll Be Home For Christmas / My Favorite Things / The Christmas Waltz / I've Got My Love To Keep Me Warm / River / What Are You Doing New Year's Eve? / A Gift Of Love

Production Information:
Produced by Robbie Buchanan and Barry Manilow
Executive Producers: Garry C. Kief and Jay Landers
Recorded at: Capitol Studios, Hollywood, CA / The Hop, Studio City, CA
Engineered by: Bill Schnee / Scott Erickson
Assistant Engineers: Charlie Paakkari / Steve Genewick / Toby Foster
Studio Assistants: Wil Donovan / Bruce Monical / James Go forth / Jay Anista
Mixed by Bill Schnee at Schnee Studios, North Hollywood, CA
Assistant Mix Engineer: Ryan Petrie
Mastered by Doug Sax and Robert Hadley at: The Mastering Lab, Hollywood, CA
Project Coordinator: Scott Erickson
Photography: Jeff Katz
Art Direction: Hooshik
Management: Garry C. Kief, Stiletto Entertainment
Assistant to Barry Manilow: Marc Hulett
Song layouts conceived by: Barry Manilow

Musicians:
Piano: Michael Lang
Keyboards: Robbie Buchanan
Bass: Chuck Berghofer
Drums: Gregg Field
Guitar: John Pisano / Dean Parks / Ken Berry / Mike Thompson
Concert Master: Bruce Dukov
Orchestra Contractor: David Low
Music Copyist: Terry Woodson Music

Singles Released From This Album:
"River" (Peaked at # 17 in the US on the Billboard Adult Contemporary Chart on January 4, 2003)

Album Data:
Highest Chart Position: # 55 on December 21, 2002
Billboard Chart: Billboard Top 200
Number of Weeks on Chart: 7

Notes & Trivia:
- This album was released on CD and multi-channel CD on November 12, 2002.
- This album was certified Gold on December 13, 2002.
- A cassette tape version was released in Indonesia by Sony Music Indonesia.
- Recording sessions for the album took place in April, August and September 2002

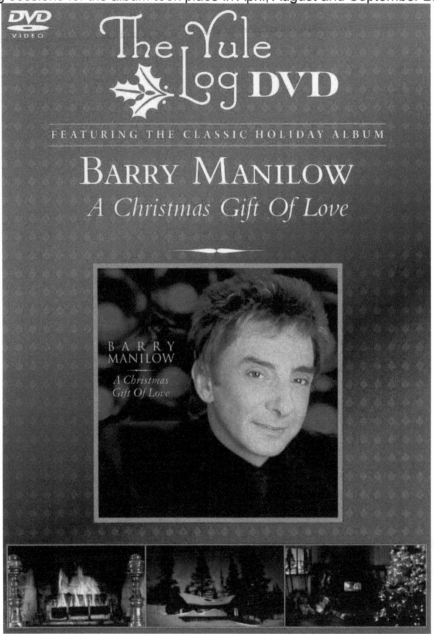

Nothing better than a warm fire and Barry Manilow's 2002 Christmas album:
"A Christmas Gift Of Love." 2010 DVD release.
Three scenes to choose from: Yule Log / Snowy Cabin / Cozy Christmas Cottage

Manilow Scores - Songs from Copacabana and Harmony
CCD-2251-2

Track Listing:
Copacabana:
Just Arrived / Dancin' Fool / Who Needs To Dream? / Sweet Heaven (I'm In Love Again) / Bolero de Amor / This Can't Be Real (duet with Olivia Newton-John) / Copacabana (At The Copa) 2005 Dance Mix
Harmony:
Harmony / And What Do You See? / Every Single Day / This Is Our Time! / Where You Go / In This World / Stars In The Night

Production Information:
Produced by: Phil Ramone and Barry Manilow
Associate Producer: David Benson
Executive Producers: Garry C. Kief and Rob Kief
Recorded at: Henson Studios, Los Angeles, CA / O'Henry Studios, Burbank, CA / Peppertree Studios, Palm Springs, CA / Sunset Studios, Los Angeles, CA
Engineered by: Dave Reitzas
Assistant Engineers: Nick Marshall / Mark Valentine
Mixed at: O'Henry Studios, Burbank, CA
Mixed by: Dave Reitzas
Assistant Mix Engineers: Nick Marshall / Scott Moore
Mastered by: Ted Jensen at Sterling Sound, NYC
Production Manager: Jill Dell'Abate
Digital Audio and Sequencing: David Benson / Greg Bartheld / Gino Finley / Steve Deutsch
Music Preparation by: Terry Woodson Music
Photography: Jeff Katz
Art Direction: Sara Zickuhr, John Adams (Stiletto Entertainment)
Production Supervisors: Abbey Anna, Kurt Sievert (Concord Records)
Personal Management: Garry C. Kief (Stiletto Enteatainment)
Publishing Administrator: Kirsten Kief (Stiletto Entertainment)
Assistant to Barry Manilow: Marc Hulett

Musicians:
Piano: Steve Welch / Ron Walters / Ron Pedley / Andy Rumble / Barry Manilow
Drums: Russ McKinnon

Synthesizers: Ron Pedley
Guitar: Mike Lent
Acoustic Bass: Chuck Berghofer
Violins: Assa Drori (Concert Master) / Bruce Dukov (Concert Master) / Charlie Bisharat / Rebecca Bunnell / Eve Butler / Darius Campo / Kevin Connolly / Joel DeRouin / Lisa Dondlinger / Ron Folsom / Berj Garabedian / Peter Kent / Raymond Kobler / Johana Krejci / Jennifer Munday / Katia Popov / Jim Stark / Haim Strum / Yan To / Olivia Tsui Irina Voloshina / Dynell Weber / Sherrie Zippert
Violas: Brett Baldacci / Bob Becker / Caroline Buckman / Kenneth Burward-Hoy / Miguel Ferguson / Vickie Miskolszy / Kazie Pitelka / Harry Shirinian
Celli: Trevor Handy / John Krovoza / Armen Ksajikian / Tim Landauer / Tina Soule / David Speltz / Cecelia Tsan
Harp: Julie Berghofer / Gayle Levant
Woodwinds: Lee Callet / Bob Carr / Gene Cipriano / Jeff Driskill / Phil Feather / Dan Higgins / Greg Huckins
Trumpets: Rick Baptist / Wayne Bergeron / Warren Luening / Larry McGuire / Frank Szabo
Trombones: Bryant Byers / Craig Gosnell / Alan Kaplan / Bob Machesney / Charlie Moriallas / Chauncey Welsch
French Horns: Dan Kelley / Paul Klintworth / John Reynolds / Trish Skye
Percussion: Mark Converse / Dan Greco
Orchestra Contractor: Joe Soldo

COPACABANA
Music by Barry Manilow
Lyrics by Bruce Sussman and Jack Feldman
Book by Jack Feldman, Bruce Sussman and Barry Manilow

"Just Arrived"
Arranged by Larry Hochman with Barry Manilow
All vocals by Barry Manilow

"Dancin' Fool"
Arranged by Andy Rumble with Barry Manilow
All vocals by Barry Manilow

"Who Needs To Dream?"
Music by Barry Manilow and Artie Butler
Arranged by Artie Butler
Originally recorded by Anthony D'Amico
Mixed by Joel Moss
Recording from the 1985 CBS Television Movie "Copacabana"
Published by Careers-BMG Music Publishing Inc./Appoggiatura Music/Camp Songs Music BMI/Artie Butler Music ASCAP

"Sweet Heaven (I'm In Love Again)"
Arranged by Artie Butler
Originally recorded by Joel Moss

"Bolero de Amor"
Arranged by Larry Hochman with Barry Manilow

"This Can't Be Real" (duet with Olivia Newton-John)

Arranged by Andy Rumble with Barry Manilow
Additional String Arrangement by J.B. Griffiths
Drums and percussion by Dave Reitzas

"Copacabana (At The Copa) (2005 Dance mix)"
Produced and arranged by david benson and Jez Colin
Original arrangement by Artie Butler
Background vocals by Lauren Evans / Barry Manilow
Copacabana Score published by Careers-BMG Music Publishing Inc./Appoggiatura Music/Camp
Songs Music BMI

HARMONY
Music by Barry Manilow
Book and Lyrics by Bruce Sussman

"Harmony"
Arranged by Don Sebesky
All vocals by Barry Manilow

"And What Do You See?"
Arranged by Don Sebesky

"Every Single Day"
Arranged by Artie Butler

"This Is Our Time!"
Arranged by Doug Walter with Barry Manilow

"Where You Go"
Arranged by Artie Butler

"In This World"
Arranged by Don Sebesky
All vocals by Barry Manilow

"Stars In The Night"
Arranged by Jonathan Tunick
Harmony Score published by Obbligato Music/Appoggiatura Music BMI

Singles Released From This Album:
"Copacabana (At The Copa)" 2005 Dance Mix (PRO–CJ–0073–1) (Peaked at # 7 in the US on the
Billboard Hot Dance Music / Club Play) (This was issued on CD-R and two 12" vinyl records)
Sweet Heaven (I'm in Love Again) (Radio promo only release)

Album Data:
Highest Chart Position: # 47 on October 16. 2004
Billboard Chart: Billboard Top 200
Number of Weeks on Chart: 8

Notes & Trivia:
- This album was released on CD on September 28, 2004.

- Olivia Newton-John appears courtesy of ONJ Productions
- Long involved as a songwriter for musical theater, "SCORES" finally gives the superstar singer-songwriter the chance to record his personal renditions of songs he has written for two of his major musical properties, *Harmony* and *Copacabana*.
- HARMONY, is based on the true story of Germany's "Comedian Harmonists." Recognized as the world's first superstar boy band, The Comedian Harmonists enjoyed worldwide album and movie success before being forced to disband by the Nazi regime. Based on a book by Bruce Sussman, the songs for HARMONY were co-written by Barry and Bruce Sussman.
- After phenomenal reviews during its regional production at the prestigious La Jolla Playhouse, HARMONY is scheduled to open on Broadway during the next season.
- COPACABANA, which Barry co-wrote along with Bruce Sussman and Jack Feldman started as a worldwide number one hit song in 1978 before morphing into an original musical movie made for CBS television in 1985 and then ultimately a musical for the stage. COPACABANA enjoyed a successful 14 month run on London's West End before an 18 month tour of the UK. Since then, there have been more than 100 productions of COPACABANA: The Musical on stage throughout the United States, the Netherlands, Canada, Europe, and India.
- Includes seven songs from each of the productions, "SCORES" is co-produced by Barry and legendary, multi-Grammy award winner Phil Ramone.

The 2005 double vinyl set of "Copacabana" Remixes / PRO-CJ-0073-1

64

The Greatest Songs of the Fifties
82876-74509-2

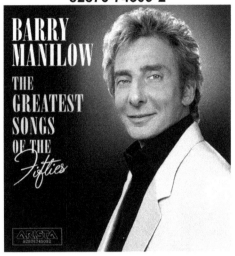

Track Listing:
US Release:
Moments to Remember / It's All in the Game / Unchained Melody / Venus / It's Not for Me to Say / Love Is a Many Splendored Thing / Rags to Riches / Sincerely - Teach Me Tonight (Medley) (duet with Phyllis McGuire) / Are You Lonesome Tonight? / Young at Heart / All I Have to Do Is Dream / What a Diff'rence a Day Made / Beyond the Sea

UK Release:
Moments to Remember / It's All in the Game / Unchained Melody / Venus / It's Not for Me to Say / Love Is a Many Splendored Thing / Rags to Riches / Sincerely - Teach Me Tonight (Medley) (duet with Phyllis McGuire) / Are You Lonesome Tonight? / Young at Heart / All I Have to Do Is Dream / What a Diff'rence a Day Made / Beyond the Sea / If You Love Me (Really Love Me) / As Time Goes By

Japanese Release:
Moments to Remember / It's All in the Game / Unchained Melody / Venus / It's Not for Me to Say / Love Is a Many Splendored Thing / Rags to Riches / Sincerely - Teach Me Tonight (Medley) (duet with Hiromi Iwasaki) / Are You Lonesome Tonight? / Young at Heart / All I Have to Do Is Dream / What a Diff'rence a Day Made / Beyond the Sea / Have I Told You Lately

Production Information:
Producers: Barry Manilow / Clive Davis / David Benson
Associate producer: Marc Hulett / Greg Bartheld
Executive producer: Garry C. Kief
Recorded at: Ocean Way Recording, Hollywood, CA / Bill Schnee Studios, Los Angeles, CA / A&M Studios, Hollywood, CA / Peppertree Studios, Palm Springs, CA / Digital Insight Recording Studios, Las Vegas, NV / Chalice Recording Studios, Los Angeles, CA / O'Henry Sound Studios, Burbank, CA.
Engineered by – Bruce Botnick / Koji Egawa / Bill Schnee
Assistant Engineers: David Benson / Don Murray / Greg Bartheld / Darius Fong / Jeff Burns
Digital editing: Koji Egawa
Pro-Tools programmed by: Koji Egawa / Greg Bartheld
Mixed at: Bill Schnee Studios
Mixed by: Bill Schnee
Mastered at: The Mastering Lab by Robert Hadley
Photography: Andrew MacPherson

Art Direction / Design: Alexis Yraola
Concertmaster: Assa Drori
Contractor: Joe Soldo
Arranged by: Barry Manilow
Artist Management: Garry C. Kief
A&R: Stephen Ferrera
Production Manager: Marsha Burns

Musicians:
Piano: Barry Manilow / Joe Melotti / Ron Pedley / Steve Welch
Drums: John Robinson / Russ McKinnon
Percussion: Dan Greco
Bass: Dave Carpenter / Dave Stone
Bassoon: John Mitchell
Flute: Dave Shostac / Sheridon Stokes
French Horn: Brad Warnaar / Danielle Ondarza / Jim Atkinson / Mark Adams / Paul Klintworth / Steve Becknell
Guitar: Ken Berry / Mike Lent
Harmonica: Tommy Morgan
Harp: Gayle Levant / Marcia Dickstein
Oboe: Earl Dumler / Joe Stone
Saxophone: Dan Higgins / Don Shelton / Gary Foster / Gene Cipriano / George Shelby / Greg Huckins
Trombone – Bryant Byers / Charles Loper / Chauncey Welsch / Craig Gosnell / Stephen Baxter*
Trumpet – Charlie Davis* / Chris Gray / Larry Lunetta / Larry McGuire / Warren Leuning / Wayne Bergeron
Woodwind: Gary Foster / Dan Higgins / George Shelby / Don Shelton / Greg Huckins / Gene Cipriano
Viola: Caroline Buckman / Carrie Holzman / Harry Shirinian / Kazi Pitelka / Ken Burward-Hoy / Miguel Ferguson / Ray Tischer / Rodney Hurtz / Sam Formicola
Violin: Alyssa Park / Armen Garabedian / Assa Drori / Barbra Porter / Brian Benning / Charles Bisharat / Synthia Moussas / David Stenske / Dynell Weber / Irina Voloshina / Jennifer Munday / Jennifer Walton / Johanna Krejci / Kevin Connolly / Liane Mautner / Margaret Wooten / Mario Deleon / Neel Hammond / Olivia Tsui / Rebecca Bunnell / Ron Clark / Ronald Folsom / Shari Zippert / Tereza Stanislav / Yan To Tsong / Yvette Devereaux
Cello: Christina Soule / David Speltz / John Krovoza / Larry Corbett / Paula Hochhalter / Rowena Hammill / Stephanie Fife /, Vanessa F. Smith
Background Vocals: Connie Nassios / Gary Stockdale / Jon Joyce / Randy Crenshaw

Singles Released From This Album:
"Unchained Melody" (Arista – 82876 77950 2 / Promo) (Peaked at # 20 in the US on the Billboard Adult Contemporary Chart on March 4, 2006)
"Love Is a Many Splendored Thing" (Arista – 82876 83134 2 / Promo) (Peaked at # 32 in the US on the Billboard Adult Contemporary Chart on April 29, 2006)

Album Data:
Highest Chart Position: # 1 on February 18, 2006
Billboard Chart: Billboard Top 200
Number of Weeks on Chart: 25

Notes & Trivia:
- This album was released on Dual-Disc, CD and Cassette on January 31, 2006
- This album was certified Gold on March 7, 2006 for sales of over 500,000 and Platinum on

March 24, 2006 for sales of over 1,000,000 copies.

- This is a Dual Disc. The CD side of the disc features the album. The DVD side has the album in enhanced stereo, an on-camera interview with Barry Manilow and behind-the-scenes video of the making of the album. This disc is intended to play on standard DVD and CD players as well as PC ROM devices.
- The album entered the Billboard 200 at #1, giving Barry the second chart-topping album of his career. His only other top of the chart album was "Barry Manilow Live," in 1977. This is also the highest-debuting album in Barry's career, selling over 150,000 copies in its opening week and surpassing the #3 opening of "Ultimate Manilow" in 2002.
- This album had Barry once again returning to his home label, Arista.
- This album had a songbook

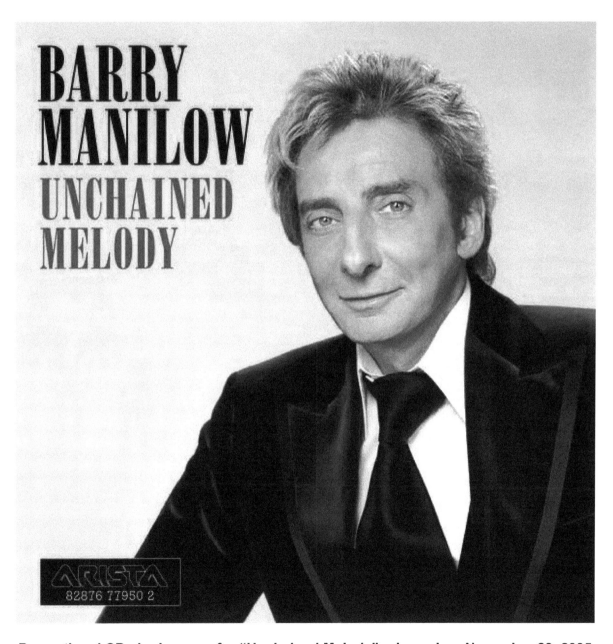

Promotional CD single cover for "Unchained Melody" released on November 29, 2005

The Greatest Songs of the Sixties
82876-82640-2

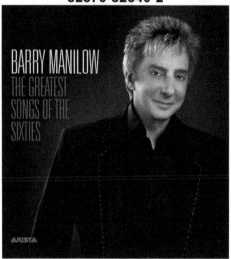

Track Listing:
US Version:
Can't Take My Eyes Off You / Cherish/Windy (duet with The Association) / Can't Help Falling In Love / There's A Kind Of Hush (All Over The World) / Blue Velvet / Raindrops Keep Falling On My Head / And I Love Her / This Guy's In Love With You / Everybody Loves Somebody Sometime / You've Lost That Lovin' Feeling / When I Fall In Love / Strangers In The Night / What The World Needs Now Is Love

UK Version (Released - Released November 27, 2006):
Can't Take My Eyes Off You / Cherish / Windy (duet with The Association) / Can't Help Falling in Love / There's a Kind of Hush (All Over the World) / And I Love Her / Blue Velvet / Raindrops Keep Falling on My Head / This Guy's in Love With You / Everybody Loves Somebody / You've Lost That Lovin' Feeling / When I Fall in Love / Strangers in the Night / What the World Needs Now Is Love / California Dreamin' / Yesterday

Production Information:
Produced by Barry Manilow / Clive Davis / David Benson
Executive Producer: Garry C. Kief
Associate Producers: Greg Bartheld / Marc Hulett
Recorded at Capitol Studios, Hollywood, CA / Peppertree Studios, Palm Springs, CA
Engineered by: Bruce Botnick
Assistant Engineers: Jimmy Hoyson / Aaron Walk / Charlie Paakkari
Additional Recording / Editing and Pro Tools by: David Benson / Greg Bartheld / Koji Egawa at Ignited Now Studios, Sylmar, CA
Mixed by Al Schmitt at: Capitol Studios, Hollywood, CA
Assistant Mix Engineers: Steve Genewick / Bill Smith
Mastered at: The Mastering Lab, Ojai, CA
Mastered by: Doug Sax / Sangwook "Sunny" Nam
Management: Garry C. Kief, Stiletto Entertainment
A&R: Stephen Ferrera
Production Management: The Marsha Burns Group
Photography: Jeff Katz
Design: Jeff Schulz @ Command-Z-Design

Musicians:
Piano: Barry Manilow / Randy Waldman
Bass: Dave Carpenter
Guitar: Ken Berry / Mike Lent
Drums: Russ McKinnon
Percussion: Dan Greco / Paulinho Da Costa
Violins: Assa Drori (Concert Master) / Darius Campo / Daphne Chen / Lisa Dondlinger / Sam Fisher / Ron Folsom / Neel Hammond / Ray Kobler / Johanna Krejci / Liane Mautner / Cynthia Moussas / Jennifer Munday / David Stenske / Yan To / Miwako Watanabe / Dynell Weber
Violas: Ken Burward-Hoy / Sam Formicola / Carrie Holzman / Andrew Picken / Harry Shiranian / Ray Tischer
Cello: Larry Corbett / Armen Ksajikian / Dane Little / Timothy Loo / Tina Soule / John Walz
Harp: Gayle Levant / Marcia Dickstein
Saxophones: Gene Cipriano / Gary Foster / Dan Higgins / Greg Huckins / Joe Stone
Flute: Steve Kujala
Trumpets: Wayne Bergeron / Gary Grant / Chris Gray / Warren Leuning
Trombone: Steve Baxter / Craig Gosnell / Charles Loper / Chauncey Welsch
Tuba: Tommy Johnson
French Horn: Mark Adams / Steve Bicknell / Paul Klintworth
Background Vocals: Randy Crenshaw (Contractor) / Ron Dante / Linda Harmon / Walt Harrah / Jon Joyce / Rick Logan / Connie Nassios / Susie Stevens / Dick Wells
Contractor: Joe Soldo
Music Preparation: Terry Woodson Music / J. Barrick Griffiths / Danny Perito / Yeli Lim / Bill Baker / Curt Berg / Bill Edwards / Gisela Garcia Brugada / Jackie Johnson

Singles Released from This Album:
"Can't Take My Eyes Off You" (Arista – 82876-89162-2 / Promo)

Album Data:
Highest Chart Position: # 2 on November 18 , 2006
Billboard Chart: Billboard Top 200
Number of Weeks on Chart: 12

Notes & Trivia:
- This album was released on CD on October 31, 2006
- This album was certified Gold on December 1, 2006 for sales in excess of of 500,000 copies.
- A Wal-Mart Exclusive CD included: One year BMIFC free membership and an exclusive download of the track, "The Shadow Of Your Smile."
- A QVC Exclusive Bonus 7-Song CD titled "More Manilow" (Arista - A701958) included "Tryin' To Get The Feeling Again" (Music and Passion Live) / "The Best Seat In The House" (Music and Passion Live) / "I Made It Through The Rain" (Music and Passion Live) / "See The Show Again" (Music and Passion Live) / "One Voice" (Music and Passion Live) / "Never My Love-I Swear" / "My Cherie Amour"
- The UK Dual-Disc version includes Exclusive Behind-The-Scenes Footage: Never My Love - I Swear / My Cherie Amour
- The QVC Dual-Disc version includes Exclusive Behind-The-Scenes Footage: California Dreamin' / Yesterday
- CD's duplicated by Sonopress in Weaverville, North Carolina
- **Original album press release:** 13 classics from the '60s – "You've Lost That Lovin' Feeling'" (Righteous Brothers), "And I Love Her" (The Beatles), "This Guy's In Love With You" (Herb

Alpert), "Can't Take My Eyes Off You" (Frankie Valli), "When I Fall In Love" (The Letterman), "What The World Needs Now Is Love" (Jackie DeShannon), "Everybody Loves Somebody Sometime" (Dean Martin), "Blue Velvet" (Bobby Vinton), "Can't Help Falling In Love" (Elvis Presley), "Strangers in the Night"(Frank Sinatra), "Raindrops Keep Falling On My Head" (Burt Bacharach), "There's A Kind of Hush (All Over The World)" (Herman's Hermits), and "Cherish"/"Windy" (The Association) THE GREATEST SONGS OF THE SIXTIES once again marks a reunion between Manilow and Clive Davis, Arista founder and BMG U.S. Chairman & CEO. The two produced The Greatest Songs Of The Fifties together, and that magic has carried over to the new album as well. Each song on THE GREATEST SONGS OF THE SIXTIES is a classic in its own right – from his remake of the Righteous Brothers "You've Lost That Lovin' Feeling'" (1965) to the Beatles' "And I Love Her"(1964), to Herb Alpert's "This Guy's In Love With You" (1968), the Lettermen's "When I Fall In Love" (1962) and Burt Bacharach's "Raindrops Keep Falling On My Head" (1969). Like the marvelous musical decade of the '60s itself, the album covers many genres, from its recollection of Herman's Hermits' "There's A Kind Of Hush (All Over The World)"(1967), to Bobby Vinton's "Blue Velvet" (1963), to Jackie DeShannon's "What The World Needs Now Is Love" (1965). Manilow also pays tribute to some of America's greatest singers, whose memories are evoked on songs that are forever associated with them, including Dean Martin on "Everybody Loves Somebody Sometime" (1964) and Frankie Valli's "Can't Take My Eyes Off You" (1967). Two artists whose legacies were recalled on The Greatest Songs Of The Fifties are again paid homage on the new album, namely Elvis Presley with "Can't Help Falling In Love" (1962) and Frank Sinatra with "Strangers In The Night" (1966). One of the highlights of the album is a great duet with The Association of their two #1 hits "Cherish" (1966) and "Windy" (1967). With THE GREATEST SONGS OF THE SIXTIES Barry Manilow pays a loving and welcome tribute to some of the songs that inspired him to become one of the most beloved performers in pop music of the past three decades.

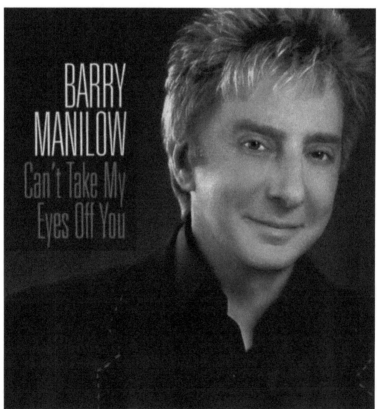

Promotional only CD single for "Can't Take My Eyes Off You" (82876-89162-2)

70

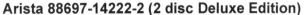

The Greatest Songs of the Seventies
Arista 88697-10034-2
Arista 88697-14222-2 (2 disc Deluxe Edition)

Track Listing:

The Way We Were / My Eyes Adored You / Bridge Over Troubled Water / How Can You Mend A Broken Heart / It Never Rains In Southern California / You've Got A Friend (duet with Melissa Manchester) / He Ain't Heavy, He's My Brother / Sailing / The Long And Winding Road / (They Long To Be) Close To You / If / Sorry Seems To Be The Hardest Word / Mandy (Acoustic version) / Weekend In New England (Acoustic version) / Copacabana (At The Copa) (Acoustic version) / Even Now (Acoustic version) / Looks Like We Made It (Acoustic version) / I Write The Songs (Acoustic version)

Production Information:

Produced by: Barry Manilow / Clive Davis / David Benson
Executive Producer: Garry C. Kief
Associate Producers: Greg Bartheld / Scott Erickson / Marc Hulett
Recorded at: Capitol Studios, Hollywood, CA / Pepper Tree Studio, Palm Springs, CA / Schnee Studio, North Hollywood, CA / Pepper Tree Studio, Las Vegas, NV / SongLee Studio, La Canada, CA / IgnitedNow Studio, Kagal Canyon, CA / Henson Studios, Hollywood, CA / Larrabee Studios North, Universal City, CA / Studio At The Palms, Las Vegas, NV
Engineered by: Bruce Botnick
Assistant Engineers: Aaron Walk / Steve Genewick / Paul Smith / Justin Pintar
Additional Engineering and Audio Editing by: Bill Schnee / Tommy Vicari / Greg Bartheld / David Benson / Koji Egawa / Scott Erickson / Brian Donovan / Barry Manilow
Mixed at: Schnee Studio, North Hollywood, CA
Mixing Engineer: Bill Schnee
Assistant Mix Engineer: Darius Fong
Mastered at: The Mastering Lab, Ojai, CA
Mastered by: Doug Sax / Sangwook "Sunny" Nam
Photography: Jeff Katz
Creative Direction: Jane Morledge
Design: Maria Marulanda
Artist Management: Garry C. Kief, Stiletto Entertainment

Musicians:

Piano: Barry Manilow / Ron Pedley / Scott Erickson / Kevin Bassinson / Randy Kerber / Ron Walters Jr.
Keyboards: Ron Pedley / Scott Erickson

Rhythm Bass: Dave Carpenter
Bass: Ian Martin
Drums: Russ McKinnon
Guitar: Ken Berry / Mike Lent / George Doering / Tim Pierce
Percussion: David Rosenblatt / Dan Greco / Luis Conte / Alex Acuna / Paulinho Da Costa
Violins: Assa Drori (Concert Master) / Liane Mautner / Miwako Watanabe / Yan To / Johana Krejci / Ron Folsom / Jennifer Munday / Cynthia Mousses / Dynell Weber / Joel Derouin / Haim Shtrum / Darius Campo / Rebecca Bunnell / Josephina Vergara / Miran Kojian / Songa Lee / Patricia Johnson / Audrey Soloman / Irina Voloshina / Brian Benning / Nina Eutuhov / Paul Tseitlin / Kevin Connolly / Yue Deng / Ron Clark / Alyssa Park / Margaret Wooten / Sam Fischer / Jennifer Walton / Anatoly Rosinsky / Lisa Dondlinger / Neel Hammond / Raymond Kobler
Violas: Ken Burward-Hoy / Harry Shirinian / Ray Tischer / Sam Formicola / Alma Fernandez / Caroline Buckman / Andrew Duckles
Celli: Larry Corbett / Christina Soule / Jon Walz / Timothy Loo / Roger Lebow / Trevor Handy / Paula Hochhalter / John Krovoza / David Speltz
Basses: Chuck Berghofer / Drew Dembowski / Oscar Hidalgo
Harp: Gayle Levant / Julie Berghofer
French Horns: Steve Becknell / Jim Atkinson / Dan Kelley / Paul Klintworth
Trumpets: Gary Grant / Warren Leuning / Chris Gray / Larry McGuire
Trombones: Steve Baxter / Chauncey Welsch / Charles Loper / Craig Gosnell
Flutes: Sheridan Stokes / Gary Foster / Greg Huckins / Brandon Fields
Oboes: David Kossoff / Joe Stone
Clarinet: Phil O'Connor
Background Vocals: Randy Crenshaw (Contractor) / Ron Dante / Bill Cantos / Scott Erickson / Susie Stevens / Karen Harper / Angie Jeree / Tim Davis (Contractor) / David Loucks
Music Preparation: TERRY WOODSON MUSIC: J. Barrick Griffiths / Danny Perito / Penny Watson-Crum / Curt Berg / Bill Edwards / Bill Baker / Yeli Lim
Additional Music Preparation: Ron Walters Jr. / Doug Walter / Ron Pedley Music Services / Christina Abaroa
Production Manager: Christina Abaroa
Contractor: Joe Soldo

Singles Released From This Album:
No single releases

Album Data:
Highest Chart Position: # 4 on October 6, 2007
Billboard Chart: Billboard Top 200
Number of Weeks on Chart: 15

Notes & Trivia:
- This album was released on CD on September 18, 2007
- The final six tracks had all originally been recorded by Barry Manilow himself.
- A QVC Exclusive: Deluxe Edition + Bonus 5-Song CD "Even More Manilow" including "If You Love Me, Really Love Me" / "As Time Goes By" / "Have I Told You Lately That I Love You" / "The Shadow Of Your Smile" / "California Dreamin'"
- The two-disc package (Deluxe Edition) of THE GREATEST SONGS OF THE SEVENTIES contains a Dual-Disc (CD + DVD) with new versions of 12 classic songs by other artists from the 1970s on the audio layer and "The Making of the Album" with Barry reflecting on the music and the decade on the video layer. The bonus CD contains acoustic versions of many of Barry Manilow's own hits.

- The UK Edition CD includes: "Solitaire" / "Somewhere In The Night (Acoustic)" / "This One's For You (Acoustic)" / "Could It Be Magic (Trevor Horn Dance Mix)" in place of "How Can You Mend A Broken Heart", "It Never Rains In Southern California", "Sailing" and "I Write The Songs (Acoustic)"
- The Greatest Songs of the Seventies "Making Of The Album" video Somewhere In The Night (Acoustic) / Can't Smile Without You (Acoustic) / This One's For You (Acoustic) / Could It Be Magic (Trevor Horn Dance Mix) / Solitaire
- This album was certified Gold on April 11, 2008 for sales of over 500,000 copies and Platinum on April 11, 2008 for sales of over 1,000,000 copies.

The Japanese CD insert. Promotional use only.

In The Swing of Christmas
XPR4172

Track Listing:
Silver Bells / Carol Of The Bells/Jingle Bells / Medley- Joy To The World/It's The Most Wonderful Time Of The Year / Have Yourself A Merry Little Christmas / Violets For Your Furs / O Tannenbaum-Winter Wonderland / Christmas Time Is Here / The Christmas Song (Chestnuts Roasting On An Open Fire) / Toyland / Count Your Blessings

Production Information:
Producer and Arranged by: Barry Manilow
Co-producer: Scott Erickson
Associate producer: Marc Hulett
Executive producer: Garry C. Kief
Recorded at: Studio At The Palms, Las Vegas, NV / Capitol Studios, Hollywood, CA / Pepper Tree Studio, Las Vegas, NV and Palm Springs, CA / SongLee Studio
Engineer: Don Murray
Assistant engineering: Greg Bartheld / Koji Egawa / Charlie Paakari / Dan Monti, Justin Pintar / Mark Gray
Technical Assistance: Greg Bartheld / Koji Egawa
Coordinator and Production Assistance: Cristina Abaroa
Mixed at: SongLee Studio / Studio At The Palms, Las Vegas, NV / Firehouse Studios, Pasadena, CA
Mixed by: Scott Erickson
Mastered at: The Mastering Lab, Ojai, CA by Doug Sax and Sangwook "Sunny" Nam
Photography by: Jeff Katz
Design & Liner Notes: Hallmark Marketing Studio
Artist Management: Garry C. Kief - Stiletto Entertainment
Music Preparation: Ron Pedley Music Services / Terry Woodson Music / J. Barrick Griffiths / Cristina Abaroa.

Musicians:
Piano: Matt Jerkewitz / Randy Kerber
Keyboards: Ron Pedley
Bass: Matt Fieldes / Mike Valerio
Drums: David Rosenblatt / Joe La Barbera
Guitar: George Doering
Saxophone / Flute: Tom Scott

Trumpet: Warren Leuning

Singles Released From This Album:
"Have Yourself A Merry Little Christmas" (Peaked at # 11 in the US on the Billboard Adult Contemporary Chart on January 5, 2008)

Album Data:
Highest Chart Position: # 127 on December 19, 2009
Billboard Chart: Billboard Top 200
Number of Weeks on Chart: 4

Notes & Trivia:
- This album was initially released on CD on November 1, 2007
- The album was manufactured and distributed in the US by Hallmark Cards.
- Re-Released in the US and Japan on October 13, 2009 by Arista Records (Arista 88697-57490-2 / SICP 2455) with two Bonus Tracks: "Rudolph The Red Nosed Reindeer" / "Christmas Is Just Around The Corner (from "Cranberry Christmas" TV special)
- Japanese liner notes by: Yuji Muraoka (村岡裕司)
- This album was nominated for a Grammy for Best Traditional Pop Vocal Album in 2009.
- This album was certified Gold on January 28, 2008 for selling in excess of 500,000 copies
- .In 2008, the album was nominated for a Grammy Award in the 'Best Traditional Pop Vocal Album' category.

The 2009 Japanese release of the album showing OBI strip (SICP 2455)

The Greatest Songs of the Eighties
88697 37161-2

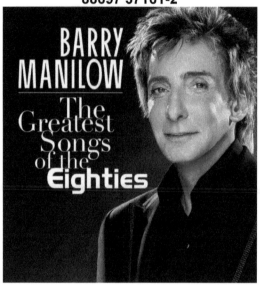

Track Listing:
Islands in the Stream (duet with Reba McEntire) / Open Arms / Never Gonna Give You Up / Have I Told You Lately / I Just Called to Say I Love You / Against All Odds (Take A Look At Me Now) / Careless Whisper / Right Here Waiting / Arthur's Theme (The Best That You Can Do) / Hard To Say I'm Sorry (with Chicago) / Time After Time / (I've Had) The Time Of My Life

Production Information:
Produced by: Barry Manilow and Clive Davis
Executive Producer: Garry C. Kief
Associate Producer: Marc Hulett
Orchestra Recorded at: Schnee Studio, North Hollywood, CA
Orchestral Engineering by: Bill Schnee
Additional Recording at: Pepper Tree Studio, Palm Springs, CA / Pepper Tree Studio, Las Vegas, NV / Song Lee Studio, La Canada, CA / The Shore, Malibu, CA / Sha Intermedia, Malibu, CA / The Studio, Beverly Hills, CA
Additional Recording and Editing Engineers: Scott Erickson / Michael Lloyd / Brian Donovan / Nathaniel Kunkel / Michael Leonard / George Leger / Ken Sluiter / Nigel Lundemo / M. Jeffrey Lloyd / Bob Kearney
Except: "Against All Odds (Take A Look At Me Now)" Mixed by Scott Erickson at Song Lee Studio, La Cañada, CA / "Never Gonna Give You Up" / "Right Here Waiting" / "Time After Time" / "Hard To Say I'm Sorry" Mixed and Vocal Overdubs Engineered by Michael Lloyd at The Studio, Beverly Hills, CA
Mixed at: Schnee Studio, North Hollywood, CA
Mixing Engineer: Bill Schnee
Assistant Mix Engineer: Darius Fong
Pro Tools Editing: Koji Egawa / Nigel Lundemo / Michael Lloyd
Mastered at: The Mastering Lab, Ojai, CA
Mastered by: Doug Sax and Robert Hadley
Music Preparation: Express Music Services / Lee Monroe / Ashley Wells / Cristina Abaroa / Terry Woodson Music / J. Barrick Griffiths / Penny Watson-Crum / John D'Andrea
Production Manager: Cristina Abaroa
Artist Development: Scott Seviour
Photography: Matthew Rolston
Art Direction & Design: Erwin Gorostiza

Styling and Make-up: Kevin Posey
Management: Garry C. Kief, Stiletto Entertainment
Dave Koz appears courtesy of Blue Note Records

Musicians:
Piano: Barry Manilow / Scott Erickson / Randy Kerber / Greg O'Connor
Keyboards: Scott Erickson / Jim Cox
Drums: Charlie Morgan / John Ferraro / John "JR" Robinson
Percussion: David Rosenblatt / Scott Erickson / Michael Lloyd
Guitar: Tim Pierce / Oscar Castro Neves / Eddie Arkin
Bass: Lee Sklar
Programming: Scott Erickson / Greg O'Connor
Violins: Assa Drori (Concert Master) / Joel Derouin / Anatoly Rosinsky / Johana Krejei / Songa Lee / Raymond Kobler / Rebecca Bunnell / Haim Shtrum / Ronald Folsom / Rita Weber / E. Samuel Fischer / Lisa Dondlinger / Liane / Mautner / Phillip Levy / Darius Campo / Tereza Stanislav / Irina Voloshina
Violas: Roland Kato / V. Miskolezy / Evan N. Wilson / Alma Fernandez
Celli: Larry Corbett / Christina Soule / Ira Glansbeek / John Walz / Armen Ksajikian / Cecilia Tsan
Harp: Marcia Dickstein
French Horns: Steven Becknell / Brian O'Connor / James Atkinson / Daniel Kelley
Flutes: Sheridon Stokes / Gary Foster / Greg Huckings
Background Vocals: Kayla Balch / Randy Crenshaw / Ron Dante / Scott Erickson / Vangie Gunn / Jeff Gunn / Michael Lloyd / Greg O'Connor / Windy Wagner / Barry Manilow
Contractor: Joe Soldo

Singles Released From This Album:
Islands In The Stream (duet with Reba McEntire)

Album Data:
Highest Chart Position: # 14 on December 13, 2008
Billboard Chart: Billboard Top 200
Number of Weeks on Chart: 6

Notes & Trivia:
- This album was released on CD on November 24, 2008
- The UK Version (Released March 16, 2009) included the tracks: "Every Time You Go Away" and "Biggest Part Of Me"
- **Original Album Press Release read:** *THE GREATEST SONGS OF THE EIGHTIES* uncovers a bounty of treasures and reignites nostalgia for these fantastic hit songs reinterpreted by Manilow in his signature style - from his duet with Reba McEntire on "Islands in the Stream," as they pay homage to Kenny Rogers & Dolly Parton's #1 duet of 1983 - to a trio of songs associated with memorable films: Phil Collins #1 hit of 1984, "Against All Odds (Take A Look At Me Now)"; Bill Medley & Jennifer Warnes' #1 hit of 1987, "I've Had the Time of My Life" (from Dirty Dancing); and Christopher Cross' Oscar-winning #1 hit of 1981, "Arthur's Theme (The Best That You Can Do)," and much more. THE GREATEST SONGS OF THE EIGHTIES is Manilow's newest addition to the mega-best-selling series of tribute albums that he masterminded with Arista founder Clive Davis. Davis has been Manilow's hit-making collaborator on virtually all his recordings, since they first worked together on "Mandy," his debut #1 single as the first artist signed to Arista by Davis in 1974, the first year of the label's existence. THE GREATEST SONGS OF THE EIGHTIES continues the series that began nearly three years ago with The Greatest Songs Of The Fifties, which was certified RIAA

platinum after entering the Billboard 200 at #1 in January 2006 (his first #1 album since Barry Manilow/Live in 1977). The Greatest Songs Of The Sixties (October 2006) entered at #2. When the RIAA platinum The Greatest Songs Of The Seventies entered at #4 (September 2007), he was distinguished as the only artist to chart three Top 5 debuts during 2006-2007. THE GREATEST SONGS OF THE EIGHTIES moves seamlessly through a selection of major hits from both sides of the Atlantic. The UK is well-represented by "Careless Whisper," the #1 hit of 1984 by Wham! featuring George Michael; Rick Astley's #1 "Never Gonna Give You Up"; and a song that Van Morrison first wrote and recorded in 1989, "Have I Told You Lately," which later became a giant hit for Rod Stewart. Manilow's impeccable performances and signature arranging style also breathe new life into a quintet of American classics: "Open Arms" by Journey; Chicago's #1 "Hard to Say I'm Sorry"; Stevie Wonder's #1 "I Just Called to Say I Love You"; Cyndi Lauper's #1 "Time After Time"; and Richard Marx's #1 "Right Here Waiting."

Barry with Reba McEntire and producer, arranger, engineer and writer Scott Erickson. Taken at the recording session for "Islands in the Stream."

The Greatest Love Songs Of All Time
88697-59777-2

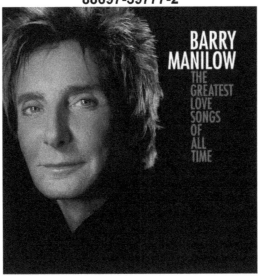

Track Listing:
Love Is Here To Stay / The Look Of Love / Theme From "Love Story" (Where Do I Begin) / I Only Have Eyes for You / I Can't Give You Anything But Love / The Twelfth Of Never / We've Only Just Begun / Nevertheless (I'm In Love With You) / Love Me Tender / You Made Me Love You / It Could Happen To You / How Deep Is The Ocean? / When You Were Sweet Sixteen

Production Information:
Produced by Barry Manilow / Michael Lloyd / Clive Davis
Executive Producer: Garry C. Kief
Associate Producer: Marc Hulett
Recorded at 20th Century Fox Scoring Stage, Los Angeles, CA / Capitol Studios, Hollywood, CA / The Studio One, Beverly Hills, CA / Peppertree Studios, Palm Springs, CA
Enginnered by: Armin Steiner / Alan Sides / Michael Lloyd / Barry Manilow / Bob Kearney
Assistant Engineers: Steve Genewick / Tim Lauber
Digital Editing by: George Leger III
Pro Tools Editing by: Nigel Lundemo / Michael Lloyd
Pro Tools Engineer at 20th Century Fox: Larry Mah
20th Century Fox Scoring Stage Manager: Tom Steele
Mixed by: Michael Lloyd
Mastered at: Dave Collins Mastering
Mastered by: Dave Collins
Artist Development: Scott Seviour
Creative Director: Erwin Gorostiza
Photography: Greg Gorman
Art Direction and Design: Erwin Gorostiza / Denise Trotman
Management: Garry C. Kief Stiletto Entertainment
Music Preparation: Terry Woodson / Gordon Berg / Daniel Perito / J.B. Griffiths / William Baker / Penny Watson

Musicians:
(Rhythm Section)
Piano: Barry Manilow / Randy Kerber / Alan Broadbent
Bass: Chuck Berghofer / Chuck Domanico / Leland Sklar

Drums: Gregg Field / Vinnie Colaiuta / Carols Vega
Guitar: Dean Parks / Laurence Juber / Tim Pierce
Percussion: Brian Kilgore / Paulinho DaCosta

(Orchestra)
Violins: Assa Drori (Concert Master) / Darius Campo / Kevin Connolly / Joel Derouin / Ron Folsom /
Anatoly Rosinsky / Liane Mautner / Miran Kojian / Becky Bunnell / Johana Krejci / Tereza Stanislav /
Jennifer Munday / Rita Weber / Irina Voloshina / Songa Lee / Cynthia Moussas / Katia Popov / Audrey
Solomon / Lisa Dondlinger / Alyssa Park / Neel Hammond / Brian Benning
Violas: Roland Kato / Victoria Miskolczy / David Walther / Harry Shirinian / Alma Fernandez / Ray
Tischer / Rodney Wirtz
Celli: Armin Ksajikian / Cecila Tsan / Tina Soule / Trevor Handy / John Walz / David Speltz / Tim Loo /
Paula Hochhalter / John Krovoza / Diego Mirillas
Contra Bass: Drew Dembowski / Nico Abandolo / Ramon Stagnaro
Harp: Gayle Levant
Woodwinds: Gary Foster / Dave Shostac / Bob Sheppard / Gene Cipriano / Greeg Huckins / Lee
Callet / Dave Hill
Trumpets: Warren Luening / Wayne Bergeron / Charles Davis / Larry McGuire
Trombones: Charles Loper / Bob McChesney / Charles Morillas / Phil Teele
French Horns: Steve Becknell / Paul Klintworth / Jim Atkinson / Justin Hageman
Contractor: Joe Soldo

Singles Released From This Album:
No Single Releases

Album Data:
Highest Chart Position: # 5 on February 13, 2010
Billboard Chart: Billboard Top 200
Number of Weeks on Chart: 6

Notes & Trivia:
- This album was released on CD on January 26, 2010
- This album was nominated for a Grammy for Best Traditional Pop Vocal Album in 2011.
- A QVC Exclusive release of the album (Released January 19, 2010) included the bonus 5-Song CD "Songs From The Vault." It contained the tracks: "Nature Boy" (Brooklyn, New York - 1948) / "Golddigger" (Outtake from "Barry" - 1980) / "Biggest Part Of Me" (Outtake from "The Greatest Songs Of The Eighties" - 2008) / "Everybody Wants To Rule The World" (Outtake from "The Greatest Songs Of The Eighties" - 2008) / "Every Breath You Take" (Outtake from "The Greatest Songs Of The Eighties" - 2008)
- **Original Album Press Release read:** Grammy, Tony, and Emmy Award-winning recording artist Barry Manilow teams up once again with his longtime collaborator, Arista Records founder Clive Davis (now Chief Creative Officer, Sony Music Entertainment) to record a brand new studio album entitled THE GREATEST LOVE SONGS OF ALL TIME, set for release on January 26th.
  On THE GREATEST LOVE SONGS OF ALL TIME, produced with Michael Lloyd (Somewhere in Time and Dirty Dancing), Manilow presents loving interpretations and arrangements of classic, nostalgic love songs for the Manilow and music fan alike. The album selections include jazz and American standards, as well as songs from the "Great White Way" and silver screen including: Irving Berlin's "How Deep Is The Ocean," "You Made Me Love You" (written by James V. Monaco), Fats Waller's "I Can't Give You Anything But Love," "When You Were Sweet Sixteen" (written by James Thornton and revived and popularized by Al Jolsen in 1929),

"The Theme From Love Story (Where Do I Begin)" (written by Francis Lai), "Nevertheless, I'm In Love With You" (written by Harry Ruby), Gershwin's "Our Love is Here To Stay," and "It Could Happen To You" (written by Johnny Burke and Jimmy Van Heusen). The album also features great renditions of "The Look Of Love" (written by Burt Bacharach and Hal David), "We've Only Just Begun" (Written by the songwriting team of Roger Nichols and Paul Williams) and "The Twelfth of Never" (written by Jerry Livingston and Paul Francis Webster).

- "The real joy in creating this album was taking these classic songs that everyone knows and using my chops as an arranger to deconstruct then recreate them to make them my own," explained Barry.
- Comments from Clive Davis: "Barry and I have a mission to bring to a new generation the great songs that are the soundtrack of our lives. This album does just that and Barry is sounding better than ever."

15 Minutes: Fame...Can You Take It?
SE0001

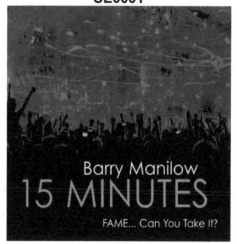

Track Listing:
15 Minutes / Work The Room / Bring On Tomorrow / Now It's For Real / Wine Song / He's A Star / Written In Stone / Letter From A Fan - So Heavy, So High / Everybody's Leavin' / Who Needs You? / Winner Go Down / Slept Through The End Of The World / Reflection / Train wreck / 15 Minutes (Reprise) / Everything's Gonna Be All Right

Production Information:
Produced and Arranged by: Barry Manilow / Michael Lloyd / Scott Erickson
Executive Producer: Garry C. Kief
Associate Producer: Marc Hulett
Recorded at: The Studio, Beverly Hills, CA / Peppertree Studios, Palm Springs, CA / The Complex Studios, Los Angeles, CA
Engineered by: Bob Kearney / Michael Lloyd / Barry Manilow / Greg Bartheld
Assistant Engineer at: The Complex Studios: James Doser
Overdubs Engineered and Mixed by: Michael Lloyd
Digital Editing by: George Legeri III / Nigel Lundemo
Mastered by: Dave Collins Mastering
Project Manager: John Adams
Original Art: James Jensen Studios/Colin Davis
Art Director: Sara Zickhur / Jason Irwin
Artist Management: Garry C. Kief, Stiletto Entertainment

Musicians:
The 15 Minutes Band:
Keyboards: Barry Manilow / Matt Rawlings / Jim Cox / Michael Lloyd
Guitars: Tim Pierce / Laurence Juber / Michael Lloyd
Bass: Matt Bissonette / Michael Lloyd / Barry Manilow
Drums: Greg Bisonette
Basic Track Drums: M.B. Gordy
Digital Programming: Barry Manilow / Michael Lloyd
Background Vocals: Randy Crenshaw / Ron Dante / Michael Lloyd / Bill Santos / Judith Hill / Navanna Holley / Carmen Echols / Keely Vasquez / Muffy Hendrix / Melanie Nyema / Kye Brackett / Barry Manilow

Singles Released From This Album:
"Bring On Tomorrow" March 14, 2011 (Digital release only)
"Now It's For Real" June 23, 2011 (Digital release only)
"Everything's Gonna Be All Right" (2012 Remix) July 10, 2012 (Digital release only)

Album Data:
Highest Chart Position: # 7 on July 2, 2011
Billboard Chart: Billboard Top 200
Number of Weeks on Chart: 9

Notes & Trivia:
- This album was released on CD on June 14, 2011 / UK Release: June 20, 2011
- A QVC Exclusive Disc Titled "On The Way To 15 Minutes" included 4 tracks: "Wandering Troubadour" (Demo) / "Star Children" (Demo) / "Something's Comin' Up" (Demo) / "I'll Get Up Again" (Demo)
- "Bring On Tomorrow" Music by Barry Manilow, Lyrics by Enoch Anderson, Published by Obbligato Music (BMI) / Catapult Music (BMI); Produced by Barry Manilow / Scott Erickson / Michael Lloyd. Orchestra arranged by Barry Manilow / Scott Erickson. Additional Programming: Scott Erickson
- "So Heavy, So High" Music by Barry Manilow, Lyrics by Enoch Anderson, Published by Obbligato Music (BMI) / Catapult Music (BMI); Produced by Barry Manilow / Greg Bartheld / Michael Lloyd. Basic Track recorded and engineered by Greg Bartheld. Second Engineer: James Doser. Recorded at the Complex Studios, Los Angeles, CA.
- "15 Minutes" / "15 Minutes (Reprise)" / "Everything's Gonna Be All Right" / "Work The Room" / "Now It's For Real" / "He's A Star" / "Written In Stone" / "Letter From A Fan" (featuring Nataly Dawn of Pomplamoose) / "Who Needs You" / "Winner Go Down" / "Slept Through The End Of The World" / "Trainwreck" Music by Barry Manilow, Lyrics by Enoch Anderson, Published by Obbligato Music (BMI) / Catapult Music (BMI)
- "Wine Song" Music by Barry Manilow, Lyrics by Adrienne Anderson, Published by Obbligato Music (BMI) / Vegavox Music (BMI)
- "Everybody's Leavin'" Music and Lyrics by Barry Manilow, Published by Obbligato Music (BMI)
- "Reflection" Music by Barry Manilow; Published by Obbligato Music (BMI)
- *15 Minutes* won Barry a Best Traditional Pop Vocal Album Grammy Award nomination in 2012.
- The album was the first independent release of Barry's career, through his Stiletto Entertainment label (distributed by Fontana/Universal Music).
- "He's a Star" was originally issued on Barry's 1975 album *Tryin' to Get the Feeling* as "She's a Star." The version released on 15 Minutes, in addition to the change in gender, was recorded in a much faster tempo compared to the original recording.

Night Songs
Stiletto Entertainment -SE0009

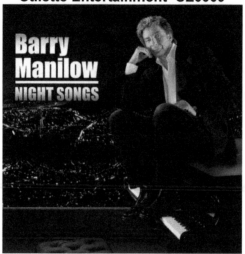

Track Listing:

I Fall In Love Too Easily / Alone Together / Blame It On My Youth / I Get Along Without You Very Well / You're Getting To Be A Habit With Me / It Amazes Me / But Not For Me / It's A New World / While We're Young / You Don't Know What Love Is / Ac-Cent-Tchu-Ate The Positive / My One And Only Love / I've Never Been In Love Before / I Walk A Little Faster / Here's That Rainy Day / Some Other Time

Production Information:

Produced and Arranged by: Barry Manilow
Executive Producer: Garry C. Kief
Associate Producer: Marc Hulett
Recorded at: Peppertree Studios, Palm Springs, CA / O'Henry Studio, Burbank, CA
Engineers: David Benson / Greg Bartheld / Jerry Napier
"It Amazes Me" / "Ac-Cent-Tchu-Ate The Positive" / "I Walk A Little Faster" / "Here's That Rainy Day" / "Some Other Time" were recorded at Ignited Now Studios, Los Angeles, CA and engineered by: Greg Bartheld
Digital Audio Editing by: Greg Bartheld
Mixed at: Schnee Studios, North Hollywood, CA
Mixed by: Bill Schnee
Mastered at: Jacob's Well Mastering, West Lebanon, NH
Mastered by: Sangwook "Sunny" Nam
Art Direction by: Dale Voelker at DigitalLava.com
Photography by Gregg Segal
Artist Management: Garry C. Kief, Stiletto Entertainment

Musicians:

Piano and Synthesized Acoustic Bass: Barry Manilow

Singles Released From This Album:

"I Fall In Love Too Easily" December 16, 2013 (Digital release only)
"Blame It On My Youth" (Digital release only)

Album Data:

Highest Chart Position: # 8 on April 12, 2014
Billboard Chart: Billboard Top 200

Number of Weeks on Chart: 4

Notes & Trivia:
- This album was released on CD and LP on March 25, 2014
- This album was nominated for a Grammy for Best Traditional Pop Vocal Album in 2015.
- 2014 album from the veteran Pop singer, songwriter and entertainer. On NIGHT SONGS, Barry Manilow strips down to nothing but a piano! "Pour yourself a glass of wine. Dim the lights. NIGHT SONGS is the perfect soundtrack for your evening. NIGHT SONGS is the most intimate album I've ever made. Just me singing and playing piano. It's filled with some of the greatest standards of all time. All of them my favorites. So pretend it's just me sitting in your living room, playing and singing for you. Just you, me and your glass of wine. I hope you enjoy Night Songs. And I hope it introduces you to some songs you may never have heard."
  ~Barry Manilow.

My Dream Duets
B0021902-01

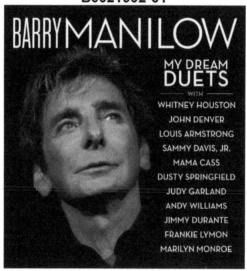

Track Listing:
The Song's Gotta Come From The Heart (duet with Jimmy Durante) / Goody Goody (duet with Frankie Lymon) / Dream A Little Dream Of Me (duet with Mama Cass) / I Believe In You And Me (duet with Whitney Houston) / Sunshine On My Shoulders (duet with John Denver) / Zing! Went The Strings Of My Heart (duet with Judy Garland) / Moon River (duet with Andy Williams) / The Look Of Love (duet with Dusty Springfield) / The Candy Man (duet with Sammy Davis, Jr.) / I Wanna Be Loved By You (duet with Marilyn Monroe) / What A Wonderful World / What A Wonderful Life (duet with Louis Armstrong)

Production Information:
Conceived and Arranged by: Barry Manilow
Produced by: Barry Manilow / David Benson
Executive Producers: Jay Landers / Garry C. Kief
Associate Producers: Greg Bartheld / Marc Hulett
Recorded at: Peppertree Studios, Palm Springs, CA / Oceanway Recording, Hollywood, CA / Ignited Now Studios, Los Angeles, CA
Engineers: Bill Schnee / Greg Bartheld / David Benson / Ryan Reault / Patrick Spain
Mixed at: Schnee Studios, Los Angeles, CA
Mix Engineer: Bill Schnee
Mastered at: Jacob's Well Mastering, West Lebanon, NH
Mastered by: Sangwook "Sunny" Nam
Original Voice Separations by: ADX Technology
Separation Engineer: Rick Silva and the Audionamix Production Team
Production Manager: Christine Telleck
Cover Photography: Dana L. Holland
Artist Management: Garry C. Keif / Stiletto Entertainment

Musicians:
Piano: Barry Manilow / Doug Walter / Curtis Brengle
Bass: Chuck Berghofer / David Benson / Greg Bartheld
Guitar: Ken Berry / Dean Parks
Drums: Gregg Field / David Benson / Greg Bartheld
Saxophones: Dan Higgins / Greg Huckins / Jeff Driskill / Terry Harrington / Gene Cipriano

Saxophone solo on "The Look of Love" by Don Shelton
Trumpets: Gary Grant / Wayne Bergeron / Chris Gray / Dan Fornero
Trombones: Dave Ryan / Charlie Morillas / Steve Baxter / Craig Gosnell
French Horns: Steve Becknell / Jim Atkinson / Justin Hageman / Danielle Ondarza
Flutes: Steve Kujala / Sara Andon
Violins: Ralph Morrison (Concert Master) / Katia Popov / Roberto Cani / Kevin Connolly / Joel Derouin / Nina Eutuhow / Neel Hammond / Radu Pieptea / Katie Sloan / Alyssa Park / Teresa Stanislav / Joel Pargman
Violas:Roland Kato / Andrew Picken Alma Fernandez / David Walther
Celli: Cecila Tsan / Trevor Handy / Vanessa F. Smith / Tim Loo
Background Vocals: Randy Crenshaw / Fletcher Sheridan / Greg Whipple / Alvin Chea / Debra Byrd / Karina Lammas / Janis Liebhart / Gabrielle Walters / Ronald L. Walters III / Bary Manilow

Rhythm Section on "Goody Goody": The Campus Five Jonathan Stout / Chris Dawson

Singles Released From This Album:
No Single Releases

Album Data:
Highest Chart Position: # 4 on November 15, 2014
Billboard Chart: Billboard Top 200
Number of Weeks on Chart: 7

Notes & Trivia:
- This album was released on CD and LP on October 27, 2014 (U.S.) / November 7, 2014 (Australia) / November 24, 2014 (U.K.)
- The LP came with a card to down a digital copy of the album.
- Album pressed in Nashville by United Record Pressing.
- An Exclusive QVC Disc: "Live in London with the Royal Philharmonic Concert Orchestra" included 4 tracks: "Tryin' To Get The Feeling Again" / "Sandra" (duet with Keely Vasquez) / "Sweet Heaven (I'm In Love Again)" / "Who's Been Sleeping In My Bed."
- This album was nominated for a Grammy for Best Traditional Pop Vocal Album in 2016.
- "The Song's Gotta Come From The Heart" (originally from the 1947 film "It Happened in Brooklyn" starring Jimmy Durante): Music by Jule Styne, Lyrics by Sammy Cahn
- "Goody Goody" (a former Top 20 hit for Frankie Lymon in 1957, Gee Records 1039): Music by Matty Malneck, Lyrics by Johnny Mercer (1936)
- "Dream A Little Dream Of Me" (a former Top 20 hit for Mama Cass of the Mamas & the Papas in 1968): Music by Fabian Andre and Wilbur Schwandt, Lyrics by Gus Kahn (1931)
- "I Believe In You And Me" (a song recorded by Whitney Houston for the 1996 film "The Preacher's Wife," also a pop single for the Four Tops featuring Levi Stubbs in 1983): Music by David Wolfert, Lyrics by Sandy Linzer (1982)
- "Sunshine On My Shoulders" (a former #1 song for singer/songwriter John Denver in 1974): Music and Lyrics by John Denver (1971)
- "Zing! Went The Strings Of My Heart" (from the 1938 film "Listen, Darling" starring Judy Garland): Music and Lyrics by James Frederick Hanley (1934)
- "Moon River" (from the 1961 film "Breakfast at Tiffany's," also a 1961 signature song for Andy Williams): Music by Henry Mancini, Lyrics by Johnny Mercer
- "The Look Of Love" (a song recorded by Dusty Springfield for the 1967 film Casino Royale): Music by Burt Bacharach, Lyrics by Hal David
- "The Candy Man" (from the 1971 film "Willy Wonka and the Chocolate Factory," also a former

#1 hit for Sammy Davis, Jr. in June 1972): Written by Anthony Newley and Leslie Bricusse
- "I Wanna Be Loved By You" as performed by Marilyn Monroe in the 1959 film "Some Like It Hot." Music by Herbert Stothart and Harry Ruby, Lyrics by Bert Kalmar (1928)
- "What A Wonderful World" (a former single for Louis Armstrong in 1967, which was also included in the 1988 film "Good Morning, Vietnam." Written by Bob Thiele and George David Weiss

This Is My Town – Songs Of New York
B0026212-01

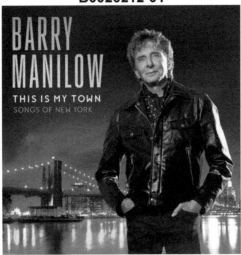

Track Listing:

This Is My Town / New York City Rhythm - On Broadway / Coney Island / Lonely Town / Lovin' At Birdland / Downtown - Uptown / On The Roof / I Dig New York / The Brooklyn Bridge (Virtual duet with Mel Tormé) / NYC Medley

Production Information:

Produced and Arranged by: Barry Manilow
Co-Produced by: David Benson (except "Coney Island," produced by Barry Manilow / Michael Lloyd, engineered and mixed by: Michael Lloyd)
Executive Producer: Garry C. Kief
Associate Producers: Marc Hulett and Greg Bartheld
Recorded at: Capitol Studios, Hollywood, CA / Peppertree Studios, Palm Springs, CA / Ignited Now Studios, Los Angeles, CA / Woodcliff Studios, Sherman Oaks, CA
Engineers: Bruce Botnick / Barry Manilow / Greg Bartheld / David Benson / Frank Rosato
Assistant Engineers: Chandler Harrod at Capitol Studios / Nolan Bateman at Ignited Now Studios
Mel Tormé Audio Isolation: Rick Silva and Audionamix. Mel Tormé Hi Resolution Audio Capture: Ed Stryker
CD Mastered by: Sangwook Sunny Nam
CD Mastered at: Jacob's Well Mastering, West Lebanon, NH
Vinyl Mastering and Cutting by: Eric Boulanger / Jett Gallindo
Mastered at: The Bakery, Los Angeles, CA
Programming and Pro Tools Editing: Greg Bartheld and David Benson
Photos: Mark Seliger
Art Direction: Josh Cheuse
Design: M. Holme
Music Librarian: J.B. Griffiths
Music Copying: J.B. Griffiths / Terry Woodson Music / Gordon Berg / William Edwards / Daniel Perito / Ron Pedley / Doug Walter and Ron Walters Jr.
A&R Admin: Evelyn Morgan
Release Coordination: Julie Johantgen
A&R Coordination: Allison Joyce
Production Manager: Mandy Dallacorte
Special Thanks to Bryan Jones at the Telos Alliance
Artist Management: Garry Kief / Stiletto Entertainment

Musicians:
Piano: Barry Manilow / Randy Kerber / Mike Lang / Greg Phillinganes
Bass: Will Lee / Chuck Berghofer / Nathan East
Guitar: Ken Berry / Jim Fox / Dean Parks / Paul Jackson Jr.
Drums: Gregg Field / John Robinson / Gregg Bissonette / Harvey Mason
Percussion: Emil Richards
Background Vocals: Barry Manilow / Ron Dante / Randy Crenshaw / Fletch Sheridan
Concert Master: Ralph Morrison
Violins: Joel Derouin / Liane Maunter / Lisa Dondlinger / Darius Campo / Ina Veli / Joel Pargman / Ron Clark / Kevin Connolly / Cynthia Moussas / Jennifer Takamatsu / Sara Parkins / Radu Pieptea / Marisa Kuney / Neil Samples / Neel Hammond / Nina Eutuhov
Violas: Robert Brophy / Alma Fernandez / Matt Funes / Luke Mauer / Rodney Wirtz
Cello: Armen Ksa Jikian / Timm Loo / John Walz / Ira Glansbeek / Christina Soule / Cecila Tsan
Harp: Julie Berghofer
Alto Sax: Dan Higgins / Don Shelton / Sal Lozano
Tenor Sax: Bob Sheppard / Vince Trombetta / Jeff Driskill / Joe Stone / Glen Berger
Baritone Sax: Gene Cipriano / Glen Berger
Trumpet: Wayne Bergeron / Gary Grant / Mike Stever / Chris Gray / Dan Fornero / Rob Schaer
Trombones: Steve Baxter / Dave Ryan / Bob McChesney / Charles Morillas
Bass Trombone: Craig Gosnell / Ben Devitt
French Horn: Jim Atkinson / Paul Klintworth
Contractor: Joe Soldo

Singles Released From This Album:
No Single Releases

Album Data:
Highest Chart Position: # 12 on May 13, 2017
Billboard Chart: Billboard Top 200
Number of Weeks on Chart: 4

Notes& Trivia:
- This album was released on CD and LP on April 21, 2017
- A Barnes & Noble Exclusive LP was released with a card to down a digital copy of the album.

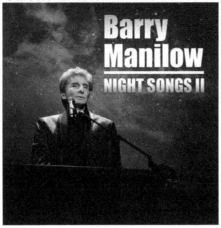

Track Listing:
Everything Happens To Me / I'm Old Fashioned / My Funny Valentine / I Had The Craziest Dream /
She Was Too Good To Me / Meditation / Lush Life / Isn't It A Pity / Moonlight Becomes You / Little Girl
Blue / Polka Dots And Moonbeams / We'll Be Together Again

Production Information:
Produced by: Barry Manilow and David Benson
Arranged by: Barry Manilow
Executive Producer: Garry C. Kief
Associate Producer: Marc Hulett
Recorded at: Ignited Now Studios, Los Angeles, CA
Engineered by: Greg Bartheld / David Benson
Assistant Engineer: Nolan Bateman
Digital Audio Editing by: Greg Bartheld
Digital and Vinyl Mastering by: Eric Boulanger
Mastered at: The Bakery, Los Angeles, CA
Project Manager: Chris Walters
Cover Photo: Dana Holland
Art Direction: Ria and Tim Photography
Management: Garry C. Kief - Stiletto Entertainment

Musicians:
Piano and Synthesized Acoustic Bass: Barry Manilow

Singles Released From This Album:
"My Funny Valentine" February 11, 2020 (Digital release only)

Album Data:
Highest Chart Position: # 32 on February 29, 2020
Billboard Chart: Billboard Top 200
Number of Weeks on Chart: 2

Notes & Trivia:
- This album was released on CD and LP on February 14, 2020
- The CD has a bonus track: "Like Someone In Love."

The Photo Gallery

MILES J. LOURIE
PERSONAL MANAGEMENT
250 West 57th Street
Suite 1028
New York, N.Y 10019

Publicity:

(212) 787-6621

A handsome Barry photo from early in his career. Used here for promotion.
This is an alternate shot taken during the photo session for his first album in 1973.
Photo by Kenn Duncan

THE ARRIVAL OF ANOTHER GREAT STAR!

BARRY MANILOW

has zoomed to the top
of the '75 charts with
his sensational hit—

"MANDY"

from his brilliant
album – an album that is
moving as fast as his
sold-out concert
appearances!

BARRY MANILOW II

includes
"MANDY" and "IT'S A MIRACLE"

The magic of this great
new star is also evident in
the tremendous sales now
being generated by the first
BARRY MANILOW
album!

BARRY MANILOW

"His Carnegie Hall Concert proved Manilow is a star in his own right and that he has
the potential to become a long-lasting superstar!—**PERFORMANCE MAGAZINE**

"He will be a star for a long time!"— **PHILADELPHIA DAILY NEWS**

"Manilow is going to make it. BIG!"— **PHILADELPHIA INQUIRER**

"When you watch Manilow, you begin to think of the categories that apply—from
entertainer to singer-songwriter to record star!—**BOSTON HERALD-TRAVELER**

A 1974 ad for Barry's first and second albums on ARISTA Records.

94

BARRY
MANILOW

bell
xxx

Publicity:

(212) 787-6621

**An early publicity photo.
Circa 1974**

Another beautiful Bell Records promotional photo.
Circa 1974

BARRY MANILOW

THE NEW SINGLE
"I Write The Songs"
ARIST 280.

Taken from the Album "MANILOW MAGIC. The Best of Barry Manilow."
Album: ARTV 2. Cassette: ARTVC 2.

ARISTA

A magazine promo ad from the UK for "I Write The Songs."

A smiling Barry in 1976
Photo by Lee Gurst

A poster for Barry's November 16, 1976 concert in Chicago, Illinois

Barry around 1976.
While growing up and collecting on Barry I could never get enough of his photos,
that hasn't changed all these years later.

Barry around 1977.
I was teased for liking Barry when I was a teenager, wearing his shirts to school, but I didn't care. I was enamored with Barry. Actually, I still am.

A beautiful man who is as talented as he is handsome.
My father wanted me to spend my money on blonde "babe"posters... nope
I wanted Barry and Barry is what I bought.

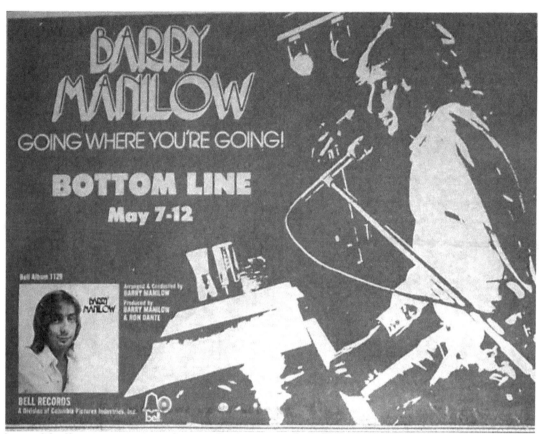

I would clip out every and any photo I found on Barry. Some of my aunts would also send them to me. I have hundreds in a filing cabinet.

A Barry Manilow pillow would have been just the thing I would have bought as a teenager. Unfortunately I don't recall ever seeing them back then.

A poster from TV Week. My walls were plastered with Barry Manilow, Marie Osmond, Karen Carpenter and John Denver.

Two of my favorite singer-songwriters while growing up.
In 1995 I was able to tell John I had a crush on him growing up and he was OK with that.
Though not gay himself he was perfectly fine with me and *very* supportive.
Two wonderfully talented and beautiful men here on Barry's 3rd CBS-TV Special!

I always wanted to thank the photographers who took such amazing photos of Barry,
but never knew who they were unless it was listed in the liner notes of an LP.

I often wondered how Barry had been so blessed. He could sing, he could write songs...
He just has so much talent.

Simply a gorgeous and vastly talented man.

No words necessary...

I loved when Barry dressed in all black. I loved his colorful outfits, but all black was extremely nice. This color suited him very well.

I recall being very sad that young men could not participate in some parts of the concerts. It was women only. Barry always put on a world class show.

112

BARRY MANILOW

ARISTA™

Personal Management:
MILES LOURIE
314 West 71st Street
New York, N.Y. 10023
(212)595-4330

Personal Agent:
ICM
International Creative Management
40 West 57th Street
New York, N.Y. 10019
(212)556-5600

Press Representatives:
SOLTERS & ROSKIN, INC.
62 West 45th Street, N.Y.C.
9255 Sunset Blvd., L.A.
(212)842-3500/(213)278-5692

Barry around 1976. One of many ARISTA Records promotional 8 x 10 photos I was able to get back in the day.

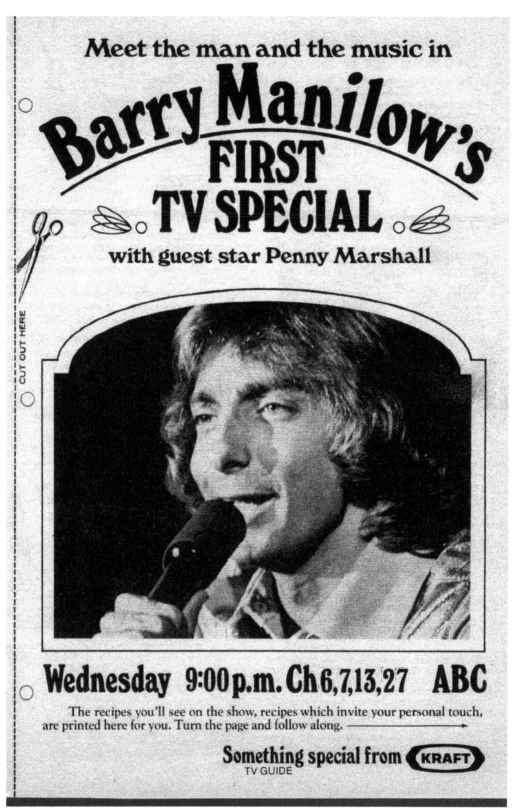

Meet the man and the music in

Barry Manilow's
FIRST
TV SPECIAL

with guest star Penny Marshall

Wednesday 9:00 p.m. Ch 6, 7, 13, 27 ABC

The recipes you'll see on the show, recipes which invite your personal touch, are printed here for you. Turn the page and follow along. ──────→

Something special from **KRAFT**
TV GUIDE

CUT OUT HERE

The 1970's were a different time. I was glad to have grown up during them. TV was so different. We had amazing TV specials. Here was a TV guide page I clipped out in 1977 for Barry's first special which I recorded on our Betamax machine.

114

So many celebrities were given TV Specials. 1979 was a great time in television.
I recorded both of these specials. I later bought Barry boxed set, but still have Cheryl's
special (all of them actually) on Beta tape transferred to DVD for home use.

A favorite ad from a favorite 1979 album!I have read Barry does not like his hair here.
I have always loved this style.

```
PG0527  404    K   4      ADULT
EVENT CODE SECTION/BOX ROW SEAT      40.00
        40.00 ENTER AISLE H
        7TH AVE 31ST & 33RD STS.
  404
SECTION/BOX
  CQ  20X     THE PARAMOUNT
  K   4
ROW  SEAT     BARRY MANILOW
MSG4B0A
16SEP91   FRI SEP 27,1991 8:00PM
```

Showstoppers certainly lived up to its name. Barry's series of 1991 concerts remain a favorite of mine. The man is a genius! From the first note to the finale it was one fantastic experience!

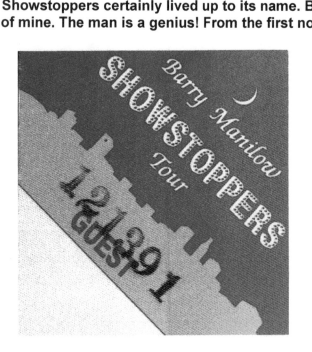

While I have collected as much as possible on Barry through the years there was always a lot of items that were not authorized, such as the plaque above. Though I wanted to buy the items I always resisted. Below is another unauthorized item. Nice, but no!

An ARISTA Records press kit used to promote Barry. These are rare and HTF.

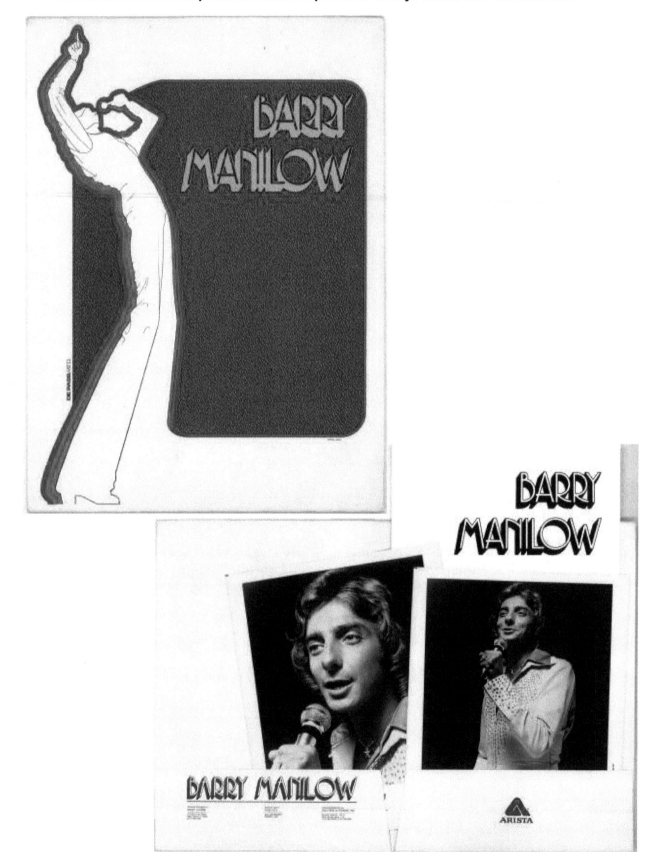

An ad for Barry's single "Looks Like We Made It" from his 1976 Arista album "This One's For You" (AL-4090)

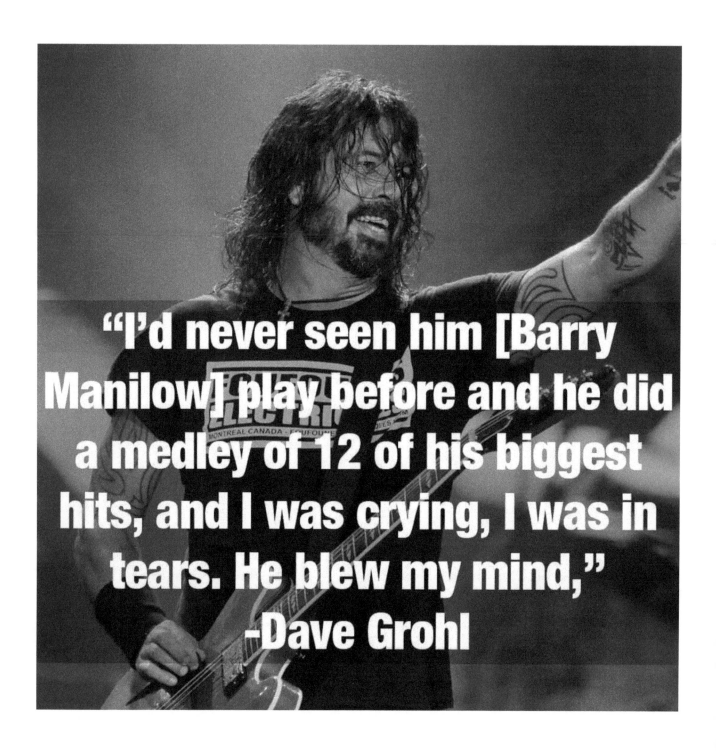

"I'd never seen him [Barry Manilow] play before and he did a medley of 12 of his biggest hits, and I was crying, I was in tears. He blew my mind,"
-Dave Grohl

I love finding out that people you don't think would appreciate Barry's music actually do. This has always reminded me not to judge a book by it's cover. Just because someone plays one style of music does not mean they can't appreciate another. Even Barry has shown his love for other genres with his albums and the material he presents in his concerts.
Good music is good music.

I've always loved to see the man smile.

Barry with longtime engineer and producer Michael DeLugg in the recording studio. This looks to be an overdub session and Barry is communicating with the musicians in the studio using the talk-back (TB) microphone. This was likely at the now shuttered Media Sound Studios in New York City. Media Sound Studios was located at 311 West 57th St, New York, NY

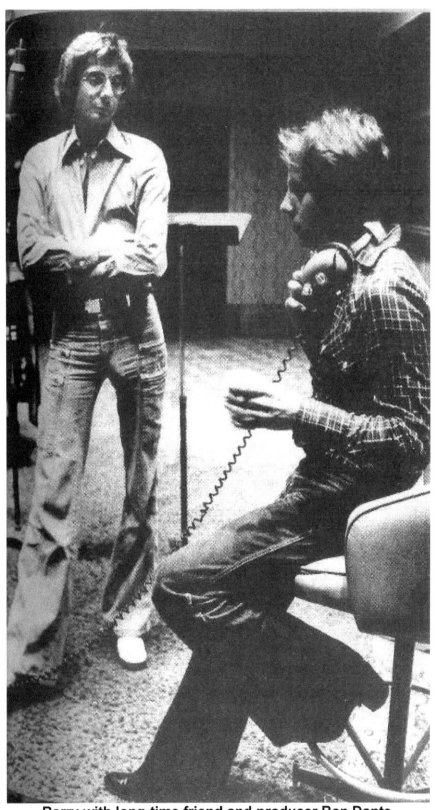

Barry with long-time friend and producer Ron Dante.
Ron co-produced with Barry, Barry's first nine albums!
I wish the image quality was better, but we work with what is available.

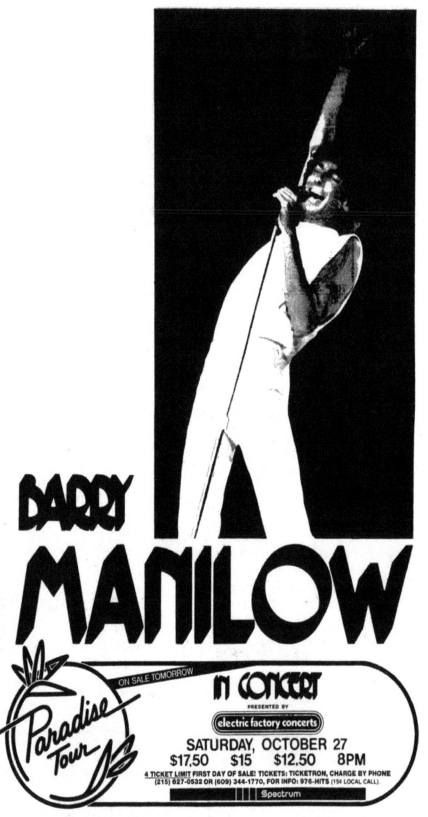

BARRY MANILOW

Paradise Tour

ON SALE TOMORROW

IN CONCERT

PRESENTED BY

electric factory concerts

SATURDAY, OCTOBER 27
$17.50 $15 $12.50   8PM

4 TICKET LIMIT FIRST DAY OF SALE! TICKETS: TICKETRON, CHARGE BY PHONE
(215) 627-0532 OR (609) 344-1770, FOR INFO: 976-HITS (15¢ LOCAL CALL).

Spectrum

Without promotion an artist will go nowhere no matter how talented. If the public doesn't hear of them they won't sell records or concert tickets. Those promoting Barry though the years knew what they were doing!

An artist at work. This looks to be a vocal overdub session.
Media Sound Studios, NY. Photo by Lee Gurst.

Barry with the fabulous Dick Clark who did so much for so many in the
entertainment world. Dick was tough, but at times you need to be.

127

BARRY MANILOW

MILES J. LOURIE
PERSONAL MANAGEMENT
250 West 57th Street
Suite 1023
New York, N. Y. 10019

A Bell Records promotional photo from 1974. Bell Records became Arista around this time.

"All the Time" is a song that was (is) so important to me and knowing now that Barry would have been OK with my crush on him makes everything I went through worth it.

A collectible plate was authorized in 1984.
(Authors collection)

130

**The greeting card included with the UK release of
"Read Em and Weep" from 1983 - Arista (ARIST-551)
(Authors Collection)**

Live
Albums

Barry Manilow Live
AL8500

Track Listing:
Riders to the Stars / Why Don't We Live Together / Looks Like We Made It / New York City Rhythm / A Very Strange Medley / Jump Shout Boogie Medley / This One's for You / Beautiful Music" (Part I) / Daybreak / Lay Me Down / Weekend in New England / Studio Musician / Beautiful Music (Part II) / Could It Be Magic – Mandy / It's a Miracle / It's Just Another New Year's Eve / I Write The Songs / Beautiful Music (Part III)

Production Information:
Produced by: Barry Manilow & Ron Dante
Recording Engineer: Michael DeLugg
Live Recording Engineer: John Venable
Mixed and assembled at: Media Sound Studios
Cover photography: Lara Donin
Interior photograph: Lee Gurst
Back Cover photographs: Lara Donin / Lee Gurst / William Redd / Bob Banks / Mark David Imburgia
Cover design and preparation: Ron Kellum & Howard Frizon
Art Direction: Bob Heimall

Musicians:
Piano: Barry Manilow
Guitar: Keith Loving
Bass Guitar: Steven Donaghey
Keyboards: Alan Axelrod
Drums: Lee Gurst
Percussion: Harold "Ricardo" Alexander
Background Vocals: Debra Byrd / Monica Burruss / Raparata

Singles Released From This Album:
"Daybreak" b/w ""Jump Shout Boogie" (ARISTA – 0273) September 9, 1977 (Peaked at # 23 in the US on the Billboard Hot 100 Chart in November 1977)

Album Data:
Highest Chart Position: # 1 on July 16, 1977
Billboard Chart: Billboard Top 200
Number of Weeks on Chart: 67

Notes & Trivia:
• This album was released on double LP, Open Reel, 8 Track and Cassette on May 11, 1977.

The first CD release was in 1986 (Arista A2CD 8049), "Beautiful Music" (Parts I, II and III) and portions of spoken material were edited from that release.

- This double album was certified Platinum 3x September 2, 1987 for sales in excess of 3,000,000 copies sold.
- This album was recorded in December 1976 at the Uris Theatre (now the The Gershwin Theatre - a Broadway theatre - located at 222 West 51st Street in New York during Barry's 12 days residency there from December 21, 1976 to January 2, 1977.) Except for "Very Strange Medley" which was recorded in Chicago at the Ravinia Festival on August 9, 1976.
- This album was a Billboard Top Album Pick on May 28, 1977
- This album was reissued on June 13, 2006 (Deluxe Legacy Edition 2-CD Arista/Legacy 82876 78552 2, 6/13/2006) includes bonus tracks "Let Me Go" / "I Am Your Child" / "Tryin' To Get The Feeling Again" / "Lady Flash Medley: Street Singin' / Nowhere To Run" and "One Of These Days." "Beautiful Music" (Parts I, II and III) was restored on this reissue as well.
- This album had a songbook released.
- Custom printed inner lyric / credit sleeve

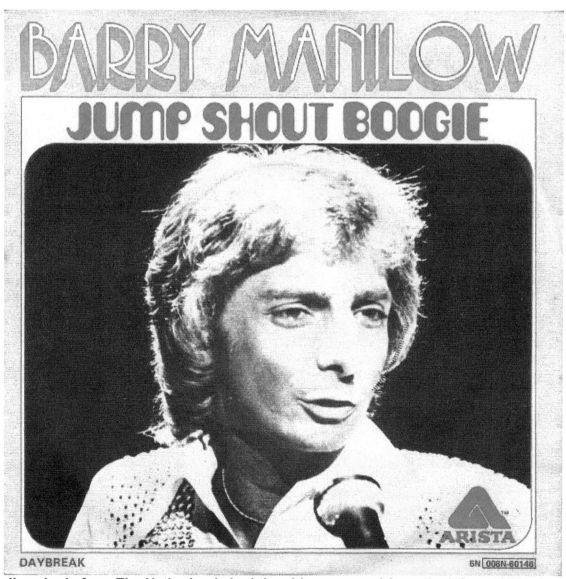

The live single from The Netherlands had the sides reversed from the US and UK releases.

Live In Britain
ARTV 4

Track Listing:
It's A Miracle - London / The Old Songs Medley (The Old Songs - I Don't Wanna Walk Without You - Let's Hang On) / Even Now / Stay (featuring Kevin DiSimone and James Jolis) / Beautiful Music Medlety (Beautiful Music - I Made It Through The Rain - Beautiful Music End) / Bermuda Triangle / Break Down The Door - Who's Been Sleeping In My Bed / Copacabana (At The Copa) / Could It Be Magic - Mandy / London - We'll Meet Again / One Voice / It's A Miracle

Production Information:
Produced by: Barry Manilow
Associate in Production and Engineer: Michael DeLugg
Assistant Engineer: Gary Boatner
Live Sound Engineer: Rick Southern
Mixed at: United-Western Studios, Los Angeles
Mastered by: Gordon Vicary
Mastered at: The Townhouse Studio, London, England
Irish release mastered at: Tape One, London, England by Jack Adams
Creative Consultant: Roberta Kent
Assistant to Barry Manilow: Roger Wall
Production Coordinator: Eric Borenstein
Contractor: Shaun Harris
Photography: Keith Morris and Richard Gray
Art Direction and Design: David Shortt

The Tour Crew: Jack Albeck / Eric Borenstein / John Borland / Harry Donovan / Holly Evans / A.J. Geigerich / Bruce George / Dean Hart / John Hill / Gary Lanvy / Charles Mercuri / Gary Rivera / Ira Seigel / Roy Shanahan / Bruce Weinstein / Gary Zipperman.
In The UK: Mick Chester / Bill Churchman / Chris Clow / Steve Croxford / Pete Edmonds / Connor Finn / Chris Harbord / Ian Purdie / Martin Rogers / Simon Tutchner. Tour Manager: Les Joyce.
Production Manager: Gary Speakman. Lights: Stig Edgren.

Musicians:
Keyboards: Robert Marullo / Victor Vanacore
Guitar: John Pondel
Bass: Carl Sealove
Drums: Bud Harner

Percussion: Robert Forte
Woodwind: Bill Page
Background Vocals: Kevin DiSimone / James Jolis / Muffy Hendricks / Becky Lopez-Porter
Additional Percussion Overdubs: Alan Estes / Emil Richards
Additional Vocal Overdubs: Eric Borenstein
Additional Guitar Overdubs: Mitch Holder
Music Director: Victor Vanacore

Singles Released From This Album:

"Stay" b/w "Nickles and Dimes" (ARIST – 464) (April 1982) (Peaked at # 23 in the UK on the UK Singles Chart.) This single was issued as a 7" picture disc as well as a picture sleeve release.

Album Data:

Highest Chart Position: # 1
Chart: Official Charts Company (UK)
Number of Weeks on Chart: 23

Notes & Trivia:

- This album was released on LP and Cassette on April 20, 1982.
- The Irish release of the LP included a flexi-disc: "BARRY Live in Ireland" Exclusive RTE Radio 2 Interview with Marty Whelan dated January 24, 1982 Limited Edition. Promotional Copy – Not For Resale.
- The album was re-issued on CD in Germany in 1991 as Arista–261 320
- The album was recorded live at the Royal Albert Hall in London January 11 and 12, 1982
- This album was certified Platinum in the UK for sales for sales in excess of 300,000 copies.
- The album came with a gate-fold sleeve and had a hype sticker on the cover that read: "BARRY MANILOW His greatest hits and more *AS SEEN ON TV.*

**The 45 single for "Stay" b/w "Nickles and Dimes" from the UK.
The single track is longer than the album track. DJ copy.**

Live On Broadway
AL-8638

Track Listing:
ACT I: Sweet Life - It's A Long Way Up / Brooklyn Blues / Memory / Up Front (Barry, Debra Byrd and Company) / God Bless The Other 99 (Barry and Company) / Mandy - It's A Miracle
ACT II: Some Good Things Never Last (duet with Debra Byrd) / If You Remember Me / Do Like I Do / The Best Seat In The House / The Gonzo Hits Medley / If I Can Dream

Production Information:
Produced by: Barry Manilow / Michael DeLugg
Engineered by: Michael DeLugg
Mixed at: The Power Station, New York City / Sound Track, Inc., New York City / Image Recording, Hollywood, CA
Mixing Engineer: Michael DeLugg
Assistant Mix Engineers: Dan Gellert / David Lebowitz / Jason Roberts
Assembled at: The Hit Factory, New York City
Assembling Engineers: Chris Tergesen / Michael DeLugg
Assistant Assembling Engineer: Paul Logus
Digitally Mastered at: The Hit Factory DMS, New York City
Mastering Enginner: Tom Coyne
Cover Photo: Barry Dahlkoetter
Montage Photos: Larry Busacca/Retna Ltd. / Mark Hulett / Kevin Roberts / Christie Sayre / Dennis Hallinan
Back Cover Photo: Steven R. Straub
Art Direction / Design: Carolyn Quan
Production Assistant: Glenn Wygant
Executive in Charge of Production: Eric Borenstein
Music Directors: Bud Harner / Ron Pedley
Assistant to Mr. Manilow: Marc Hulett
Artist Management: Garry C. Kief / Steve Wax / Eric Borenstein / Stiletto Management, Inc. Hollywood, CA

The Stage Show:
Directed by: Kevin Carlisle
Original Production Created and Produced by: Joe Gannon

Written by: Ken and Mitzie Welch, Roberta Kent, Barry Manilow
Production Designer: Jeremy Railton
Lighting Designer: J.T. McDonald
Visual Images: Julio Campos / Kevin Roberts

The Tour Crew:
Tour Manager: Les Joyce
Assistant Tour Manager: Victor Bridgers
Production Manager: Gary Speakman
Stage Manager: Jack Albeck
Tour Advance: Charlie Robertson
Production Assistants: Randy Doney / Kathy Carey
Music Copyist & Librarian: Karen Smith
Wardrobe Master: Phillip Dennis
Drum Technician: John Bunker
Keyboard Technician: Terry Lawless
Head Carpenter: Dana Vanella
Carpenter: Kevin Spinks
Lighting Director: Jonathan Holt
Lighting Contractor: Peter Clarke / John Lee (Supermick Lights, Inc.)
Head Electrician: James Geoghegan
Electrician: John Harper
Gel-Jet Operator / Electrician: Mary Malley
Sound Contractor: Rikki Farr & Pierre D'Astugues (Electrotec Productions, Inc.)
House Engineer: Russell Fischer
Monitor Engineer: Michael Graphix
Head Audio Technician: Billy Chrysler
Audio Technician: Mark Tooch
Visual Images (Slide Programmer): Kevin Roberts
Projectionist: Andy Jackson
Musical Instruments Furnished by: **Yamaha International**

Musicians:
Drums: Bud Harner
Keyboards: Ron Pedley
Bass Guitar / Cello / Vocals : Marc Levine
Guitar / Vocals: John Pondel
Keyboards / Vocals: Joe Melotti / Billy Kidd
Percussion / Violin / Vocals: Vanessa Brown
Woodwinds / Vocals: Dana Robbins
Vocals: Debra Byrd

Singles Released From This Album:
"If I Can Dream" b/w "Even Now" (Arista / BMG 113 025) (Peaked at # 81 in the UK on the UK Singles
Chart.) Side B: ©1978 Arista Records.
"If You Remember Me" (ASCD–9948) (Peaked at # 41 in the US on the Billboard Adult Contemporary
Singles Chart.)

Album Data:
Highest Chart Position: # 196 on June 30, 1990
Billboard Chart: Billboard Top 200

Notes & Trivia:

- This album was released on 2 LPs / 1 CD / 1 Cassette on April 17, 1990
- A UK double Cassette version was also released.
- A VHS videotape and LaserDisc were released of the concert in 1990. A DVD was released in 1991.
- Recorded December 2-3, 1989 at the Chicago Theatre, Chicago, Illinois
- A 1993 CD release titled: "Memory" (Distributed by: SAAR - srl # CD-12051 / Italy) includes ten of these 1990 live tracks but in a different order: "Mandy" - "It's A Miracle" / "Brooklin Blues" (spelled incorrectly on the insert) / 'If You Remember Me" / "Memory" / "The Gonzo Hits Medley" / "If I Can Dream" / "Sweet Life" - "It's A Long Way Up" / "Up Front" / 'Do Like I Do" / "God Bless The Other 99"
- "Up Front" (songwriters - Barry Manilow, Bruce Sussman), Kamakazi Music Corp./Appoggiatura Music (BMI)
- "God Bless The Other 99" (songwriters - Ken & Mitzie Welch), Little Jug Music, Inc. (ASCAP), Townsway Music (BMI)
- "If You Remember Me" (songwriters - Marvin Hamlisch, Carole Bayer Sager), Begonia Melodies, Inc. (BMI), Chappell & Co., Inc., Red Bullet Music (ASCAP)
- "Do Like I Do" (songwriters - Hammer and Slater), EMI Music (ASCAP)
- "The Best Seat In The House" (songwriters Dave Grusin, Alan & Marilyn Bergman), Roaring Fork Music (BMI), Threesome Music, Co. (ASCAP)
- "If I Can Dream" (songwriter - Walter Earl Brown), Gladys Music, Chappell & Co., Inc. (ASCAP)

A promotional poster for the *Live on Broadway* album.

2Nights Live
BMG 82876 59478 2

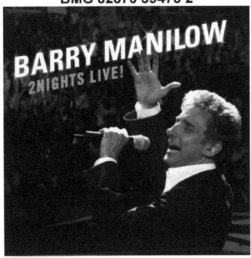

Track Listing:
Night One:
The Walk To The Stage / Gonzo Opening: Ready To Take A Chance Again - Daybreak - Somewhere In The Night - This One's For You / Looks Like We Made It / Can't Smile Without You / Bandstand Boogie / Mandy / Even Now / Dialogue #1 / Harmony (from "Harmony") / Turn The Radio Up / Dialogue #2 / The Best Of Me / Weekend In New England / Could It Be Magic (Play Off) / Let Freedom Ring / It's A Miracle / Dialogue #3 / You're There / We Live On Borrowed Time / Could It Be Magic (Play Off)
Night Two:
Fanfare - I'm Comin' Back / Sweet Heaven (I'm In Love Again) / Who's Been Sleeping In My Bed / Tryin' To Get The Feeling Again / Somewhere Down The Road / Dialogue #4 / That's Life / Dialogue #5 / Every Single Day (from "Harmony") / New York City Rhythm (Intro) / New York City Rhythm / I Made It Through The Rain / She Should'a Been Mine / They Dance! / Dialogue #6 / When October Goes / If Tomorrow Never Comes / Copacabana (At The Copa) / I Write The Songs / Old Friends / Forever And A Day

Production Information:
Produced by: Garry C. Kief / Barry Manilow
Assistant to Mr. Kief: Lynn Michelson
Assistant to Mr. Manilow: Marc Hulett
Written by: Barry Manilow / Mitzie and Ken Welch
Set Design by: Seth Jackson
Lighting Design by: Seth Jackson
Sound Design by: Ken Newman
Wardrobe Design by: Phillip Dennis
Choreography by: Kye Brackett
Special Material by: Larry Amoros

Musicians:
Musical Director / Keyboards / Vocals: Steve Welch
Percussion: Mike Faue
Guitars / Vocals: Michael Lent
Keyboards: Ron Pedley
Bass / Vocals: Larry Antonino / Stan Sargeant
Drums: Russ McKinnon

141

Reeds: Ed Joffe / Dan Willis / John Winder
Trumpet: David Rogers / David Gale / Larry Lunetta
Trombone: Keith O'Quinn / Herb Besson
French Horn: Lisa Pike
Choir: New Jersey One Love Choir
Tour Choir Directors: Byron Motley / Ron Walters / Debra Byrd

Singles Released From This Album:
No Single Releases

Album Data:
Highest Chart Position: # 27 on April 24, 2004
Billboard Chart: Billboard Top 200
Number of Weeks on Chart: 2

Notes & Trivia:
- This album was released on CD on April 6, 2004
- Released in the UK on CD on August 22, 2005 as "Ultimate Live" BMG-82876719142
- This album was certified Gold on May 11, 2004 for sales of of over 500,000 copies
- Recorded August 3 - 4, 2002 at: PNC Bank Arts Center in Holmdel, NJ. Recorded during the last two days of the *Barry Manilow Live 2002!* tour.

Tour program from the *Barry Manilow Live 2002!* tour

Barry Manilow With The Royal Philharmonic Concert Orchestra – Live In London
Stiletto Entertainment -SE0004

Track Listing:
Overture / Fanfare - I'm Comin' Back / Riders To The Stars / Opening Medley: Daybreak - Somewhere In The Night - Looks Like We Made It / Can't Smile Without You / Stay (UK release only) / Even Now / New York City Rhythm / Bermuda Triangle (UK / Germany releases only) / Studio Musician / Bring On Tomorrow (UK / US releases only) / The Best Seat In The House (UK / US releases only) / Talk To Me (US Only) / Sandra (UK release only) / Mandy / Copacabana (At The Copa) (UK / US release only) / I Write The Songs / One Voice - It's A Miracle / Old Friends - Forever And A Day (UK / US releases only) / Mandy (Alex Christensen's Radio Edit. Germany release only) / Copacabana (At The Copa) (Bonus Mix – Germany release only) / Can't Smile Without You (Alex Christensen's Radio Edit – Germany release only)

Production Information:
CD produced by: Barry Manilow / Michael Lloyd
Executive Producer: Garry C. Kief
Associate Producer: Marc Hulett
Engineered by: Tom Davis
Digital Editing: George Legeri III / Nigel Lundemo
Mixed at: The Studio One, Los Angeles, CA
Mixed by: Michael Lloyd
Mastered at: The Mastering Lab, Inc., Ojai, CA
Mastered by: Doug Sax and Sanwook "Sunny" Nam
DVD produced by: Barry Manilow / Garry C. Kief
Executive Producers: Mark C. Grove / Troy P. Queen / Rob Kief
Directed and Edited by: Rob Kief
Audio portion engineered by: Tom Davis
Audio mixed at: The Studio One, Los Angeles, CA
Audio mixed by: Michael Lloyd
DVD audio Mixed and Mastering by: Tom Davis
Audio Digital Editing by: George Legeri III / Nigel Lundemo

Album Data:
Highest Chart Position: # 24 on May 12, 2012
Billboard Chart: Billboard Top 200
Number of Weeks on Chart: 2

Notes & Trivia:

- This album was released on CD in the US on April 24, 2012
- This album was released with a DVD in the UK and US only. The DVD could be purchased separately in Germany.
- The UK version was released April 23, 2012
- Germany version was released March 23, 2012 as a 2 CD set titled "Forever and Beyond." The Germany release includes the 2011 album *15 Minutes* in its entirety as Disk 1. Disk 2 - *Live in London*, includes "Bermuda Triangle" (Live in London) / "Mandy" (Alex Christensen's Radio Edit) / "Copacabana (At The Copa)" (Bonus Mix) and the track "Can't Smile Without You" (Alex Christensen's Radio Edit) in place of US Release "Bring On Tomorrow" (Live in London) / "The Best Seat In The House" (Live in London) / "Talk To Me" (Live in London) / "Copacabana (At The Copa)" (Live in London) / "Old Friends - Forever And A Day" (Live in London)
- Recorded live at The O2 Arena in London, England, May 4 -7, 2011
- UK Release includes "Stay" / "Bermuda Triangle" / "Sandra" in place of US Release "Talk To Me."
- The DVD included: Overture / Fanfare - I'm Comin' Back / Riders To The Stars / Opening Medley: Daybreak - Somewhere In The Night - Looks Like We Made It / Can't Smile Without You / Stay / Even Now / Studio Musician / Bring On Tomorrow / Mandy - Could It Be Magic / Copacabana (At The Copa) / I Write The Songs / Old Friends - Forever And A Day

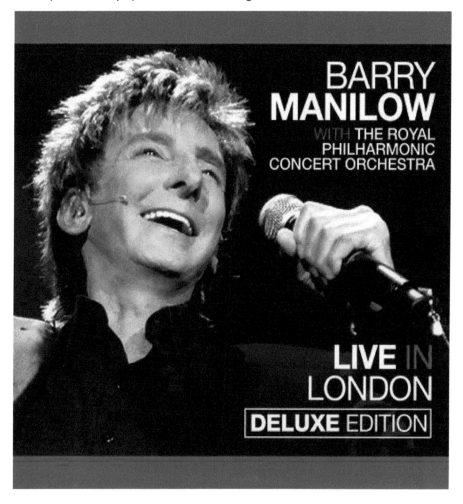

The Deluxe edition above with the DVD

The single disc version is pictured above.

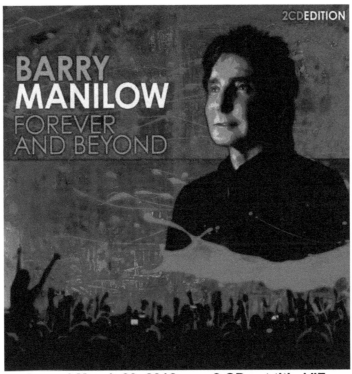

Germany version released March 23, 2012 as a 2 CD set titled "Forever and Beyond"
Includes the 2011 album *15 Minutes*

Critical Compilation Albums

Many compilation albums have been released on Barry world-wide since the start of his career, far too many to compile here. These are, in my opinion, the best of the best in terms of material and graphic design.

Greatest Hits
A2L-8601

Track Listing:
Mandy / New York City Rhythm / Ready To Take A Chance Again (in Mono - from the film "Foul Play") / Looks Like We Made It / Daybreak (Live) / Can't Smile Without You / It's A Miracle / Even Now / Bandstand Boogie / Tryin' To Get The Feeling Again / Could It Be Magic / Somewhere In The Night / Jump Shout Boogie / Weekend In New England / All The Time / This One's For You / Copacabana (Disco) / Beautiful Music / I Write The Songs

Production Information:
Produced by: Barry Manilow and Ron Dante
Engineer: Michael DeLugg
Cover Photography by: Ron Harris
Interior Photos by: Lee Gurst
Back Cover Photography by: John Ford
Art Direction by: Donn Davenport

Musicians:
Please see individual albums tracks are culled from; "Barry Manilow I" / "Barry Manilow II"/ "Tryin' To Get The Feeling" / "This One's For You" / "Even Now"

Singles Released From This Album:
N/A

Album Data:
Highest Chart Position: # 7 on February 10, 1979
Billboard Chart: Billboard Top 200
Number of Weeks on Chart: 75

Notes & Trivia:
- This album was released on LP, Open Reel, Cassette and 8 Track on November 1, 1978.
- Released as picture discs.
- This album was certified Gold on November 27, 1978 for sales in excess of 500,000 copies. Certified Platinum on November 27, 1978 for sales in excess of 1,000,000 copies and triple Platinum on September 2, 1987 for sales in excess of 3,000,000 copies.

- Custom printed inner lyric / credit sleeve.
- This album has a songbook
- Three CD versions have been issued with various changes:
- (1) ARCD 8039 DIDY 479 (total time 70:50) has disco version of "Copacabana" (5:45) / Live version of "Daybreak" (3:49) and the slightly shorter album version of "It's A Miracle" (3:45)
- (2) ARCD 8039 DIDY 479 (total time 68:49) has original version of "Copacabana" (4:01) / Studio version of "Daybreak" (3:09) and a remixed version of "It's A Miracle" (3:56)
- (3) ARCD 8039 DIDX 162 (Japanese issue) (total time 69:06) has original version of "Copacabana" (4:00) / Live version of "Daybreak" (3:49) and shorter album version of "It's A Miracle" (3:44)
- Single CD release is missing "Jump Shout Boogie."
- Japanese LP version has rearranged track order and contains 20 tracks instead of 19. Includes "Bermuda Triangle" / "(Why Don't We Try) A Slow Dance" / "Ships" / "I Made It Through The Rain" instead of "Bandstand Boogie" / "Somewhere In The Night" / "This One's For You."
- In some European countries this album was released as "Manilow Magic: The Best of Barry Manilow," "The Very Best of Barry Manilow," or "The Best Of Barry Manilow." These releases are a single LP with only 11 or 12 tracks. The albums had nearly identical artwork. It was initially available on LP and cassette and was later issued on CD in Hong Kong as "Greatest Hits." The cover below is the European "Manilow Magic" LP cover.

A Touch More Magic
Arista 610 101-222

Track Listing:
+You're Looking Hot Tonight / Let's Hang On / I Wanna Do It With You / I'm Gonna Sit Right Down And Write Myself A Letter / Bermuda Triangle / Some Kind Of Friend / Stay (Live) / *Put A Quarter In The Jukebox (with Ronnie Milsap) / Read 'Em And Weep / The Old Songs / Lonely Together / Even Now / Memory / I Made It Through The Rain / One Voice

+Production Information "You're Looking Hot Tonight":
Produced and Arranged by: Arif Mardin / Barry Manilow
Recorded at: Recorded at: Sunset Sound, Los Angeles, CA / Atlantic Studios, New York, NY / Right Track Recording, New York, NY
Engineered by: Jeremy Smith
 Assistant Engineer: Terry Christian
Additional recording and mixed by: Michael O'Reilly, Assisted by Dan Nash
Mixed at: Atlantic Studios, New York
Mixed by: Michael O'Reilly
Assistant Mix Engineer: Dan Nash
Contractor: Frank Dicaro
Concertmaster: Gene Orloff
Ronnie Milsap appears courtesy of RCA Records
Cover design by: David Shortt

+Musicians "You're Looking Hot Tonight":
Synthesizers: Michael Boddicker
Guitar: Paul M. Jackson, Jr
Bass: Leland Sklar
Drums: Carlos Vega / Mike Baird

*Production Information: "Put A Quarter In The Juke Box":
Produced by: Jack White + Arranged by: Barry Manilow / Michael Boddicker
Recorded at: Sunset Sound, Los Angeles, CA / Westlake Recorders, Los Angeles, CA / Bodifications, Los Angeles, CA
Engineer: Humberto Gatica
Mixed by: Juergen Koppers

*Musicians: "Put A Quarter In The Juke Box":
Piano: Barry Manilow
Yamaha JS-1 Synthesizers: David Foster
Guitar: Dan Huff
Bass: Neil Stubenhaus
Drums: Carol Vega
Additional Synclavier: Bob Christianson
Simmons Drum Programmer: Reek Havok
Tamborine: Joe Mardin
Background Vocals: Tom Kelly / Jon Joyce / Tom Funderburk / Barry Manilow

Album Data:
N/A

Notes & Trivia:

- Released on November 28, 1983 on LP, Cassette and CD
- Lacquer cut by Jack Adams at Strawberry Mastering and was one of the last albums mastered at the cutting facility.
- European Import follow-up to "Manilow Magic/The Best Of Barry Manilow"; equivalent to the US release of "Greatest Hits Vol. II".
- Manufactured by Sonopress, Gutersloh, West Germany.
- Distributed by Polygram Records Operations, Ltd.
- The album was mostly compilation, with the exception of three new tracks: "You're Looking Hot Tonight" / "Put a Quarter in the Jukebox" / "Read 'Em and Weep" (last is a cover of the Meat Loaf song of the same name which was recorded for his 1981 album, "Dead Ringer," although with an amended second verse and different instrumental arrangement. The song was written and produced for Meat Loaf by the late Jim Steinman. Barry's recordings was also produced by Jim Steinman)
- Available in US only as an import item / special order
- Other Producers: Ron Dante / John Jansen / Michael DeLugg
- "Let's Hang On" from the album "If I Should Love Again" (1981) / "I Wanna Do It With You" from the album "I Wanna Do It With You" (1982) / "I'm Gonna Sit Down And Write Myself A Letter" from the album "I Wanna Do It With You" (1982) / "Bermuda Triangle" from the album "Barry" (1980) / "Some Kind Of Friend" from the album "I Wanna Do It With You" (1982) / "Stay" (Live) from the album "Live In Britain" (1982) / "The Old Songs" from the album "If I Should Love Again" (1981) / "Lonely Together" from the album "Barry" (1980) / "Even Now" from the album "Even Now" (1978) / "Memory" from the album "I Wanna Do It With You" (1982) / "I Made It Through The Rain" from the album "Barry" (1980) / "One Voice" from the album "One Voice" (1979)

The Magic of Barry Manilow
SMM-109

Track Listing:

A1 Bermuda Triangle / A2 Copacabana / A3 The Old Songs / A4 I Don't Wanna Walk Without You / A5 Let's Hang On / A6 You're Looking Hot Tonight / B1 Stay / B2 Could It Be Magic / B3 If I Should Love Again / B4 I Made It Through The Rain / B5 I Wanna Do It With You / B6 Somewhere Down The Road

Production Information:

Produced by Barry Manilow

Associate producer and engineer: Michael DeLugg on tracks A1-A5 / B2 / B3 / B4 / B6 - Bill Drescher on tracks B1 / B5

Notes & Trivia:

- All original sound recordings made by Arista Records Inc. Released 1984.
- Tracks A1-A5 recorded live at the Royal Albert Hall in January 1982
- Track A6 recorded live at Blenheim Palace in August 1983
- Compiled for Lever Brothers by Stiletto Music Marketing Limited
- Manufactured in the UK by Stiletto Music Marketing Limited, 122 Holland Park Avenue, London, W11 4UA
- Side one contained live concert recordings and side two was material recorded in the studio.
- Also released on Cassette as shown below.

The Manilow Collection / Twenty Classic Hits
Arista AL9-8274

Track Listing:

Mandy / This One's For You / Weekend In New England / Even Now / I Made It Through The Rain / It's A Miracle / Can't Smile Without You / Ready To Take A Chance Again / Looks Like We Made It / Somewhere In The Night / Copacabana (At The Copa) / Some Kind Of Friend / Read 'Em And Weep / Memory / Run To Me (duet with Dionne Warwick) / When October Goes / Tryin' To Get The Feelin' / I Write The Songs / Could It Be Magic / One Voice

Production Information:

Art Direction / Design: Ria Lewerke
Illustration: Terry Taylor
Original Logo Design: Ben Cziller

Notes & Trivia:

- This album was released on May 30, 1985 on LP, Cassette and 8 Track. Later re-released in 1992 on CD with a slight cover redesign and fewer tracks. The CD does not have "I Made It Through The Rain" / "Memory" / "When October Goes" / "Tryin' To Get The Feeling." The LP does not contain "Paradise Cafe" and "You're Looking Hot Tonight." The CD has the original album version of "Could It Be Magic" and LP contains the single release version.
- This album was certified Gold on September 2, 1987
- All songs previously released except for: "Run To Me" (duet with Dionne Warwick) which was produced by Barry Manilow. Engineer / Associate in Production: Michael DeLugg
- One version of the cover artwork in the US has no cover text as seen below and a longer tie.

Barry Manilow Especial
404.7232

Track Listing:

Can't Smile Without You / Copacabana (At The Copa) / Daybreak / Escrevo As Canqoes (I Write The Songs) / It's A Miracle / Qualquer Dia (Twenty Four Hours A Day) (duet with Joanna) / This One's For You / Mandy / I Made It Through The Rain / Magia (Could It Be Magic)

Notes & Trivia:

- Released on LP on September 27, 1985
- Brazilian edition with Barry singing 5 songs in Portuguese.
- This release is available as a digital download from various digital providers.

Back jacket.

EOLIA/LOVE SONGS
Arista A32D-95

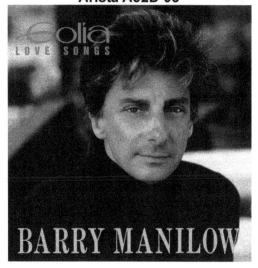

Track Listing:

Eolia / Mandy / I Write The Songs / Ready To Take A Chance Again / The Old Songs / Weekend In New England / Here Comes The Night / Looks Like We Made It / Even Now / Stay / One Voice / This One's For You / Memory / Somewhere In The Night / In Search Of Love (duet with Hideki Saijo)

Production Information:

Produced by Barry Manilow and Ron Dante, except: "The Old Songs" (produced by Barry Manilow) / "Eolia" (produced by Barry Manilow and J. Pasquale) / "Here Comes The Night" (produced by Barry Manilow) / "Stay" (produced by Barry Manilow) / "Memory" (produced by Barry Manilow) / "In Search Of Love" (produced by Tasuku Okamura, Barry Manilow and Howie Rice)

Singles Released From This Album:

"Eolia" / "You Begin Again" (Arista – A10D-143) December 16, 1989

Notes & Trivia:

- Japanese only release.
- All songs previously released except; "Eolia" and "In Search Of Love" (duet with Hideki Saijo)

The Japanese promotional 7" single insert for "Eolia"
PRTD-3068

The Songs 1975-1990
2LP Arista-503 868 / 2CD-2CT Arista-353 868

Track Listing:
I Write The Songs / One Voice / The Old Songs / I Don't Want To Walk Without You / Some Good Things Never Last (duet with Debra Byrd - featuring Dana Robbins from "Live on Broadway" - edit) / Somewhere Down The Road / When I Wanted You / Stay (featuring Kevin Di Simone and James Jolis - Live in Britain) / Even Now / Read 'Em And Weep / Somewhere In The Night / I Made It Through The Rain / Daybreak (Live) / Please Don't Be Scared / Looks Like We Made It / Some Kind Of Friend / Bermuda Triangle / This One's For You / Mandy / If I Should Love Again (Live) / All The Time / Copacabana (At The Copa) / Keep Each Other Warm / Weekend In New England / Lonely Together / Can't Smile Without You / Tryin' To Get The Feeling Again / Could It Be Magic / Brooklyn Blues - (Featuring Tom Scott) / Who Needs To Dream / Ready To Take A Chance Again / If I Can Dream (from "Live on Broadway") / Ships / London

Production Information:
Direction: Stiletto, Hollywood, California, Stiletto Management U.K. Ltd. (London)
Design: John Rimmer / Pointblanc
Centrefold photography: John Barton / Lucy Waters / Lynn Killick (Memorabilia)

Notes & Trivia:
- Released in July 1990 on 2 LPs / 2 CDs / 2 Cassettes. European only release.
- The songs "Some Kind Of Friend" / "Bermuda Triangle" / "This One's For You" / "Ships" / "London" are not on the vinyl or tape releases.
- The album reached the top 20 of the UK sales charts in 1990.

Inner graphic design for LP / CD / Cassette

The Complete Collection and Then Some...
Arista 82876 69272 / 4CD+DVD

Track Listing:

The Best Of Me (Intro only) (0:45) / Sweet Life (Unreleased Live Performance at Carnegie Hall) (4:12) / I Am Your Child (Unreleased Live Performance at Continental Baths) (2:35) / Could It Be Magic (Featherbed) (2:34) / Could It Be Magic (6:50) / Brandy (Scott English) (edit) (1:30) / Mandy (Unreleased Original First Take) (3:47) / It's A Miracle (4:01) / Sandra / (Unreleased Live from Carnegie Hall) (4:33) / I Write The Songs (3:55) / As Sure As I'm Standing Here (4:54) / New York City Rhythm (4:44) / Tryin' To Get The Feeling Again (Unreleased Alternate Take) (4:45) / All The Time (3:17) / Ready To Take A Chance Again (from the motion picture "Foul Play") (3:02) / Somewhere In The Night (3:29) / The Old Songs (Unreleased Alternate Take) (4:53) / I Don't Want To Walk Without You (3:57) / If I Should Love Again (Unreleased Alternate Take) (5:02) / Copacabana (Home cassette edit) (1:33) / Copacabana (At The Copa) (4:05) / Dancin' Fool (from Big Fun on Swing Street) (1:18) / I'm Your Man (4:48) Hey Mambo (2:51) / Big Fun (3:55) / Riders To The Stars (Live) (4:52) / I Wanna Be Somebody's Baby (Unreleased Live Outtake) (4:17) / Daybreak (Live) (3:51) / Even Now (Unreleased Live in Tokyo) (3:37) / Life Will Go On (Unreleased Live in London) (3:44) / Memory (Live on Broadway) (4:28) / Ships (Live on Broadway) (4:00) / If I Can Dream (Live on Broadway) (4:51) / One Voice (Live in Britain) (3:02) / This One's For You (Unreleased Demo) (3:09) / Lay Me Down (4:22) / Big City Blues (duet with Mel Tormé) (4:20) / Somewhere Down The Road (Unreleased Demo) (4:07) / A Little Travelling Music, Please (4:26) / You Could Show Me (1:49) / Ave Maria (4:00) / Look To The Rainbow (duet with Barbara Cook) (4:34) / Joey (Unreleased Demo) (3:15) / Please Don't Be Scared (5:37) / Baby, It's Cold Outside (duet with K.T. Oslin) (5:26) / When October Goes (4:03) / Ain't It A Shame (Unreleased Outtake) (3:37) / Brooklyn Blues (5:12) / How Do I Stop Loving You? (Unreleased Demo) (5:04) / Just Remember / Unreleased Live from Los Angeles) (3:22) / I Can't Teach My Old Heart New Tricks (4:03) / Weekend In New England (3:45) / Give My Regards To Broadway (Live from Atlantic City) (3:47) / Send In The Clowns/Looks Like We Made It (Live from Atlantic City) (5:50) / Can't Smile Without You (Unreleased Alternate First Take) (3:07) / Beautiful Music (4:40) / Fugue For Tinhorns (Trio with Michael Crawford and Hinton Battle) (2:50) / My Girl/No

One In This World (with Melissa Manchester) (5:25) / Don't Talk To Me Of Love (with Mirielle Mattieu) (4:11) / The Last Duet (duet with Lily Tomlin) (4:02) / Wild Places (4:14) / Never Met A Man I Didn't Like (5:00) / Who Needs To Dream (3:55) / Read 'Em And Weep (5:12) / Let Freedom Ring (4:07) / Let Me Be Your Wings (solo) (3:46) / If Tomorrow Never Comes (5:04) Another Life (4:20) / I Made It Through The Rain (Unreleased Alternate Take) (4:21) / The Best Of Me (4:07)

Production Information:
Produced and compiled by: Marc Hulett and Barry Manilow
Executive Produced by: Garry Kief
Engineering supervised by: Don Murray at Sunset Sound, Los Angeles, CA
Digitally edited by: Robert Vosgien at: CMS Digital, Pasadena, CA
Digitally re-mastered by: Wally Traugott at: Capitol Studios, Hollywood, CA
Tape restoration / baking by: Ran Ballard for Hydratech
Creative Direction by: Ken Levy
Art Direction by: Susan Mendola
Book Design by: Carolyn Quan / Studio Q
Text edited by: Maureen Lasher
Production Supervision by: Milton Sincoff
Production Coordination by: Andrea Doornheim
Music Administration by: Melanie Baldwin
Booklet Photography by: Timothy White
Other photographs courtesy of: Linda Allen / Bobby Bank / Peter Borsari . Larry Busacca / The Chicago Tribute Company / Cashbox Magazine / Ann Flood / Greg Gorman / Lee Gurst / Leon Lecash / David Leshay / Jack Hoffman / Michael Jacobs / Robin Platzer / Record World / Matthew Rolston / Jay Thompson / Randee St. Nicholas / The Sunday Mail / US Magazine ... apologies for any omissions.
Artist Management: Stiletto Management: Garry Kief / Steve Wax / Edna Collison

Notes & Trivia:
- Originally released on 4 CDs / 4 Cassettes on October 11, 1992 with VHS tape.
- It was certified Gold on May 24, 2002 for sales in excess of 500,000 copies.
- Re-released on September 13, 2005 with a DVD of the same material as the original VHS video tape.
- This collection features 70 tracks, including unreleased songs and five new recordings and comes with a 65 page booklet.
- A set called "Hidden Treasures" was released containing 15 tracks from this collections.
- "Sweet Life" (Recorded at Carnegie Hall, NYC, June 23, 1972) Careers-BMG Music Publishing, Inc. (BMI) / Piano: Barry Manilow / Guitar: Dick Frank / Bass & Vocals: Michael Federal / Drums: Kevin Ellman / Background Vocals: Melissa Manchester / Gail Kantor / Merle Miller
- "I Am Your Child" (Recorded at the Continental Baths, NYC, June 2, 1973) Careers-BMG Music Publishing, Inc. (BMI) / Piano: Barry Manilow / Guitar: Stu Scharff
- "Could It Be Magic" (Featherbed featuring Barry Manilow) 1971 Careers-BMG Music Publishing, Inc. (BMI) / Produced by Tony Orlando
- "Could It Be Magic" Recorded at A&R Studios, New York (see album "Barry Manilow I")
- "Brandy" (Original Scott English Single) 1971 Screen Gems-EMI Music (BMI), Morris Music (BMI), Grahple Music (PRS)
- "Mandy" (Unreleased Original First Take) (Recorded at Media Sound Studios, NYC, 8/20/74)
- "It's A Miracle" (see album "Barry Manilow II")
- "I Write The Songs" / "As Sure As I'm Standing Here" / "New York City Rhythm" / "Tryin' To Get

The Feeling Again" (Unreleased Alternate Take) / "Lay Me Down" / "Beautiful Music" (see album "Tryin' To Get The Feeling")

- "All The Time" / "Weekend In New England" (see album "This One's For You")
- "Riders To The Stars" / "Daybreak" (see album "Barry Manilow Live")
- "Somewhere In The Night" / "Copacabana (At The Copa)" / "Can't Smile Without You" (Unreleased Alternate First Take) (see album "Even Now")
- "I Don't Want To Walk Without You" / "You Could Show Me" (see album "One Voice")
- "The Last Duet" / "I Made It Through The Rain" (Unreleased Alternate Take) (see album "Barry")
- "One Voice" (see album "Live In Britain")
- "Read 'Em And Weep" (see album "Greatest Hits Vol. II")
- "Big City Blues" / "When October Goes" (see album "2:00 AM Paradise Café")
- "I'm Your Man" (see album "Manilow")
- "Who Needs To Dream" (see "Copacabana Soundtrack" album)
- "Hey Mambo" / "Big Fun" / "Brooklyn Blues" (see album "Swing Street")
- "A Little Travelin' Music, Please" / "Please Don't Be Scared" (see album "Barry Manilow" - 1989)
- "Memory" / "If I Can Dream" (see album "Live On Broadway")
- "Baby, It's Cold Outside" (see album "Because It's Christmas")
- "Look To The Rainbow" / "Fugue For Tinhorns" / "Never Met A Man I Didn't Like" (see album "Showstoppers")
- "Ready To Take A Chance Again" 7/12/78 Careers-BMG Music Publishing, Inc., Ensign Music Corporation (BMI) / Produced by: Barry Manilow / Ron Dante / Engineered by: Michael DeLugg / Arranged by: Barry Manilow / Orchestration by: Dick Behrke; (see "Foul Play" Soundtrack)
- "Sandra" (Recorded at Carnegie Hall, NYC, 11/21/74) Careers-BMG Music Publishing, Inc. (BMI) / Piano: Barry Manilow / Bass: Steve Donaghey / Keyboards: Alan Axelrod / Drums: Lee Gurst
- "The Old Songs" (Unreleased Alternate Take) "If I Should Love Again" (Unreleased Alternate Take)
- "Copacabana" (Home Cassette of Composing the Song) 1977 Careers-BMG Music Publishing, Inc. (BMI)
- "Dancin' Fool" (from the CBS Television Special "BIG FUN ON SWING STREET", March 1988), Careers-BMG Music Publishing, Inc. (BMI) Produced by: Barry Manilow / Eddie Arkin / Synthesizer and synthesizer programming: Eddie Arkin / Background Vocals: Full Swing (Lorraine Feather / Charlotte Crossley / Augie Johnson)
- "I Wanna Be Somebody's Baby" (Unreleased Outtake from "Barry Manilow Live"), 1977 Careers-BMG Music Publishing, Inc. (BMI)
- "Even Now" (Unreleased Live Performance) (Recorded at The Budokan, Tokyo, Japan, 3/29/83) Careers-BMG Music Publishing, Inc. (BMI); Mixed by Don Murray at: Sunset Sound, Los Angeles, CA in July 1992 / Assisted by Mike Kloster / Keyboards: Victor Vanacore / Robert Marullo / Guitar: Art Phillips / Drums: John Ferraro / Bass: Leon Gaer / Percussion: Ken Park / Woodwinds: Bill Page / Background Vocals: James Jolis / Muffy Hendricks / Freeman Clemente / Donna Fein
- "Life Will Go On" (Unreleased Live Performance) (Recorded at Wembley Arena, London, England, 11/27/80) Sweet Harmony Music (ASCAP), Irving Music, Inc. (BMI); Mixed by Don Murray at Sunset Sound, Los Angeles, CA in July 1992 / Assisted by: Mike Kloster / Keyboards: Victor Vanacore / Robert Marullo / Guitar: John Pondel / Bass: Lou Shoch / Drums: Bud Harner / Percussion: Ken Park / Background Vocals: Robin Grean / Pat Henderson / James Jolis / Kevin DiSimone

- "Ships" (from the Video "Live On Broadway") (Recorded at: The Gershwin Theatre, NYC, May 1989), EMI-April Music, Ian Hunter Music (ASCAP)
- "This One's For You" (Unreleased Demo) 1976 Careers-BMG Music Publishing, Inc. (BMI); Piano: Barry Manilow
- "Somewhere Down The Road" (Unreleased Demo) (Recorded at: Dirk Dalton Recorders, Santa Monica, CA, 2/2/81), 1981 ATV Music Corp, Mann & Weill Songs, Snow Music (BMI) / Piano: Barry Manilow
- "Ave Maria" (Originally released on "The Christmas Album...A Gift Of Hope" benefiting Hospitals for Children, 1990)
- "Joey" (Unreleased Demo) (Recorded at: United Western Studios, Hollywood, California) 1981 Careers-BMG Music Publishing, Inc. (BMI) / Piano: Barry Manilow
- "Ain't It A Shame" (Unreleased Outtake from "If I Should Love Again") 1981 Careers-BMG Music Publishing, Inc. (BMI)
- "How Do I Stop Loving You" (Unreleased Demo, 1984), Artie Butler Music (ASCAP), Norman Martin Music, admin. by Royce Music (BMI) / Piano / Synthesizer: Randy Kerber
- "Just Remember" (Unreleased Live Performance) (Recorded at: The Dorothy Chandler Pavillion, Los Angeles, April 28, 1992 at "The Singers Salute to the Songwriter, honoring Johnny Mercer and benefiting The Betty Clooney Foundation") Careers-BMG Music Publishing, Inc. (BMI) / Produced by: Barry Manilow / Eddie Arkin / Mixed by: Don Murray at Sunset Sound, Los Angeles, CA / Assisted by: Mike Kloster / Orchestra conducted by: Peter Matz / Arranged by: Eddie Arkin / Acoustic Guitar: Eddie Arkin / Harmonica: Tommy Morgan
- "I Can't Teach My Old Heart New Tricks" 1992 Careers-BMG Music Publishing, Inc. (BMI) / Produced by: Barry Manilow / Eddie Arkin / Arranged by: Eddie Arkin / Recorded at: Sunset Sound, Los Angeles, CA / Engineers: Don Murray / Tommy Vicari / Assisted by: Mike Kloster / Mixed at: The Record Plant, Los Angeles, CA by Tommy Vicari / Piano: Randy Kerber / Synthesizers / Synthesizer programming: Eddie Arkin / Bass: Neil Steubenhaus / Drums: Harvey Mason / Guitar: Paul Jackson, Jr. / Saxophone: Sam Riney / Background Vocals: Randy Crenshaw / Jon Joyce / Susan Boyd / Pattie Brooks
- "Give My Regards To Broadway" / "Send In The Clowns" / "Looks Like We Made It" (Recorded in Atlantic City, NJ, May 1992 / George M. Cohan Music, BMPI Music-BMG Songs (BMI), Appoggiatura Music (BMI); Produced by: Barry Manilow / Keyboards: Kevin Bassinson / Wally Minko / Steve Welch / Guitar: Ken Berry / Bass: Kevin Axt / Drums: Mark Scholl / Percussion: Billy Hulting / Vocals: Debra Byrd / Donna Cherry / Craig Meyer / Kevin Brackett
- My Girl" / "No One In This World" (duet with Melissa Manchester) (Unreleased Outtake from "This One's For You"), 1976 Jobete Music (ASCAP), Careers-BMG Music Publishing, Inc. (BMI)
- "Don't Talk To Me Of Love" (from the French Release of "Manilow" November 1985), Copyright Control; Produced by: Tim Smit / Charlie Skarbek / Arranged by: Charlie Skarbek / Claude Ermelin
- "Wild Places" (Unreleased Demo, 1981), Logo Songs, Blue Lkae Music (BMI)
- "Let Freedom Ring" (Unreleased Outtake from "Showstoppers"), 1991 Careers-BMG Music Publishing, Inc. (BMI) / Produced by: Barry Manilow / Eddie Arkin / Arranged by: Barry Manilow / Eddie Arkin / Artie Butler / Horn Arrangement by: Jerry Hey / Choral Arrangement by: Barry Manilow / Choir Directed and Conducted by: Debra Byrd / Piano: Rander Kerber / Bass: Abe Laboriel / Drums: Carlos Vega / Thanks to The Doretha Wilkerson Choral Ensemble / The Power of Prayer Ensemble / The Tower of Praise Church / Vocal solo: Debra Byrd / Engineered and mixed by Don Murray at Rumbo Recorders, Canoga Park, CA / Smoke Tree Ranch, Chatsworth, CA / Assisted by Squeak Stone / Shawn Berman
- "Let Me Be Your Wings' (from "Thumbelina") 1992 Jodi-Lynn Music, Appoggiatura Music, Camp Songs Music, Inc. (BMI) / Produced / Arranged by: Barry Manilow / Eddie Arkin

- "If Tomorrow Never Comes" 1992 Evanlee Music, Major Bob Music (ASCAP) / Produced by: Barry Manilow & Bob / Co-Produced by: Eddie Arkin / Recorded by: Alan Abrahamson at Conway, Los Angeles, CA / Sunset Sound, Los Angeles, CA / Mixed by David Cole at: Ground Control, Santa Monica, CA / Assistant Engineers: Marnie Riley / Mike Kloster / Gabriel Sutter / Keyboards and Synthesizers: Randy Kerber / Tim Heintz / Jay Mitchell / Ren Klyce / Guitar: Michael Landau / Bass: Michael Porcaro / Drums: Jonathon Moffett / Background Vocals: Jon Joyce / Joe Pizzulo / Phillip Ingram / Production Coordination by: Suzanne Marie Edgren for Humble Heart Music
- "Another Life" 1992 Pillarview B.V. c/o Chrysalis Songs (BMI), Chrysalis Music (ASCAP) / Produced by: Barry Manilow and Bob / Co-Produced by: Eddie Arkin / Engineered by: Alan Abrahamson at Conway, Los Angeles, CA / Sunset Sound, Los Angeles, CA / Mixed by: David Cole at: Ground Control, Santa Monica, CA / Assistant Engineers: Marnie Riley / Mike Kloster / Gabriel Sutter / Keyboards and Synthesizers: Randy Kerber / Tim Heintz / Jay Mitchell / Ren Klyce / Guitar: Michael Landau / Bass: Michael Porcaro / Drums: Jonathon Moffett / Background Vocals: Jon Joyce / Joe Pizzulo / Phillip Ingram / Production Coordination by: Suzanne Marie Edgren for Humble Heart Music
- "The Best Of Me" 1992 Warner-Tamerlane Publishing Corp. (BMI), Foster Frees Music (BMI), Neropub Music (BMI), Hollisongs (BMI), Security Hogg Music (ASCAP) Produced by: David Foster / Co-Produced by: Jeremy Lubbock / Arranged by: Jeremy Lubbock / David Foster / Barry Manilow / Strings arranged and conducted by: Jeremy Lubbock / Recorded at: Devonshire, Hollywood, CA / The Record Plant, Los Angeles, CA / Cherokee, Los Angeles, CA / Post Logic Studios, Los Angeles, CA in June & July 1992 / Engineered by: Will Rogers / Simon Franglen / Dave Reitzas / Mixed by: Dave Reitzas / Keyboards: Jeremy Lubbock / Synth Bass: David Foster / Guitar: Michael Thompson / Synclavier programming: Simon Franglen / Keyboards and Synthesizers: Randy Kerber / Additional Synth programming: Claude Gaudette

VHS / DVD included the following video clips:

- "Chapel of Love" (performed with Bette Midler at The Continental Baths - Videotaped September 5, 1971) (Jeff Barry/Ellie Greenwich / Phil Spector)
- "Very Strange Medley" (performed on "The Mike Douglas Show." Aired on Group W / June 10, 1974) (arr. by Manilow)
- "Mandy / Could It Be Magic" (performed on The Midnight Special. Aired on NBC-TV / March 14, 1975) (English/Kerr/Manilow/Anderson)
- "I Write the Songs" (performed on "Saturday Night Live" with Howard Cosell as the host. Aired on ABC-TV / October 11, 1975) (Johnston)
- "It's a Miracle/This One's for You" (performed on "The Barry Manilow Special," Aired on ABC-TV / March 2, 1977) (Manilow/Panzer)
- Emmy Award Presentation for Best Comedy / Variety Special: 1977 ("29th Annual Emmy Awards." Aired on NBC-TV / September 11, 1977)
- "Daybreak" (performed on "The Second Barry Manilow Special." Aired on ABC-TV / November 16, 1977) (Manilow/Anderson)
- "Copacabana (At the Copa)" (performed during "Barry Manilow In Concert at The Greek Theatre." Cablecast on HBO / February 11, 1979) (Manilow/Sussman/Feldman)
- "Weekend in New England" (performed on "The Third Barry Manilow Special." Aired on ABC-TV / May 23, 1979) (Edelman)
- "The Old Songs Medley" (performed during "The Concert At Blenheim Palace." Videotaped on August 27, 1983. Previously not available) (arr. by Manilow)
- "When October Goes" (filmed during the making of "2:00 AM Paradise Cafe." Videotaped July,

1984) (Manilow/Mercer)
- "Keep Each Other Warm" (performed during "Barry Manilow Live On Broadway." Cablecast on Showtime / October 8, 1989) (Pete Sinfield/Hill)
- Video program content ©1992 by GRAMERCY PARK PRODUCTIONS

"The Complete Collection And Then Some..." re-release with the DVD.

Coming soon to your video screen

BARRY MANILOW

Performances

Volumes II, III, IV, V AND VI*

Each volume is a full-length feature....with Barry's
greatest moments from the video archives.
Just a few of the highlights.......

VOLUME II
Beautiful Music
Don Kirshner's Rock Concert - 1975
Tryin' To Get The Feeling Again
Midnight Special - 1976
I Am Your Child
Sound Stage - 1975

VOLUME III
Here We Go Again
Greek Theater - 1979
All The Time
ABC Special - 1977
New York City Rhythm
From THE TONY AWARDS - 1977

VOLUME IV
VSM (Very Strange Medley)
Pittsburgh - In Concert - 1981
Documentary
Bleinheim - In Concert - 1983
Outtakes Medley
Bleinheim - In Concert - 1983

VOLUME V
Come With Me
Japan - In Concert - 1985
That's Why They Call Her Sugar
England - In Concert - 1984
Who Needs To Dream
From COPA - The Movie - 1985

VOLUME VI
Dirt Cheap
From LIVE ON BROADWAY - 1988
In Search Of Love
Duet with Hideki Saijo - 1985
It's Just Another New Year's Eve
Includes "The Toast"
In Concert - Los Angeles - 1991

*Scheduled track listing at time
of publication

To find out more about these upcoming home video releases...just call
1-800-423-1851 or **213-461-5881** and ask for information about
BARRY MANILOW - PERFORMANCES.

ARISTA

8714-2/4 © 1992 Arista Records, Inc., a Bertelsmann Music Group Company.

**Information card that came with the VHS video tape of "The Complete Collection And Then
Some..." detailing the other videos that were due out in the future.
It is unknown if these videos were released or if these numbers are still active.
This was pre-Internet so there was no email address to contact.**

The Music of Barry Manilow
88697 77708 2

Track Listing:

I Am Your Child / Could It Be Magic / Mandy / It's A Miracle / I Write The Songs / Tryin' To Get The Feeling Again / Lay Me Down / Beautiful Music / This One's For You / Weekend In New England / Looks Like We Made It / All The Time / Daybreak (Live) / New York City Rhythm (Live) / Can't Smile Without You / Even Now / Copacabana (At The Copa) / Ready To Take A Chance Again / Somewhere In The Night / Ships / One Voice / Who's Been Sleeping In My Bed / Lonely Together / I Made It Through The Rain / The Old Songs / If I Should Love Again / Somewhere Down The Road / No Other Love / Memory / Some Kind Of Friend / Stay / Read 'Em And Weep / When October Goes / Who Needs To Dream / Brooklyn Blues / A Little Travelling Music, Please / The Best Seat In The House / The Best Of Me / Let Freedom Ring / Singin' With The Big Bands / Unchained Melody / Love Is A Many Splendored Thing / Can't Take My Eyes Off You / When I Fall In Love / The Way We Were / (They Long To Be) Close To You / Islands In The Stream (duet with Reba McEntire) / Never Gonna Give You Up / The Look Of Love / You Made Me Love You

Production Information:

Producers: Barry Manilow / Clive Davis / David Benson / David Foster / Eddie Arkin / Greg O'Connor / Jeremy Lubbock / Jim Steinman / Michael DeLugg / Michael Lloyd / Phil Ramone / Ron Dante / Scott Erickson
Compilation Producer: Al Quaglieri
Mastered At: Battery Studios, New York, NY
Mastered By: Maria Triana / Mark Wilder

Notes & Trivia:
- Released in 2010 originally as a 3 disc set in the US. Re-released in the US (Cat. # 88883771662) as a 4 disc set in 2013
- Released as a 4 disc set in 2014 in Europe and Australia (Cat.# 88875020222)

Track Listing:
You've Got A friend (Melissa Manchester) / Hey Mambo (Kid Creole and The Coconuts) / Let Me Be Your Wings (Debra Byrd) / Cherish-Windy (The Association) / Look To The Rainbow (Barbara Cook) / Islands In The Stream (Reba McEntire) / Big City Blues (Mel Tormé) / On A Slow Boat To China (Bette Midler) / Run To Me (Dionne Warwick) / Summertime (Diane Schuur) / Sincerely-Teach Me Tonight (Phyllis McGuire) / Blue (Sarah Vaughan) / Now and Forever (Sheena Easton) / I Won't Be The One To Let You Go (Barbra Streisand) / The Last Duet (Lilly Tomlin)

Production Information:
Compilation produced by: Barry Manilow and Al Quaglieri
Mastered at: Battery Studios, New York, NY
Mastered by: Mark Wilder
Additional mastering engineering by: Maria Triana
Master tape research by: Mike Kull
Photography: Courtesy of Stiletto Entertainment
Art Direction & Design: Sara Zickuhr for Stiletto Entertainment
Project Direction: Gretchen Brennison and John Adams for Stiletto Entertainment
A&R: Rob Santos
Marketing: Mandy Eidgah

Notes & Trivia:
- This album was released on CD on May 3, 2011.
- "You've Got A Friend" (with Melissa Manchester) written by Carole King; produced by Barry Manilow, Clive Davis and David Benson. Previously unreleased mix
- "Hey Mambo" (with Kid Creole and the Coconuts) written by Barry Manilow, Tom Kelly, Bruce Sussman, and Jack Feldman; produced by Barry Manilow, Eddie Arkin and Emilio and The Jerks (Emilio Estefan, Jr., Joe Galdo and Lawrence Dermer); from "Swing Street" (1987)
- "Let Me Be Your Wings" (End Title Duet) (with Debra Byrd) written by Barry Manilow, Bruce Sussman, and Jack Feldman / Produced by: Robbie Buchanan; from "Thumbelina: Original Motion Picture Soundtrack" (1994)
- "Cherish / Windy" (with The Association) written by Terry Kirkman / Ruthann Friedman; produced by Barry Manilow, Clive Davis and David Benson; from "The Greatest Songs Of The Sixties" (2006)

- "Look To The Rainbow" (with Barbara Cook) written by E.Y. Harburg and Burton Lane; produced by Barry Manilow and Eddie Arkin; from "Showstoppers" (1991)
- "Islands In The Stream" (with Reba McIntire) written by Barry Gibb, Robin Gibb, and Maurice Gibb; produced by Barry Manilow and Scott Erickson; from "The Greatest Songs Of The Eighties" (2008)
- "Big City Blues" (with Mel Tormé (featuring Gerry Mulligan) written by Barry Manilow and Adrienne Anderson; produced by Barry Manilow; from "2:00 AM Paradise Café" (1984)
- "On A Slow Boat To China" (with Bette Midler) written by Frank Loesser; produced by Barry Manilow and Robbie Buchanan; from the Bette Midler album "Bette Midler Sings The Rosemary Clooney Songbook" (2003)
- "Run To Me" (with Dionne Warwick) written by Barry Gibb, Robin Gibb, and Maurice Gibb; produced by Barry Manilow; from the Dionne Warwick album "Finder Of Lost Loves" (1985) and Barry's album "The Manilow Collection / Twenty Classic Hits"
- "Summertime" (with Diane Schuur (featuring Stan Getz) written by George Gershwin and Dubose Heyward; produced by Barry Manilow and Eddie Arkin; from "Swing Street" (1987)
- "Sincerely / Teach Me Tonight" (with Phyllis McGuire) written by Alan Freed and Harvey Fuqua / Sammy Cahn and Gene DePaul; produced by Barry Manilow, Clive Davis and David Benson; from "The Greatest Songs Of The Fifties" (2006)
- "Blue" (with Sarah Vaughan) written by Barry Manilow, Bruce Sussman, and Jack Feldman; produced by Barry Manilow; from "2:00 AM Paradise Café" (1984)
- "Now And Forever" (with Sheena Easton) written by Barry Manilow and Bruce Sussman; produced by Barry Manilow; from the Motion Picture release "The Pebble And The Penguin" (1995)
- "I Won't Be The One To Let Go" (with Barbra Streisand) written by Richard Marx and Barry Manilow; produced by Richard Marx and Walter Afanasieff; from the Barbra Streisand album "Duets" (2002)
- "The Last Duet" (with Lily Tomlin) written by Barry Manilow, Bruce Sussman, and Jack Feldman; produced by Barry Manilow and Ron Dante; from the album "Barry" (1980)

Soundtrack Albums

Foul Play
AL-9501

Track Listing:
Ready To Take A Chance Again (Lyrics by: Norman Gimbel / Music by: Charles Fox / Vocal by: Barry Manilow) / Help / Beware Of The Dwarf / Love Theme Instrumental (Ready To Take A Chance Again) / Copacabana (Lyrics By: Bruce Sussman / Jack Feldman - Music and Vocal by: Barry Manilow) / Gloria Falls For Trap / Foul Play (Disco) / Scarface / Gloria Escapes / Houseboat (Love Theme) / Get Me To The Opera On Time / End Title: Ready To Take A Chance Again (Lyrics by: Norman Gimbel / Music by: Charles Fox / Vocal Barry Manilow)

Production Information:
All selections composed, conducted and produced by Charles Fox except "Copacabana" and "Ready To Take A Chance Again" produced by Barry Manilow & Ron Dante. Orchestrations by Ruby Raskin. Mastered at: Kendun Recorders, Los Angeles, CA

Singles Released from This Album:
"Ready To Take A Chance Again" b/w "Sweet Life" (AS-0357) August 24, 1978 (Peaked at # 11 in the US on the Billboard Hot 100 Chart in October 1978) Side B ©1975 Arista Records, from the LP "Barry Manilow I" (Arista - AL-4007)

Notes & Trivia:
- This album was released on LP, 8 Track and Cassette on March 1, 1978.
- CD Soundtrack released by: Intrada Special Collection Volume 88 on April 28, 2009
- The film's theme song, "Ready to Take a Chance Again," was composed by famed writer Charles Fox, with lyrics by Fox's writing partner, the equally famous Norman Gimbel. It was performed by Barry Manilow, who conceived and supervised the song's recording in partnership with Ron Dante. The soundtrack also includes "Copacabana" written by Barry Manilow, Jack Feldman and Bruce Sussman. It, too, was performed by Barry Manilow.
- The soundtrack was released a third time by Varese Sarabande in 2016, with Charles Fox's theme for the television series of *Foul Play* as a bonus track.
- "Ready to Take a Chance Again" was nominated for Best Song at the 1978 Academy Awards. It, however, lost out to Donna Summer's "Last Dance" from the movie, *Thank God It's Friday*. In Germany, the single "Ready to Take a Chance Again" was backed with a re-release of 1974's "Mandy," which had been only a minor hit on its prior release.
- A little Goldie Hawn Trivia: In Sweden, the connection made of *Foul Play* to *The Man Who Knew Too Much* led to the movie being called *Tjejen som visste för mycket* or *The Girl Who Knew Too Much*. After that, the Swedish editions of several movies starring Goldie Hawn were given titles starting with "Tjejen som..." "The girl who..." as a kind of trademark, example:

"Private Benjamin: Tjejen som gjorde lumpen" "Private Benjamin: The girl who joined the army" and Overboard "Tjejen som föll överbord" "The girl who fell overboard."

- *Foul Play* is an homage to director Alfred Hitchcock, several of whose films are referenced in the film. The idea of an innocent person becoming intertwined in a web of intrigue is one common in Hitchcock films such as *The 39 Steps*, *Saboteur*, *North by Northwest* and, most notably, *The Man Who Knew Too Much*, which inspired the opera house sequence in *Foul Play*. When Gloria is attacked in her home by a man attempting to strangle her with a scarf and she defends herself with a household object, both are references to *Dial M for Murder*. Other Hitchcock films which receive a nod from screenwriter/director Colin Higgins include *Notorious*, *Vertigo*, and *Psycho*. In addition, the plot includes a "MacGuffin" or an object that initially is the central focus of the film but declines in importance until it is forgotten and unexplained by the end—in the form of the roll of film concealed in the pack of cigarettes. Hitchcock popularized the term "MacGuffin" and used the technique in many of his films.

  The script was originally written under the name *Killing Lydia* with Goldie Hawn in mind for the lead. Higgins had met Hawn through their mutual friend, Hal Ashby. However the project did not take off. After Silver Streak came out Higgins rewrote the script. He and the producers took the project to Paramount who hoped to star Farrah Fawcett. However Fawcett was in the middle of a legal battle with the producers of *Charlie's Angels* so in the end it was decided to go with Hawn.

- The name "Gloria Mundy" is a reference to "Sic transit gloria mundi," a Latin phrase meaning "Thus passes the glory of the world." It was included in the ritual of papal coronation ceremonies until 1963. Higgins had written the role of Stanley Tibbets for Tim Conway, but when the actor turned it down he offered it to Dudley Moore instead. It was Moore's American film debut and led to his being cast in *10* by Blake Edwards the following year. Higgins says when he sold the script he wanted to direct it so badly he did not care who was going to play the lead roles. His first choice for the male lead was Harrison Ford (who had once been Higgins' carpenter) who turned it down. Steve Martin was also offered the role but ended up passing on it. Eventually Chevy Chase was cast and it was his first motion picture role. The film was shot on location in and around San Francisco, including Noe Valley, the Mission District, Hallidie Plaza, Telegraph Hill, Hayes Valley, Nob Hill, Pacific Heights, Fort Mason in the Golden Gate National Recreation Area, the Marina District, the Presidio, Potrero Hill, Nihonmachi, and the War Memorial Opera House. The lobby scenes of the Opera House were filmed in the rotunda of the City Hall across the street. The Nuart Theater, in which Bob Scott dies early in the film, is an art house located on Santa Monica Boulevard in West Los Angeles. The houseboat, "Galatea," was located at 15 Yellow Ferry Harbor in Sausalito, CA. More on Goldie Hawn with Barry Manilow in the video section of the book.

- An hour long prime-time TV special titled "A Weekend of Foul Play" celebrating the gala world premiere of the movie aired on CBS-TV on July 26, 1978. The star-filled flight from Los Angeles to San Francisco highlights this special. It stars Goldie Hawn and Chevy Chase with the amazing talents of Wayland Flowers & Madam, Henry Winkler, Martin Mull, Burgess Meredith, Billy Barty, Johnny Mathis, Kristy McNichol, Jimmy McNichol, Meatloaf, Dudley Moore, John Ritter, Joey Travolta, Anson William, Parker Stevenson, Peter Brown, Erin Moran, The Village People (who performs two songs), The Spinners and many more. The author of this book had to review his personal copy that he recorded on Beta tape when the show originally aired. Sadly, Barry Manilow does not appear on the special.

"Tribute" 1980 Film – No soundtrack released

Soundtrack Information:
"We Still Have Time"
Music by: Barry Manilow
Lyrics by: Bruce Sussman & Jack Feldman
Sung by: Barry Manilow
Produced by: Barry Manilow and Ron Dante
Recording engineer: Michael DeLugg
℗1980 Manilow Music (BMI) / Appogiatura Music Inc. (BMI) / Camp Sngs Music Inc. (BMI)
This track appears on Barry's 1980 album "Barry" (AL-9537), released November 19, 1980. As a single in Japan (Arista – 7RS-21) in 1981 with "Lonely Together" on Side B and a one sided promo single in the UK (Arista – FILM 1).

Film Plot:
Scottie Templeton is a show-business veteran, based in New York and well known in the theatrical community there. He has many acquaintances, but is divorced from his wife and estranged from his only son. Scottie learns that he has leukemia and is dying. His ex-wife Maggie, in town for a school reunion, comes to visit and reflect on their time together. Scottie makes an effort to reconnect with his son, Jud, who still has anger issues. A young model who Scottie met in the hospital, Sally Haines, strikes Scottie as someone who might be a good romantic match for his son. As a testimonial dinner is organized in Scottie's honor, he attempts to repair some of his past relationships in the time he has left.

Film released on December 15, 1980 by 20ᵗʰ Century Fox . Directed by Bob Clark. Stars: Jack Lemmon / Robby Benson / Lee Remick / Colleen Dew Hurst / John Marley / Kim Cattrall / Gale Garnett / Teri Keane

Copacabana (TV) Soundtrack
RCA SML1-7178

Track Listing:
Overture – Orchestra / Copacabana (At the Copa) – Barry Manilow / Let's Go Steppin' – Chorus / Changing My Tune – Barry Manilow / Blue – Orchestra / Lola – Barry Manilow / Who Needs to Dream – Barry Manilow / Man Wanted – Annette O'Toole / ¡Aye Caramba! – Chorus / Call Me Mr. Lucky – Barry Manilow / Big City Blues – Barry Manilow / Sweet Heaven (I'm in Love Again) – Barry Manilow / El Bravo – Annette O'Toole and Chorus / Copacabana (At the Copa) 1985 – Barry Manilow / Who Needs To Dream (Reprise) – Barry Manilow / ¡Aye Caramba! (Reprise) – Barry Manilow

Production Information:
Produced by: Barry Manilow / Bob Gaudio; except the original version of Copacabana (At The Copa) produced by: Barry Manilow and Ron Dante.
Recorded at: Evergreen Studios, Burbank, CA
Engineers: Joel Moss / Anthony V. D'Amico
Mixed at: Sound Labs, Hollywood, CA
Mixing Engineer: Joel Moss
Contractor: Shaun Harris
Assistant to Barry Manilow: Marc Hulett
Production Assistant to Bob Gaudio: Bob Sutton
Executive in Charge of Album Production: Eric Borenstein
New version of Copacabana (At The Copa) arranged by: Bob Gaudio / John P. Shenale
Musical Score Adapted / Supervised by: Artie Butler
Original Art Concept: Penelope Gottlieb
Illustration: Tim Wild
Design: RIA Images

Notes & Trivia:
- This album was released on LP, 8 Track and Cassette on December 3, 1985 to tie in with the television movie of the same name which aired that night on CBS-TV.
- The film starred: Barry Manilow / Annette O'Toole / Joseph Bologna / Estelle Getty. It was directed by Waris Hussein and written by James Lipton.
- The film was produced by: Dick Clark Cinema Productions in association with Stiletto, LTD.
- This album was released on CD in Japan (RCA R32P-1083) and later by Barry's own Stiletto Entertainment.
- The track "Blue" is an instrumental version and "Big City Blues" a piano/vocal version. These two songs Barry originally recorded for the album *2:00 AM Paradise Cafe* in 1984.

- At the 38th Primetime Emmy Awards, *Copacabana* was nominated for Outstanding Achievement in Choreography (Grover Dale) and Outstanding Directing in a Variety or Music Program (Waris Hussein), and won the Emmy for the latter category.
- The film inspired a 1990 stage show at Caesars in Atlantic City, which was based heavily on the film, as well as the 1994 musical, Copacabana, which was based more loosely on the film, which played in London's West End and elsewhere. The film has been issued on VHS tape and DVD
- A tour program was printed to tie in with the film for the 1985 tour.

The 1989 UK VHS tape edition in clam shell case released by CBS / FOX

Thumbelina
K2-29126

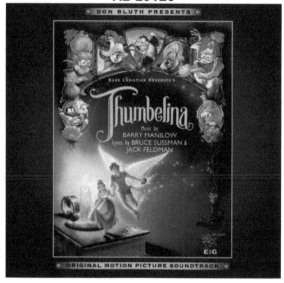

Track Listing:

Let Me Be Your Wings / Follow Your Heart (Intro) Gino Conforti / Jacquimo Tells The Story / Thumbelina - Jodi Benson & Anúna / Soon - Jodi Benson / Entrance of the Faeries / Let Me Be Your Wings - Jodi Benson & Gary Inhofe / Mama Toad Kidnaps Thumbelina / On the Road - Charo, Jodi Benson / Joe Lynch / Danny Mann & Loren Lester / Over The Waterfall / Follow Your Heart - Gino Conforti & Anúna / Yer Beautiful, Baby - Randy Crenshaw & Anúna / Cornelius Searches for Thumbelina / Soon (Reprise) - Barbara Cook / Let Me Be Your Wings (Reprise) - Jodi Benson / Marry the Mole - Carol Channing / Thumbelina Escapes / Finale: Let Me Be Your Wings - Follow Your Heart - Jodi Benson & Anúna / *Let Me Be Your Wings (End Title) - Barry Manilow & Debra Byrd

Production Information:

Produced by: Barry Manilow; except *Let Me Be Your Wings* (End Title) produced by Robbie Buchanan for Robbie Buchanan, Inc
Recorded at: Sunset Sound, Hollywood, CA / Group IV Recording Studios, Hollywood, CA / Windmill Lane Studios, Dunlin, Ireland
Engineers: Don Murray / Dana Jon Chappelle / David Reitzas / Paul McKenna
Assistant Engineers: Willie Mannion / Mike Kloster
Mixed by: Don Murray
*Mixed at: The Record Plant, Los Angeles, CA
Digital Editing by: Robert Vosgien at CMS Digital , Pasadena, CA
Mastered by: Wally Traugott
Mastered at: Capitol Studios, Hollywood, CA
Music Editor: Jim Harrison
Music Copyist: Vic Fraser
Art Direction: Henry Marquez
Package Design: Diane Cuddy
Lyrics by: Bruce Sussman, Jack Feldman
Music by, Score [Original Underscore]: Barry Manilow
Score [Original Underscore] / Orchestrated by / Conductor: William Ross
Presenter: Don Bluth
Orchestra Manager: Bill Whelan
Choral Arrangements: Earl Brown
Performed by: The Anuna Choir under the direction of: Michael McGlynn

Assistant to Barry Manilow: Marc Hulett

Musicians:
The Irish Film Orchestra
*Drum Programming / Bass / Keyboards: Robbie Buchanan
*Guitar: Michael Thompson

Singles Released From This Album:
Let Me Be Your wings (S7-17906)

Notes & Trivia:
- This album was released on CD and Cassette on April 5, 1994
- All music by Barry Manilow / All lyrics by: Bruce Sussman & Jack Feldman
- The wedding reprise of "Let Me Be Your Wings" is not on the soundtrack
- The song "Marry The Mole," sung by Carol Channing, was the recipient of a Razzie award, making *Thumbelina* the first animated film to "win" a Razzie.
- The CD / Cassette was a limited release and has long been out of print.

From "Thumbelina: Original Motion Picture Soundtrack" (1994 – Juke Box Only)
Side A: Let Me Be Your Wings by Barry Manilow / Debra Byrd
Side B: Follow Your Heart by Gino Conforti

The Pebble and The Penguin
R2 71996

Track Listing:
Original Songs:
Prologue/Now And Forever / Sometimes I Wonder / The Good Ship Misery / Helpless, Hopeless Romantic / Don't Make Me Laugh / Sometimes I Wonder (Reprise) / Looks Like I Got Me A Friend / Now And Forever (Finale)
Score:
The Mating Ceremony / Hubie Finds The Pebble / Hubie Gazes Into The Pebble / Humans At Play / Full Speed Ahead / Beneath The Ice / Killer Whales / Rocko's Return And Drake's Defeat / Now And Forever (Finale)

Production Information:
Producer: Barry Manilow
Soundtrack Producers: Barry Manilow / Marc Hulett
Arranged by: Barry Manilow
Music by: Barry Manilow
Lyrics by: Bruce Sussman
Recorded at: Sunset Sound, Hollywood, CA / Record Plant, Los Angeles, CA / Enterprise Studios, Burbank, CA / Windmill Lane Studios, Dublin, Ireland
Recorded and Mixed by: Don Murray (tracks: 1 to 3, 5 to 17) / Rick Winquest (track: 4)
Assistant Engineers: Mike Kloster / Robert Kirwan
Sonic Solutions Sequencing by Kevin Reeves at Tower Mastering
Mastered at: Tower Mastering
Mastered by: Wally Traugott
Music Performed by: The Irish Film Orchestra
The Penguins: Andrea Robinson / B.J. Ward / Bob Joyce / Hamilton Camp / Joe Pizullo / Jon Joyce / Kevin Bassinson / Kevin Dorsey / Louise Vallance / Maggie Roswell / Maxine Waters / Randy Crenshaw / Sally Stevens / Stephen Amerson / Steve Lively / Tampa Lann / Will Ryan / Yvonne Williams
The Singing Cast: Drake – Tim Curry / Hubie – Martin Short / Marina – Annie Golden / Narrator – Shani Wallis / Rocko – James Belushi / The Beachmaster – Jon Joyce

Notes & Trivia:
- This album was released on CD and Cassette on April 11, 1995
- The version of "Now and Forever" sung by Barry Manilow and Sheena Easton is not on the soundtrack, but was later released on Barry Manilow's album *Duets* and a later reissue of the soundtrack as a bonus track when Kid Rhino reacquired the rights in 2012.

Specialty Albums

There were some albums that were manufactured just for radio or promotional use.
Some others shown were for the serious audiophiles.
Here are a few of both types.

Dick Clark Presents
Labor Day Special Presented by Mutual Broadcasting System
DCBM – HR-2

Track Listing:
Record One: Bandstand Boogie Manilow Medley / Ships - The Old Songs / Could It Be Magic / I Made It Through The Rain / Where Are They Now / Something's Comin' Up / Ready To Take A Chance Again / New York City Rhythm / Can't Smile Without You / The Last Duet (with Lily Tomlin) / A Very Strange Medley

Record Two: Friends (with Bette Midler) / When I Wanted You / Even Now / It's A Miracle / Sing It / I Don't Want To Walk Without You / Mandy / See The Show Again / Somewhere In The Night / Copacabana

Record Three: Daybreak / Weekend In England / This One's For You / Tryin' To Get The Feeling Again / Deja Vu - I'll Never Love This Way Again (Dionne Warwick) / I Write The Songs / Let's Hang On / If I Should Love Again / Looks Like We Made It

Notes & Trivia:
- This 3 LP set is a specially released 1981 Labor Day three-hour radio program narrated by Dick Clark. These were to be played one time only on the date specified. The set featured interview snippets with Barry and many of his full-length songs. Also with the set is a seven page outline for each program segment and its running time, the commercial breaks and song titles. Each album contains narration by Dick Clark, interviews with Barry Manilow, full-length songs by Barry and radio commercials which ran with the program (examples are Ford Lincoln-Mercury, Delco Electronics, K-Mart Records, Tenneco, Stay-Free Maxi Pads, Campbell's V-8 Juice, etc.)
- These sets are not easily found, primarily because the radio stations were instructed to destroy these records after airplay (see record label close-up below), and with radios station storage space being limited, most of these were indeed destroyed after airplay. Usually incinerated.
- The paperwork enclosed reads in part: DATE: July 29, 1981: FROM: Glenn R. Morgan TO: "DICK CLARK PRESENTS BARRY MANILOW" - Clearing Stations.
  Subj: "DICK CLARK PRESENTS BARRY MANILLOW" - Program Discs
  Enclosed is your station's copy of Mutual's "DICK CLARK PRESENTS BARRY MANILOW" which is to be broadcast by your station on Monday, September 7th, 1981, between 6:00 AM and 12:00 Midnight, local time, according to your station's agreement.
  The program discs are produced in stereo. Each hour's format is enclosed and the commercial schedule is included on the format sheets. There are a total of five :06 second commercial positions for local sale by your station in each hour. These times are not covered on the program discs and must be filled by your station in order for the program to time out properly.

PLEASE AUDITION EACH DISC IMMEDIATELY. If you have any questions, or if there is a problem with the recordings, please contact Mutual Station Relations at:
Washington, D.C. (703) 685-2050
Los Angeles (213) 277-7700
Dallas (214) 827-2800
The program is the exclusive property of the Mutual Broadcasting System, Inc. and is intended for broadcast only in accordance with your program agreement. Any other use of this program in whole or in part without the express written consent of the Mutual Broadcasting System, Inc. is prohibited.

- Several of these packages were made following a similar format each time. Others made included: "The Rolling Stones- Past And Present" in 1982.

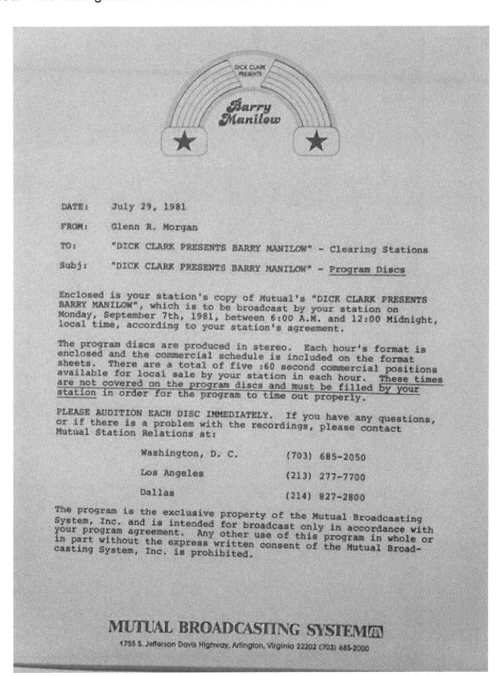

HOUR: ONE

SHOW   DICK CLARK PRESENTS
        BARRY MANILOW

AIR DATE: Labor Day Weekend

All music features Barry Manilow
unless otherwise noted.

PROGRAM SEGMENT 1 - RUNNING TIME: 5:36

IN: Tympani roll - music open
MUSIC: BANDSTAND BOOGIE
                        MANILOW MEDLEY

NETWORK POSITION: Ford (Lincoln-Mercury) :60
OUTCUE TO STN POS: Music out
STATION POSITION: :60

PROGRAM SEGMENT 2 - RUNNING TIME: 9:30

IN: Music open
MUSIC: SHIPS
                        THE OLD SONGS

NETWORK POSITION: Delco Electronics :60
OUTCUE TO STN POS: "...the battery."
STATION POSITION: :60

PROGRAM SEGMENT 3 - RUNNING TIME: 6:38

IN: Music open
MUSIC: COULD IT BE MAGIC

NETWORK POSITION: Campbells V-8 Juice :30 - Stay Free Maxi Pads :30
OUTCUE TO STN POS: "...extra comfortable." (music to conc)
STATION POSITION: :60

MUTUAL BROADCASTING SYSTEM 🅜

1755 S. Jefferson Davis Highway, Arlington, Virginia 22202 (703) 685-2000

178

HOUR: ONE

SHOW   DICK CLARK PRESENTS
        BARRY MANILOW

AIR DATE: Labor Day Weekend

PROGRAM SEGMENT 4 - RUNNING TIME: 9:19

IN: Music open
MUSIC: I MADE IT THROUGH THE RAIN
                   WHERE ARE THEY NOW

NETWORK POSITION: K-Mart Records (Eddie Rabbitt) :60
OUTCUE TO STN POS: "...music place."
STATION POSITION: :60

PROGRAM SEGMENT 5 - RUNNING TIME: 7:50

IN: Music open
MUSIC: SOMETHING'S COMIN' UP
                   READY TO TAKE A CHANCE AGAIN
                   NEW YORK CITY RHYTHM

NETWORK POSITION: Delco Electronics :60
OUTCUE TO STN POS: "...good choice." (stinger)
STATION POSITION: :60

PROGRAM SEGMENT 6 - RUNNING TIME: 4:36

IN: Music open
MUSIC: CAN'T SMILE WITHOUT YOU

OUTCUE: Music out

HOUR: TWO

SHOW   DICK CLARK PRESENTS
        BARRY MANILOW

AIR DATE: Labor Day Weekend

PROGRAM SEGMENT 1 - RUNNING TIME: 8:12

IN:	Music open
MUSIC:	THE LAST DUET - Manilow/Lily Tomlin
	A VERY STRANGE MEDLEY

NETWORK POSITION:	Walker Mufflers (Tenneco) :60
OUTCUE TO STN POS:	"...quiet as me."
STATION POSITION:	:60

PROGRAM SEGMENT 2 - RUNNING TIME: 8:23

IN:	Music open
MUSIC:	FRIENDS - Bette Midler
	WHEN I WANTED YOU

NETWORK POSITION:	K-Mart Records (Eddie Rabbitt) :60
OUTCUE TO STN POS:	"...music place."
STATION POSITION:	:60

PROGRAM SEGMENT 3 - RUNNING TIME: 7:57

IN:	Music open
MUSIC:	EVEN NOW
	IT'S A MIRACLE

NETWORK POSITION:	Ford (Lincoln-Mercury) :60
OUTCUE TO STN POS:	Music out
STATION POSITION:	:60

MUTUAL BROADCASTING SYSTEMⓜ

1755 S. Jefferson Davis Highway, Arlington, Virginia 22202 (703) 685-2000

HOUR: TWO

SHOW   DICK CLARK PRESENTS
        BARRY MANILOW

AIR DATE: Labor Day Weekend

PROGRAM SEGMENT 4 - RUNNING TIME: 10:26

IN: Music open
MUSIC: SING IT
                     I DON'T WANT TO WALK WITHOUT YOU
                     MANDY

NETWORK POSITION: Delco Electronics :60
OUTCUE TO STN POS: "...in Porches, no."
STATION POSITION: :60

PROGRAM SEGMENT 5 - RUNNING TIME: 4:32

IN: Music open
MUSIC: SEE THE SHOW AGAIN
                     SOMEWHERE IN THE NIGHT

NETWORK POSITION: Stay Free Maxi Pads :30 - Campbell's V-8 :30
OUTCUE TO STN POS: "...have a V-8." (stinger)
STATION POSITION: :60

PROGRAM SEGMENT 6 - RUNNING TIME: 4:00

IN: Music open
MUSIC: COPACABANA

OUTCUE: Music out

HOUR: THREE

SHOW   DICK CLARK PRESENTS
        BARRY MANILOW

AIR DATE: Labor Day Weekend

PROGRAM SEGMENT 1 - RUNNING TIME: 8:18

IN: Music open
MUSIC: DAYBREAK
                       WEEKEND IN NEW ENGLAND

NETWORK POSITION: Delco Electronics
OUTCUE TO STN POS: "...the battery."
STATION POSITION: :60

PROGRAM SEGMENT 2 - RUNNING TIME: 8:46

IN: Music open
MUSIC: THIS ONE'S FOR YOU
                       TRYIN' TO GET THE FEELING AGAIN

NETWORK POSITION: Campbell's V-8 :30 - Stay Free Maxi-Pads :30
OUTCUE TO STN POS: "...extra comfortable." (music to conc)
STATION POSITION: :60

PROGRAM SEGMENT 3 - RUNNING TIME: 7:49

IN: Music open
MUSIC: DEJA VU - Dionne Warwick
                       I'LL NEVER LOVE THIS WAY AGAIN - Dionne Warwick

NETWORK POSITION: K-Mart Records (Eddie Rabbitt) :60
OUTCUE TO STN POS: "...music place."
STATION POSITION: :60

MUTUAL BROADCASTING SYSTEM

1755 S. Jefferson Davis Highway, Arlington, Virginia 22202 (703) 685-2000

182

HOUR: THREE

SHOW   DICK CLARK PRESENTS
             BARRY MANILOW
AIR DATE: Labor Day Weekend

PROGRAM SEGMENT 4 - RUNNING TIME: 4:42

IN: Music open
MUSIC: I WRITE THE SONGS

NETWORK POSITION: Ford (Lincoln-Mercury) :60
OUTCUE TO STN POS: Music out
STATION POSITION: :60

PROGRAM SEGMENT 5 - RUNNING TIME: 9:02

IN: Music open
MUSIC: LET'S HANG ON
                           IF I SHOULD LOVE AGAIN

NETWORK POSITION: Monroe Shock Absorbers (Tenneco) :60
OUTCUE TO STN POS: Music out
STATION POSITION: :60

PROGRAM SEGMENT 6 - RUNNING TIME: 4:55

IN: Music open
MUSIC: LOOKS LIKE WE MADE IT

OUTCUE: Music out

DICK CLARK
PRESENTS

Barry Manilow

Labor Day Special
Hour 2, Side 2

©the dick clark company, inc. 1981. All rights reserved. This
copyrighted material may not be reproduced or broadcast in
whole or part without the prior express written permission of the
dick clark company, inc. and must be destroyed immediately
after broadcast.

Each of the six labels in the 3 LP set look the same except for the Hour and Side indicators.

Barry Manilow I / Original Master Recording
MFSL1-097

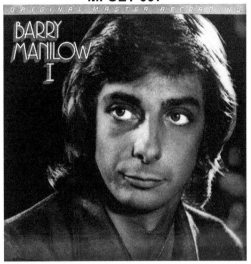

Track Listing:
Sing It (Barry with his grandfather, Joseph Manilow, in a Times Square Self-Recording Booth, 1948) / *Sweet Water Jones / Cloudburst / One Of These Days / Oh My Lady / *I Am Your Child / Could It Be Magic (Inspired By Prelude In C Minor, F. Chopin) / Seven More Years / Flashy Lady / Friends / *Sweet Life

Production Information:
Please see the 1973 LP on page 11.

Notes & Trivia:
- This version of BARRY MANILOW I is a 1982 product from the Victor Company of Japan. It is a state of the art audiophile pressings of Barry's first album from 1973, but using the 1975 remixes. This MFSL LP was pressed in Japan before Mobile Fidelity Sound Labs eventually began pressing their LP's in the United States. The LP was Half-Speed Mastered with the Ortofon Cutting System using the Original Stereo Mastering Tapes.

Tryin' To Get The Feeling
AQ-4060

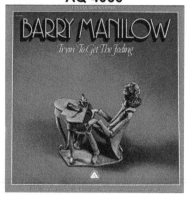

Track Listing:

New York City Rhythm / Tryin' To Get The Feeling Again / Why Don't We Live Together / Bandstand Boogie / You're Leaving Too Soon / She's A Star / I Write The Songs / As Sure As I'm Standing Here / A Nice Boy Like Me / Lay Me Down / Beautiful Music

Production Information:

Please see the 1975 LP on page 15.

Notes & Trivia:

- This album was one of several Barry Manilow album to be released in the quadraphonic format. Others Included "Barry Manilow II" and "This One's For You."

The label with the 4 Arista "Echos" for Quadraphonic.

Greatest Hits
A2L-8601

Track Listing:
Mandy / New York City Rhythm / Ready To Take A Chance Again / Looks Like We Made It / Daybreak (Live) / Can't Smile Without You / It's A Miracle / Even Now / Bandstand Boogie / Tryin' To Get The Feeling Again / Could It Be Magic / Somewhere In The Night / Jump Shout Boogie / Weekend In New England / All The Time / This One's For You / Copacabana (Disco) / Beautiful Music / I Write The Songs

Production Information:
Please see the 1978 LP on page 147.

Notes & Trivia:
- This two LP picture disc set has the same catalog number as the regular release. The set uses no labels and instead relies on the simple text of Side One, Side Two, etc centered at the lower part of the image.

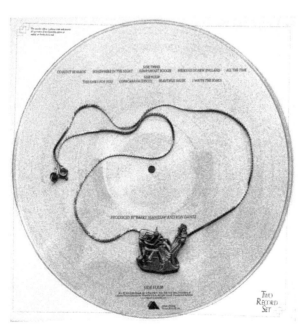

The back sides of the picture discs contain the photo found on the back of the regular jacket.

Christmas Seals Campaign 1980
ALA-8086

Track Listing:

Side One: Christmas Song:

1-1 Barry Manilow introduces Judy Garland singing Have Yourself A Merry Little Christmas / 1-2 Vikki Carr: It Came Upon A Midnight Clear / 1-3 Frank Sinatra: Mistletoe And Holly

Side Two: Bob Hope / Kids / Special Shows & Disc Jockey Introduction Spots:

2-1 Bob Hope: National Chairman / 2-2 Bob Hope: National Chairman / 2-3 Bob Hope: Partridge Music / 2-4 Bob Hope: Partridge Music / 2-5 Bob Hope: Snowman ID / 2-6 Bob Hope: Deck The Halls / 2-7 Bob Hope: Deck The Halls / 2-8 Bob Hope: Deck The Halls / (DJ Introductions): 2-9 Hank Williams Jr.: Disc Jockey Intro's / 2-10 Bill Harrell: Disc Jockey Intro's / 2-11 Larry Gatlin: Disc Jockey Intro's / 2-12 Barbara Cook: Disc Jockey Intro's / 2-13 Barry Manilow: Disc Jockey Intro's / 2-14 Vikki Carr: Disc Jockey Intro's / 2-15 Ray Charles: Disc Jockey Intro's / 2-16 Kenny Rogers: Disc Jockey Intro's / 2-17 Lynn Anderson: Disc Jockey Intro's

Production Information:

Produced By: A & J Recordings, New York, NY for the American Lung Association 1740 Broadway, New York, NY 10019

Notes & Trivia:

- This LP was made available to radio stations in August and September of 1980 in preparation for the upcoming 1980 Christmas season.
- It featured many well-known music personalities singing Christmas songs and / or providing introductions to DJ to read prepared and provided scripts for the American Lung Association.

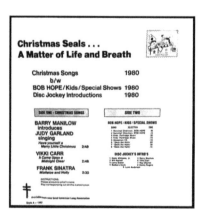

Back jacket in the center flanked by Side One (L) and Side Two (R) labels

The Singles

Barry Manilow Singles / EP's
PS – Picture Sleeve / Picture Slip (Japan) / PC – Picture Case (Cassette Singles)
7" singles unless noted

1971

Amy / Morning (as Featherbed featuring Barry Manilow) – 971 (Bell) (US) DJ Copy / White Label - Not For Sale / Stereo / March 1971

Amy / Morning (as Featherbed featuring Barry Manilow) – 971 (Bell) (US) / March 1971

Could It Be Magic / Could It Be Magic (as Featherbed featuring Barry Manilow) – 45-133 (Bell) (US) DJ Copy / White Label – Not For Sale / Mono-Stereo / October 1971

Could It Be Magic / Morning (as Featherbed featuring Barry Manilow) – 45-133 (Bell) (US) / October 1971

1973

Sweet Water Jones / Sweet Water Jones – 34-357 (Bell) (US) DJ Copy / White Label – Not For Sale / Mono-Stereo / June 1973

Sweet Water Jones / One Of These Days – 34-357 (Bell) (US) / June 1973

Cloudburst / Could It Be Magic – 45-422 (Bell) (US) DJ Copy / White Label – Not For Sale / Mono / November 1973

Versâo Reduzida (Could It Be Magic) / Versâo Reduzida (Could It Be Magic) – SDP-607 (Arista / Odeon) (Brazil) / Promotional Copy

1974

Let's Take Some Time To Say Goodbye / Let's Take Some Time To Say Goodbye – 45-443 (Bell) (US) DJ Copy / White Label – Not For Sale / Mono-Stereo / January 1974

Let's Take Some Time To Say Goodbye / Seven More Years – 45-443 (Bell) (US) / January 1974

Mandy / Mandy – 45-613 (Bell) (US) / DJ Copy / White Label – Not For Sale / Mono-Stereo / October 1974
Mandy / Something's Coming Up – 45-613 (Bell) (US) / DJ Copy / White Label – Not For Sale / Mono-Stereo / October 1974
Mandy / Something's Coming Up – 2008 295 (Bell) (Germany) (PS)
Mandy / Something's Coming Up – 2008 295 (Bell) (Netherlands) (PS)
Mandy / Something's Coming Up – 2008 295 (Bell) (Portugal) (PS)
Mandy / Something's Coming Up – 01.22.448 (Bell) (Peru)
Mandy / Something's Coming Up – BLPB-240-AR (Arista) (Japan) (PS)
Mandy / Something's Coming Up – 20 08 295 (Bell) (Spain) (PS)
Mandy / Something's Coming Up – 2008 295 (Bell) (Australia)
Mandy / Something's Coming Up – 2008 295 (Bell) (New Zealand)
Mandy / Something's Coming Up – PS.385 (Bell) (Africa)
Mandy / Something's Coming Up – PGP RTB – S 53 837 / Bell Records – S 53 837 (Yugoslavia) (PS)
Mandy / Something's Coming Up – ARISTA-1 (UK)

Mandy / Something's Coming Up – 45-494 (Bell) (Mexico)
Mandy / Algo Va A Suceder (Somethin's Comin' Up) – 494 (Arista) (Guatemala)
Mandy / Algo Se Nos Viene (Something's Comin' Up) – 1183 (Arista) (Argentina)
Mandy / Something's Coming Up – 2008 295 (Bell) (France) (PS)
Mandy / Something's Coming Up – 2008 295 (Bell) (Brazil)
Mandy / Something's Coming Up – 72-080 (Bell) (Philippines)

哀しみのマンディ (Mandy) / 愛は奇跡のように (It's A Miracle) – IER-20212 (Arista) (Japan) (PS)

It's A Miracle / One Of These Days – 2008 314 (Bell) (Germany) (PS)

Sandra / The Two Of Us – 72-096 (Bell) (Philippines)

1975

It's A Miracle / It's A Miracle – ASDJ-0108 (Arista) (US) / White Label – Promotional Not For Sale / Mono-Stereo / February 1975
It's A Miracle / One Of These Days – AS-0108 (Arista) (US) / February 1975
It's A Miracle / One Of These Days – AS-0108 (Arista) (Canada) / February 1975
It's A Miracle / One Of These Days – 5C 006-96361 (Arista) (Netherlands) (PS)
Es Un Milagro (It's A Miracle) / Uno De Estos Días (One Of These Days) – 473 (Arista) (Guatemala)
It's A Miracle / One Of These Days – BLPB-242-AR (Arista) (Japan) (PS)
It's A Miracle / One Of These Days – ARISTA 9 (Arista) (UK) / April 1975
It's A Miracle / One Of These Days – ATA-108 (Arista) (New Zealand)
It's A Miracle / One Of These Days – 3C 006 96361 (Arista) (Italy) (PS)
It's A Miracle / One Of These Days – ARISTA-10838 (Arista) (Australia)
It's A Miracle / One Of These Days – 8E 006 96361 F (Arista) (Portugal) (PS)

It's A Miracle / Avenue C – SP-382 (Bell) (France) (Marked: "Vente au public interdite" ("Sale to the public prohibited") and "Tirage limité réservé aux exploitants et à la promotion" ("Limited edition reserved for operators and promotion")

Could It Be Magic / Could It Be Magic – ASDJ-0126 (Arista) (US) / White Label – Promotional Not For Sale / Mono-Stereo
Could It Be Magic / I Am Your Child – AS-0126 (Arista) (US)
Could It Be Magic / I Am Your Child – AS-0126 (Arista) (Canada)
Could It Be Magic / I Am Your Child – 4C 006-96 806 (Arista) (Belgium) (PS)
Could It Be Magic / I Am Your Child – 2C 010-96806 (Arista) (France) (PS)
Could It Be Magic / I Am Your Child – SAR-88859 (Jugoton / Arista) (Yugoslavia) (PS)
Pudiera Ser Mágico (Could It Be Magic) / Soy Tu Niño (I Am Your Child) – J006-96.806 (Arista) (Spain) (PS)
Could It Be Magic / I Am Your Child – ARIST 229 (Arista) (France) (PS)
Could It Be Magic / I Am Your Child – 3C 006-96806 (Arista) (Italy) (PS)
Could It Be Magic / I Am Your Child – ARIST 20 (Arista) (UK) / White Label – Demo Record Not For Sale on center punch out
Could It Be Magic / I Am Your Child – ARIST 229 (Arista) (Ireland)
Could It Be Magic / I Am Your Child – ARIST 20 (Arista) (UK)
Could It Be Magic / I Am Your Child – 1C 006-96 806 (Germany) (PS)
Could It Be Magic / I Am Your Child – 5C 006-98806 (Netherlands) (PS)
Could It Be Magic / I Am Your Child – ARISTA-10862 (Arista) (Australia) / September 15, 1975
Side A above: Inspired by "Prelude In C Minor" by F. Chopin.

Mandy / Mandy – SP-398 (Bell) (France) ("Tirage limité réservé aux exploitants et à la promotion" – "Limited edition reserved for operators and promotion") 1975

Mandy / Something's Coming Up – 3C 006-97195 (Arista) (Italy) (PS) / November 1975

I Write The Songs / I Write The Songs – AS-0157 (Arista) (US) / DJ Copy / White Label – Not For Sale / Mono-Stereo
I Write The Songs / A Nice Boy Like Me – AS-0157 (Arista) (US)
I Write The Songs / A Nice Boy Like Me – AS-0157 (Arista) (US) / Blue Label / Pressed by PRC
I Write The Songs / A Nice Boy Like Me – AS-0157 (Arista) (Canada)
I Write The Songs / A Nice Boy Like Me – AR-10988 (Arista) (Australia) / November 24, 1975
I Write The Songs / A Nice Boy Like Me – ATA-157 (Arista) (New Zealand)
I Write The Songs / A Nice Boy Like Me – ATA-706 (Arista) (New Zealand) / DJ Copy / White Label – Not For Sale
I Write The Songs / A Nice Boy Like Me – C 010-97208 / 2C 010-97208 (Arista) (France) (PS)
I Write The Songs / A Nice Boy Like Me – 8E 006-97 208 F (Arista) (Portugal) (PS)
I Write The Songs / A Nice Boy Like Me – IER-10892 (Arista) (Japan) (PS) / December 20, 1975
I Write The Songs / A Nice Boy Like Me – IER-10892 (Arista) (Japan) (PS) / Promotional Copy / White Label – Not For Sale / December 20, 1975 / Marked: 見本 ("Sample Copy") and 非売品 ("Not For Sale")
I Write The Songs / A Nice Boy Like Me – 1C 006-97 208 (Arista) / 1C 006-97 208 (EMI-Electrola) (Germany) (PS)
Escribo Las Canciones (I Write The Songs) / Un Buen Chico Como Yo (A Nice Boy Like Me) – 01.22.657 (Arista) (Peru)
Escribo Mis Canciones (I Write The Songs) / Un Buen Chico Como Yo (A Nice Boy Like Me) – 7867 (Arista) (Mexico)
I Write The Songs / A Nice Boy Like Me – 4C006-97208 (Arista) (Belgium) (PS)
Escribo Mis Canciones (I Write The Songs) / Un Buen Chico Como Yo (A Nice Boy Like Me) –
I Write The Songs / A Nice Boy Like Me – 1 J 006-97208 (Arista) (Spain) (PS)

Tryin' To Get The Feeling Again /Tryin' To Get The Feeling Again – AS-0172 (Arista) (US) / DJ Copy / White Label – Not For Sale / Mono-Stereo
Tryin' To Get The Feeling Again / Beautiful Music – AS-0172 (Arista) (US)
Tryin' To Get The Feeling Again / Beautiful Music – AS-0172 (Arista) (US) / Styrene / Blue Label
Tryin' To Get The Feeling Again / Beautiful Music – AS-0172 (Arista) (US) / Styrene / Terre Haute pressing
Tryin' To Get The Feeling Again / Beautiful Music – AS-0172 (Arista) (Canada)
うつろな想い (Tryin' To Get The Feeling Again) / 愛しのミュージック (Beautiful Music) - IER-10961 (Arista) (Japan) (PS)
Tryin' To Get The Feeling Again / Beautiful Music – AR-11094 (Arista) (Australia)
Tryin' To Get The Feeling Again / Beautiful Music – 5C 06 97681 (Arista) (Netherlands) (PS)

As Sure As I'm Standing Here / Beautiful Music – AR-30132 (Arista) (Philippines)

1976

I Write The Songs / As Sure As I'm Standin' Here – ARISTA 40 (Arista) (UK) / White Label – Not For Sale / January 1976
I Write The Songs / As Sure As I'm Standin' Here – ARISTA 40 (Arista) (UK) / January 1976

Side A: Andrea E Nicole- La Prima Volta / Side B: Barry Manilow- I Write The Songs – 3C 000 – 70063 (Arista / Odeon) (Italy) / Marked: "Edizione Speciale Juke Box - vietata la vendita al pubblico" ("Juke

Box Special Edition - Not for sale to the public")

I Write The Songs / A Nice Boy Like Me – 5C 006-97208 (Arista) (Netherlands) (PS)
I Write The Songs / A Nice Boy Like Me – 3C 006-97208 (Arista) (Italy) (PS)

New York City Rhythm / Tryin' To Get The Feeling Again – 1 J 006-97925 (Arista / Odeon) (Spain) (PS)
Ritmo De La Ciudad De Nueva York (New York City Rhythm) / Intentando Sentir Nuevamente (Tryin' To Get The Feeling Again) – 7913 (Arista) (Mexico) (PS) / Promotional Copy / White Label – Not For Sale
Ritmo De La Ciudad De Nueva York (New York City Rhythm) / Intentando Sentir Nuevamente (Tryin' To Get The Feeling Again) – 7913 (Arista) (Mexico) (PS) / Labeling error: Both sides marked "Side A."

Tryin' To Get The Feeling Again / Beautiful Music – 1C 006-97 681 (Arista) (Germany) (PS)

Mandy / Could It Be Magic / It's A Miracle - 5C 006-98004 (Arista) (Netherlands) (PS) 3 track EP

Weekend In New England / Riders To The Stars – ARISTA 77 (Arista) (UK) White Label – "Demo Record - Not For Sale" on center punch out
Weekend In New England / Riders To The Stars – ARISTA 77 (Arista) (UK)

Tryin' To Get The Feeling Again / Beautiful Music – AR-11094 (Arista) (Australia) / June 26, 1976

This One's For You / This One's For You – AS-0206 (Arista) (US) DJ Copy / White Label – Not For Sale / Mono-Stereo
This One's For You / This One's For You – AS-0206 (Arista) (US) Test Pressing – Full Labels / White Label – Not For Sale / Mono-Stereo
This One's For You / Riders To The Stars – AS-0206 (Arista) (US)
This One's For You / Riders To The Stars – AS-0206 (Arista) (US) / PCR Pressing / Blue Label
This One's For You / Riders To The Stars – AS-0206 (Arista) (Canada)
This One's For You / Riders To The Stars – IER-20110 (Arista) (Japan) (PS)
This One's For You / Riders To The Stars – AS-0206 (Arista) (Guatemala)
This One's For You / Riders To The Stars – 1C 006-98253 (Arista) (Germany) (PS)
This One's For You / Riders To The Stars – NG-777 (Arista) (Netherlands) (PS)
This One's For You / Riders To The Stars – AR-11275 (Arista) (Australia)
This One's For You / Riders To The Stars – AR-11275 (Arista) (Australia) / Marked: Sample Record – Not For Sale

Weekend In New England / Weekend In New England AS-0212 (US) DJ Copy / White Label – Not For Sale / Mono-Stereo
Weekend In New England / Say The Words – AS-0212 (Arista) (US)
Weekend In New England / Say The Words – AS-0212 (Arista) (US) / White Label – Blue Logo
Weekend In New England / Say The Words – AS-0212 (Arista) (US) / Black Label
Weekend In New England / Say The Words – AS-0212 (Arista) (Canada) / Blue Label
Weekend In New England / Say The Words – AS-0212 (Arista) (Canada) / Black Label – Blue Logo
Weekend In New England / Say The Words – AR-11330 (Arista) (Australia)

Queen– Somebody To Love / Barry Manilow– This One's For You – SDP-702 (EMI) (Brazil) White label promo / Marked: Disco Promocional Invendavel (Unsaleable Promotional Disc)

Looks Like We Made It / Weekend in New England / I Write The Songs – ARISTA-120 (Arista) (UK) (PS) / 3 track EP.

Ritmo De New York (New York City Rhythm) / Te Marchas Demasiado Pronto (You're Leaving Too Soon) – AR-609 (Arista) (Venezuela)

Looks Like We Made It / Looks Like We Made It – AS-0244 (Arista) (US) DJ Copy / White Label – Not For Sale / Mono-Stereo
Looks Like We Made It / New York City Rhythm (Live Version) – AS-0244 (Arista) (US)
Looks Like We Made It / New York City Rhythm (Live Version) – ATA-244 (Arista) (New Zealand)
Looks Like We Made It / New York City Rhythm (Live Version) – NG-868 (Arista) (Netherlands) (PS)
Looks Like We Made It / New York City Rhythm (Live Version) – IER-20286 (Arista) (Japan) (PS)
Looks Like We Made It / New York City Rhythm (Live Version) – 1 C 006-99119 (Arista / EMI Electrola) (Germany) (PS)
Looks Like We Made It / New York City Rhythm (Live Version) – 4AR-616 (Arista) (Venezuela)
Se Parece A Como Lo Hicimos (Looks Like We Made It) / New York City Rhythm (Live Version) – 10 C 006-99119 (Arista) (Spain) (PS) / Marked: Depósito Legal: B. 31258-1977
Looks Like We Made It / New York City Rhythm (Live Version) – 2C 006 – 99119 (Arista) (France) (PS)
Looks Like We Made It / New York City Rhythm (Live Version) – 3C 006 99119 (Arista) (Italy) (PS)

Daybreak / Daybreak – AS-0273 (Arista) (US) DJ Copy / White Label – Not For Sale / Mono-Stereo
Daybreak / Jump Shout Boogie – AS-0273 (Arista) (US)
Daybreak / Jump Shout Boogie – AS-0273 (Arista) (Canada)
Daybreak / Jump Shout Boogie – 5N 006-60146 (Arista) (Netherlands) (PS)

Jump Shout Boogie / Daybreak – 5N 006N 60146 (Arista) (Netherlands) (PS)

1977

Looks Like We Made It / New York City Rhythm (Live Version) – 4C 006 99119 (Arista) (Belgium) (PS)

It's Just Another New Year's Eve (Stereo) / It's Just Another New Year's Eve (Mono) – SP-11 (Arista) (US) (PS) / White Label – Not For Sale / Mono-Stereo
It's Just Another New Year's Eve (Stereo) / It's Just Another New Year's Eve (Mono) – SP-11 (Arista) (Canada) / White Label – Not For Sale / Mono-Stereo

Mandy / I Write The Songs / Looks Like We Made It / Could It Be Magic – EPS 6 (Arista) (New Zealand) (PS) / 4 track EP

Weekend In New England / Looks Like We Made It / Mandy / I Write The Songs – BCM 3 (Arista) (UK) (PS) / 4 track EP / Marked: For Radio Use Only. Taken from the album "Barry Manilow Live" Arista DARTY 3

I Write The Songs / Mandy / Looks Like We Made It / A Very Special Medley – PRP-4013 (Arista / EMI) (Japan) (PS) / 4 track EP / White Label promo only. Taken from the album "Barry Manilow Live" Arista IES-67127-28

This One's For You / Mandy / Looks Like We Made It – NFS 1 (Arista) (Netherlands) (PS) / 3 track EP / Marked: Promotion Sample – Not For Sale

Weekend In New England / Say The Words – AR1133 (Arista) (Australia) / February 14, 1977

1978

Amanecer (Daybreak) / Parece Que Lo Hemos Logrado (Looks Like We Made It) – 8121 (Arista) (Mexico) (PS) / Taken from the album "Barry Manilow Live" (SLEMB-722)

涙色の微笑 (Can't Smile Without You) / サンライズ (Sunrise) – IER-20398 (Arista) (Japan) (PS) / March 5, 1978
Can't Smile Without You / Can't Smile Without You – AS-0305 (Arista) (US) / White Label – Not For Sale / Mono-Stereo
Can't Smile Without You / Sunrise – AS-0305 (Arista) (US) / March 31, 1978
Can't Smile Without You / Sunrise – AS-0305 (Arista) (Canada) / March 31, 1978
Can't Smile Without You / Sunrise – Arist-176 (Arista) (UK) (PS)
Can't Smile Without You / Sunrise – 31C 006 60505 (Arista) (Brazil)
Can't Smile Without You / Sunrise – 8E 006-60505 G (Arista) (Portugal) (PS)
Can't Smile Without You / Sunrise – AR-11665 (Arista) (Australia)
No Puedo Sonreir Sin Ti (Can't Smile Without You) / Amanecer (Sunrise) – 4400 (Arista) (Guatemala) / Marked: Discos de Centroamérica (Records from Central America)
No Puedo Sonreir Sin Ti (Can't Smile Without You) / Amanecer (Sunrise) – 01.22.1209 (Arista) (Peru)
Can't Smile Without You / Sunrise – 2C 008 60505 (Arista) (France) (PS)
Can't Smile Without You / Sunrise – 5N 006N 60505 (Arista) (Netherlands) (PS) / March 18, 1978
Can't Smile Without You / Sunrise – ATA-704 (Arista) (New Zealand)
Can't Smile Without You / Sunrise – ARIST-176 (Arista) (Ireland)
Can't Smile Without You / Sunrise – AAJ-1042 (Arista) (South Africa)
No Puedo Sonreir Sin Ti (Can't Smile Without You) / Amanece (Sunrise) – 8134 (Arista) (Mexico) (PS)

Even Now / Even Now – AS-0330 (Arista) (US) DJ Copy / White Label – Not For Sale / Mono-Stereo
Even Now / I Was A Fool To Let You Go – AS-0330 (Arista) (US) (PS)
Even Now / I Was A Fool To Let You Go – AS-0330 (Arista) (Canada)
Even Now / I Was A Fool To Let You Go – ARIST-220 (UK) (PS)
Hasta Ahora (Even Now) / Fui Un Tonto Al Dejarte Ir (I Was A Fool To Let You Go) – 4416 (Arista) (Guatemala) / Marked: Discos de Centroamérica (Records from Central America)
Even Now / I Was A Fool To Let You Go – 4C 006-61864 (Arista / EMI) (Belgium) (PS) / Marked: "Unique Concert in Brussels (Forest National) 18th October 78"
Even Now / I Was A Fool To Let You Go – ATA-330 (Arista) (New Zealand)

Even Now / Can't Smile Without You – 3C 006-60606 (Italy) (PS) / Marked: "Tratti dall LP: Even Now" ("Taken from the LP: Even Now") Arista 3C 064 - 60423

Even Now / Sunrise – AR-11802 (Australia) / September 18, 1978

No Puedo Sonreir Sin Ti (Can´T Smile Without You) / Sonrisa (Sunrise) – 114-0030 (Arista) (Ecuador)

Copacabana (At The Copa) (Spanish Version) / Copacabana (At The Copa) (English Version) – ED-9 (Arista) (Australia) 12" 45 RPM single

Copacabana / Can't Smile Without You / Even Now / Sunrise – BOD-5465 (EMI International / Odeon) / (Bolivia) (PS) / 33⅓ RPM, Maxi-Single

Copacabana / Ready To Take A Chance Again – 6RS-4 (Arista) (Japan) (PS)

Copacabana (At The Copa) (Long Version) / Ready To Take A Chance Again – 7RS-1501 (Arista)

(Japan) (PS)

Copacabana (At The Copa) Short Version / Copacabana (At The Copa) Long Version AS-0339 (Arista) (US) / DJ Copy / White Label – Not For Sale

Copacabana (At The Copa) Short Version / Copacabana (At The Copa) Long Version – 33C 066-61325 (Arista) (Mexico)

Copacabana (At The Copa) (Disco Version) – SP-18 (Arista) (US) / 12" 45 RPM single sided promo
Copacabana (At The Copa) (Disco Version) – SP-18 (Arista) (Canada) / 12" 45 RPM Maxi-Single sided promo

En El Copa (Long Spanish Version) / En El Copa (Short Spanish Version) – SP-21 (Arista) (US) / 12" RPM Maxi-Single

Copacabana (At The Copa) Short Version / Copacabana (At The Copa) Long Version – 18(0941)00014 (Arista) (Colombia) 12" 45 RPM single – various colors spattered vinyl

Copacabana (At The Copa) / Copacabana (At The Copa) – 8187-Z (Arista) (Mexico) / 12" RPM Maxi-Single / Red Vinyl

Copacabana (At The Copa) / Copacabana (At The Copa) – 8187 Z / 33C 052 61326 Z (Arista) (Mexico) / 12" RPM Maxi-Single / Red Vinyl

Copacabana (Versión En Español) [Spanish Vocals – Barry Manilow] Version Larga / Copacabana (Versión En Español) Version Corta / Mandy – SL-7050 / 102.517 (Arista) (Mexico) / 12" 45 RPM maxi-single EP

Copacabana – At The Copa (Long Version) / Copacabana – At The Cop (Short Version) – AS-0339 (Arista) (US)
Copacabana – At The Copa (Long Version) / Copacabana – At The Cop (Short Version) – AS-0339 (Arista) (Canada)
Copacabana – At The Copa (Long Version) / Copacabana – At The Cop (Short Version) – AS-0339 (Arista) (Jamaica)
Copacabana (At The Copa) Long Version / Copacabana (At The Copa) Short Version – AR-11741 (Arista) (Australia)
Copacabana – At The Copa (Long Version) / Copacabana – At The Cop (Short Version) – 0339-AS (Arista) (Guatemala)
Copacabana – At The Copa (Long Version) / Copacabana – At The Cop (Short Version) – 0339-AS (Arista) (Panama)

En El Copa (Long Version) [Spanish Vocals – Barry Manilow] / En El Copa (Short Version) [Spanish Vocals – Barry Manilow] – 4436 (Arista) (Guatemala)

En El Copa (Canta en Español) [Spanish Vocals – Barry Manilow] / En El Copa (Canta en Español) [Spanish Vocals – Barry Manilow] – 46951 (EMI Records) (Colombia)

Copacabana (At The Copa) / En El Copa (At The Copa) [Spanish Vocals – Barry Manilow] – AR-30186 (ARIST-196) (Arista) (Philippines)
Copacabana (At The Copa) / En El Copa (At The Copa) [Spanish Vocals – Barry Manilow] – 14C 006 61533 (Arista) (Greece) / Marked: "Made in Greece by EMI."

Copacabana (En El Copa) [Spanish Vocals – Barry Manilow] / Copacabana (At The Copa) – 10C006-061533 (Arista) (Spain) (PS) / Marked: "Cantado en español" ("Sung in Spanish")
Copacabana (At The Copa) / En El Copa (At The Copa) [Spanish Vocals – Barry Manilow] – POP5001 (POP Records) (Turkey) (PS)

Copacabana (At The Copa) (En Ingles) / Copacabana (At The Copa) (En Castellano) – 1425 (Arista) (Chile)

Copacabana (At The Copa) Long Version / Copacabana (At The Copa) Short Version – 4433 (Arista) (Guatemala) / Marked: Discos De Centroamérica S.A. (Records of Central America S.A.)

En El Copa [Spanish Vocals – Barry Manilow] / A Linda Song – 2C 008 – 61717 (Arista) (France) (PS)
Copacabana (At The Copa) / A Linda Song – SC-1 (Arista) (France) (PS) / Green vinyl / Marked: "Imprimé en France" ("Made in France")
Copacabana (At The Copa) / A Linda Song – 2C 006 61163 (Arista) (France) (PS)
Copacabana (At The Copa) / A Linda Song – 4C 006 61163 (Arista) (Portugal) (PS)
Copacabana (At The Copa) / A Linda Song – 4C 006 61163 (Arista) (Belgium) (PS) Marked: "Unique Concert in Brussels (Forest National) 18th October 78"
Copacabana (At The Copa) / A Linda Song – 5C 006 61163 (Arista) (Netherlands) (PS)
Copacabana (At The Copa) / A Linda Song – 5N 006 61163 (Arista) (Netherlands) (PS)
Copacabana (At The Copa) / Una Cancion Para Linda (A Linda Song) – 114-0032 (Arista) (Ecuador)
Copacabana (At The Copa) / A Linda Song – AAJ-1046 (Arista) (South Africa)
Copacabana (At The Copa) / A Linda Song – 3C 052-61163 Z (Arista) (Italy) / 12" Maxi-Single
Copacabana (At The Copa) / A Linda Song – 2C 052-52809 Z (Arista) (France) (PS) / 12" 45 RPM Maxi-Single

En El Copa (Versión En Castellano) [Spanish Vocals – Barry Manilow] / Somewhere In The Night – 01.22.1299 (Arista) (Peru)

Copacabana (At The Copa) / Somewhere In The Night – BL-354 (Arista) (New Zealand)
Copacabana (At The Copa) / Somewhere In The Night – 3C 006 61163 (Arista) (Italy) (PS)
Copacabana (At The Copa) / Somewhere In The Night – 31C 006 61421 (Arista) (Brazil)

Copacabana (At The Copa) / Starting Over – IER-20446 (Arista) (Japan) (PS)

Copacabana (At The Copa) / Can't Smile Without You – 1C 006-60507 (Arista) (Germany) (PS)
Copacabana (At The Copa) / Can't Smile Without You – 1C 006-60507YZ (Arista) (Germany) / PS / 12" RPM Maxi-Single
Copacabana (At The Copa) / Can't Smile Without You – 7C 006-60507 (Arista) (Sweden) (PS)
Copacabana (At The Copa) / Can't Smile Without You – 7C 006-60507 (Arista) (Sweden) / 12" Maxi-Single

Copacabana (At The Copa) / Mandy – 1C 052-62 470 YZ (Arista) (Germany) /12" Maxi-Single / Red vinyl

Copacabana / Hasta Ahora (Even Now) – 01.22.1265 (Arista) (Peru) / Marked: Fabricado por: Industrias Electricas Y Musicales Peruanas S.A. (Manufactured by: Electrical and Musical Industries Peruanas S.A.)
Copacabana / Aun Ahora (Even Now) – S-6004 (Helicón Internacional) (Cuba)

Copacabana (At Copa) / Can't Smile Without You / Somewhere In The Night / Even Now – 31C 016

62229 9 (Arista) (Brazil) (PS)

Barry Manilow– Copacabana (At The Copa) / The Rolling Stones– Respectable – 3C 000 - 79039 (Arista / Rolling Stones Records) / Marked: "Edizione Speciale Juke Box - vietata la vendita al pubblico" ("Juke Box Special Edition - not for sale to the public") Made in Italy. Stones: ℗ 1978 Promotone B.V

Mandy / En El Copa (At The Copa) – 114-0033 (Arista) (Ecuador)

Ready To Take A Chance Again / Ready To Take A Chance Again – AS-0357 (Arista) (US) DJ Copy / White Label – Not For Sale / Mono-Stereo
Ready To Take A Chance Again / Sweet Life – AS-0357 (Arista) (US) August 24, 1978
Ready To Take A Chance Again / Sweet Life – AS-0357 (Arista) (Canada)
Ready To Take A Chance Again / Sweet Life – ARIST 242 (Arista) (UK) (PS)
Ready To Take A Chance Again / Sweet Life (Mama Can Ya' Hear Me) – 31C 006 61777 (Arista) (Brazil)
Ready To Take A Chance Again / Sweet Life – AR-11860 (Arista) (Australia)
Ready To Take A Chance Again / Sweet Life – IER 20499 (Arista) (Japan) (PS)

Ready To Take A Chance Again / Mandy – 7C 006-61918 (Arista) (Sweden) (PS) / The film *Foul Play* was released in Sweden as "Tjejen som visste för mycket" ("The Girl Who Knew Too Much")

Ready To Take A Chance Again – SP-25 (Arista) (US) (PS) / Single sided promotional single. Cover shows black and white Original Motion Picture Soundtrack Album "Foul Play" graphics.

Somewhere In The Night / Somewhere In The Night – AS-0382 (Arista) (US) DJ Copy / White Label – Not For Sale / Mono-Stereo
Somewhere In The Night / Leavin' In The Morning – AS-0382 (Arista) (US)
Somewhere In The Night / Leavin' In The Morning – AS-0382 (Arista) (Canada)
Somewhere In The Night / Leavin' In The Morning – AR-11886 (Arista) (Australia)
Somewhere In The Night / Leavin' In The Morning – 6RS-3 (Arista) (Japan) (PS)
Somewhere In The Night / Leavin' In The Morning – ATA-382 (Arista) (New Zealand)

Somewhere in the Night / Copacabana – ARIST-196 (Arista) (UK) (PS) / Marked: Taken from the album "Even Now" SPART 1047 / July 1978 / Double A side single
Somewhere in the Night / Copacabana (Disco version) – ARIST 12196 (Arista) (UK) / Marked: Taken from the album 'Even Now' SPART 1047 / DJ use only – 12" Double A sided single

Dispuesto A Arriesgarme Otra Vez (Ready To Take A Chance Again) / Algun Lugar En La Noche (Somewhere In The Night) – FLB-104 (Arista) (Argentina)

Mandy / Ready To Take A Chance Again – 1C 006-61918 (Arista) / 1C 006-61 918 (EMI Electrola) (Germany) (PS)

Barry Manilow– Even Now / Samantha Sang– Emotion – 3C 000-79031 (Arista / Private Stock) (Italy) / Double A sided Juke box only release. Marked: "Disco Promozionale Vietata la Vendita" ("Promotional Disc Sale prohibited")

Could It Be Magic / I Am Your Child – 4C 006-96806 (Arista) (Belgium) (PS) (Reissue)
Could It Be Magic / I Am Your Child – 1C 006-96 806 (Arista) (Germany) (PS) (Reissue)
Could It Be Magic / I Am Your Child – ARIST 229 (Arista) (UK) (PS) (Reissue)

1979

Ships / Ships – AS-0464 (Arista) (US) / DJ Copy / White Label – Not For Sale / Mono-Stereo
Ships / They Gave In To The Blues – AS-0464 (Arista) (US)
Ships / They Gave In To The Blues – AS-0464 (Arista) (Canada)
Ships / They Gave In To The Blues – 6RS-36 (Arista) (Japan) (PS)
Ships / They Gave In To The Blues – 101206 (Arista) (Netherlands) (PS)
Ships / They Gave In To The Blues – 2 C 008-63346 (Arista / EMI) (France) (PS)
Ships / They Gave In To The Blues – AR-134 (Arista) (Australia)

Ships / Sunday Father – ARIST 307 (Arista) (UK) (PS) / September 1979
Ships / Sunday Father – ARIST 307 (Arista) (Ireland)
Ships / Sunday Father – 31C 006 63389 (Arista) (Brazil)
Ships / Sunday Father – 101 952 (Arista) (Brazil) (PS)

When I Wanted You / When I Wanted You – AS-0481 (Arista) (US) DJ Copy / White Label – Not For Sale / Mono-Stereo
When I Wanted You / Bobbie Lee (What's The Difference, I Gotta Live) – AS-0481 Arista (US)
When I Wanted You / Bobbie Lee (What's The Difference, I Gotta Live) – AS-0481 Arista (Canada)
When I Wanted You / Bobbie Lee (What's The Difference, I Gotta Live) – 7C 006-63708 (Arista) (Sweden) (PS)
When I Wanted You / Bobbie Lee (What's The Difference, I Gotta Live) – K7778 (Arista) (Australia)
When I Wanted You / Bobbie Lee (What's The Difference, I Gotta Live) – AR-45-001 (Arista) (Philippines)

I Don't Want To Walk Without You / I Don't Want To Walk Without You – AS-0501 (Arista) (US) / DJ Copy / White Label – Not For Sale / Mono-Stereo
I Don't Want To Walk Without You / One Voice – AS-0501 (Arista) (US)
I Don't Want To Walk Without You / One Voice – AS-0501 (Arista) (Canada)
I Don't Want To Walk Without You / One Voice – ATA-713 (Arista) (New Zealand)
No Quiero Estar Sin Ti (I Don't Want To Walk Without You) / Una Voz (One Voice) – 3003 (Arista / Ariola) (Peru)
I Don't Want To Walk Without You / One Voice – K-7909 (Arista) (Australia)

I Don't Want To Walk Without You / It's A Miracle – 101 869 / 101 869 - 100 (Arista) (Germany) (PS) / A-Side Taken from the Arista album: "One Voice" - 201 154-320 / B-Side Taken from the Arista album: "Manilow Magic" - 201 222-320

Who's Been Sleeping In My Bed / They Gave In To The Blues – BARRY 1 (Arista) (UK) (PS) / December 1979
Who's Been Sleeping In My Bed / They Gave In To The Blues – 101197 (Arista) (France) (PS)

Mandy / Could It Be Magic – 10C006-062.395 (Arista) (Spain) (PS) (Reissue)
Mandy / Could It Be Magic – 2C008-62395 (Arista) (France) (PS) (Reissue)

涙色の微笑 (Can't Smile Without You) / サンライズ (Sunrise) – 6RS-19 (Arista) (Japan) (PS) January 22, 1979 / Taken from the album "Barry Manilow Greatest Story" (Arista / 25RS-7)

I Write The Songs / As Sure As I'm Standin' Here – ARIST-280 (Arista) (UK) / June 1979 (Reissue)

Copacabana / Esta Es Tu Cancion (This One's For You) / No Puedo Sonreir Sin Ti (I Can't Smile

Without You) / Amanecer (Sunrise) – EPEM-10870 (Arista) (Mexico) (PS) / 4 track EP

One Voice / Ships / Who's Been Sleeping In My Bed / Where Are They Now – BARRY 4 (Arista) (UK) / 33-⅓ 4 track EP / Marked: Record Dealers Only

Barry Manilow "4 Hits" - Ships / One Voice / Ready To Take A Chance Again / Somewhere In The Night – 696 006 (Arista) (Brazil) (PS) / 33-⅓ 4 track EP

1980

We Still Have Time – FILM-1 (Arista) (UK) / Single sided promotional disc / Theme song taken from the 1980 motion picture "Tribute" / Taken from the Arista LP "Barry" (DLART-2)

We Still Have Time / Lonely Together – 7RS-21 (Arista) (Japan) (PS) / Theme song taken from the motion picture "Tribute" also from the Arista LP "Barry" (25RS-106)

It's A Miracle / I Don't Want To Walk Without You – ARIST-337 (Arista) (UK) (PS) / April 1980 re-issue / Double A side release / "It's A Miracle" Taken From The Album "Barry Manilow II" ARTY 100 - 1974 / "I Don't To Walk Without You" Taken From The Album "One Voice" SPART 1106 - 1979 / Sides marked A and A1

Lonely Together / Lonely Together – AS-0596 (Arista) (US) / DJ Copy / White Label – Not For Sale / Mono-Stereo
Lonely Together / The Last Duet (with Lily Tomlin) – AS-0596 (Arista) (US)
Lonely Together / The Last Duet (with Lily Tomlin) – AS-0596z (Arista) (Canada)

Lonely Together / London – ARIST- 373 (Arista) (Ireland)

Who's Been Sleeping In My Bed / Rain – A-100 724 (Arista) (Spain) (PS)

Life Will Go On / 24 Hours A Day – AR-45-036 (Arista) (Philippines)

Bermuda Triangle / I Don't Want To Walk Without You – 7RS-8 (Arista) (Japan) (PS)
Bermuda Triangle / I Don't Want To Walk Without You – 7RS-8 (Arista) (Japan) (PS) / Marked: 見本盤 ("Sample Copy") / White Label promotional copy

Bermuda Triangle / One Voice – ARIST-406 (Arista) (UK) (PS) / Limited Edition Free Poster Included

Bermuda Triangle / Beautiful Music – K-8296 (Arista) (Australia)

Why Don't We Try A Slow Dance / When I Wanted You – 6RS-54 (Arista) (Japan) (PS)

When I Wanted You / Ships – ARS 37012 (Arista) (Italy) (PS) March 4, 1980
When I Wanted You / Ships – 101 287 / 101 287–100 (Arista) (Germany) (PS)

Mandy / I Write The Songs – 101 851 / 101851 - 100 (Arista) (Germany) (PS) / Reissue

Copacabana (At The Cop) / Mandy – 102.323 (Arista) (Netherlands) (PS) / Original Double Hit Reissue Series
Copacabana (At The Cop) / Mandy – 102.323 (Arista) (Netherlands) (PS) / Special Edition pushing an alcoholic drink called "Copacabana." Picture sleeve does not feature Barry Manilow.

Copacabana (At The Cop) / Mandy – 102.323 (Arista) (Germany) (PS) / Original Double Hit Reissue Series

Bermuda Triangle / Lonely Together – 102 658 / 102 658-100 (Arista) (Germany) (PS)

Bermuda Triangle / I Made It Through The Rain – 102 860 (Arista) (France) (PS)

Copacabana (At The Cop) / Mandy – 106 716 (Arista) (Europe) (PS) / Golden Oldies Reissue Series

1981

The Old Songs / The Old Songs – AS-0633 (Arista) (US) Advance Copy / Green Label – Not For Sale / Mono-Stereo
The Old Songs / Don't Fall In Love With Me – AS-0633 (Arista) (US)
ふたりのオールド・ソング (The Old Songs) / 恋は移り気 (Don't Fall In Love With Me) – 7RS-31 (Arista) (Japan) (PS) / October 10, 1981
The Old Songs / Don't Fall In Love With Me – ARI-8205 (Arista) (Scandinavia) (PS)

The Old Songs / Let's Take All Night To Say Goodbye – K8478 (Arista) (Australia)

The Old Songs / Just Another New Year's Eve (Live version) – ARIST-443 (Arista) (France) (PS) / Side A taken from the Album "If I Should Love Again" (BMAN1) - 1981 / Side B taken from the album "Barry Manilow Live" (DARTY3) - 1977

Let's Hang On / Let's Hang On – AS-0675 (Arista) (US) DJ Copy / Blue Label – Not For Sale / Mono-Stereo
Let's Hang On / No Other Love – AS-0675 (Arista) (US)
Let's Hang On / No Other Love – AS-0675 (Arista) (Canada)
Let's Hang On / No Other Love – ARIST-429 (Arista) (Ireland) (PS)
Let's Hang On / No Other Love – ARI-8115 (Arista) (Sweden) / Picture Label Side A
Let's Hang On / No Other Love – ARIST-429 (Arista) (UK) / September 1981
Let's Hang On / No Other Love – 7RS-45 (Arista) (Japan) (PS)

Let's Hang On / The Old Songs – 0257 (Ariola / Arista) (Spain) (PS) / Marked: Disco Promocional. Prohibida Su Venta (Promotional disc. Sale Prohibited)

Let's Hang On / Don't Fall In Love With Me – 103 625 / 103 625 – 100 (Arista) (Germany) (PS) / January 1981
Let's Hang On / Don't Fall In Love With Me – K-8512 (Arista) (Australia)
Let's Hang On / Don't Fall In Love With Me – 103 625 (Arista) (France) (PS) / January 1981
Let's Hang On / Don't Fall In Love With Me – 103 625 (Arista) (Netherlands) (PS) / January 1981

Mandy / Copacabana – (Arista) 103 855 / 103 855-100 (Germany) (PS) - Taken From The Album: *Manilow Magic - The Best Of Barry Manilow* Arista 201 222-320

Somewhere Down The Road / Somewhere Down The Road – AS-0658 (Arista) (US) DJ Copy / White Label – Not For Sale / Mono-Stereo
Somewhere Down The Road / Let's Take All Night (To Say Goodbye) – AS-0658 (Arista) (US)
Somewhere Down The Road / Let's Take All Night (To Say Goodbye) – ASO-0658 (Arista) (Canada)
Somewhere Down The Road / Let's Take All Night (To Say Goodbye) – ATA-658 (Arista) (New Zealand)

1982

Somewhere Down The Road / The Old Songs – 104 095 / 104 095-100 (Arista) (Germany) (PS)

Memory / Memory – AS-1025 (Arista) (US) / Advance Copy / Green Label – Not For Sale / Mono-Stereo
Memory / Memory – AS-1025 (Arista) (US) / DJ Copy / Blue promotional Label – Not For Sale / Mono-Stereo
Memory / Heart Of Steel – AS-1025 (Arista) (US)
Memory / Heart Of Steel – AS-1025 (Arista) (Canada)
Memory / Heart Of Steel – 6198 668 (Arista) (Brazil) (PS) / 33 ⅓ RPM

Some Kind Of Friend / Here Comes The Night – 7RS-65 (Arista) (Japan) (PS)

Memory / I Wanna Do It With You – 7RS-81 (Arista) (Japan) (PS)

Memory / Read 'Em and Weep – 03.101006.11 (Arista) (Portugal) (PS)

If I Should Love Again / Let's Take All Night (To Say Goodbye) – ARIST-453 (Arista) (UK) (PS) / February 1982
If I Should Love Again / Let's Take All Night (To Say Goodbye) – ARIST-453 (Arista) (Ireland)

If I Should Love Again / If I Should Love Again (Live) – ARILE-453 (Arista) (UK) / Side A taken from the LP "If I Should Love Again" (BMAN1) - 1981 / Side B recorded live at The Royal Albert Hall in London, England.

I Wanna Do It With You / Heaven – ARIST-495 (Arista) (UK) (PS)
I Wanna Do It With You / Heaven – 104 859 (Arista) (France) (PS)
I Wanna Do It With You / Heaven – ARIST-495 (Arista) (Ireland)
I Wanna Do It With You / Heaven – ARI-8253 (Arista) (Germany) (PS)
I Wanna Do It With You / Heaven – 5104 859 (Arista) (Portugal) (PS)
I Wanna Do It With You / Heaven – AAJ-1142 (Arista) (South Africa)
I Wanna Do It With You / Heaven – ATA-744 (Arista) (New Zealand)
I Wanna Do It With You / Heaven – 104 859 / 104 859-100 (Arista) (Europe)
I Wanna Do It With You / Heaven – K-8930 (Arista) (Australia)
Quiero Hacerlo Contigo (I Wanna Do It With You) / Heaven – B-104859 (Arista) (Spain) (PS)

Quiero Hacerlo Contigo (I Wanna Do It With You) / Corazon de Acero (Heart Of Steel) – S-785 (Arista) (Mexico)

Some Kind Of Friend / Some Kind Of Friend – AS-1046 (Arista) (US) / DJ Copy / White Label – Not For Sale / Mono-Stereo
Some Kind Of Friend / Heaven – AS-1046 (Arista) (US)
Some Kind Of Friend / Heaven – AS1-9003 (Arista) (US)
Some Kind Of Friend / Heaven – AS-1046 (Arista) (Canada)

Some Kind Of Friend / Heart Of Steel – K 8971 (Arista) (New Zealand) / Includes Limited Edition Poster
Some Kind Of Friend / Heart Of Steel – K 8971 (Arista) (Australia) / Includes Limited Edition Poster

Some Kind Of Friend / Oh, Julie – 2500P (Arista) (Portugal) (PS)

Some Kind Of Friend / Oh, Julie – ARIST-516 (Arista) (UK) (PS) / June 3, 1983

Stay / Nickels and Dimes – ARIST-464 (Arista) (UK) (PS) / April 1982 / Taken from the Arista album "Barry Live in Britain" (ARTV4) – 1982
Stay / Nickels and Dimes – ARIST-464 (Arista) (UK) / April 1982 / Taken from the Arista album "Barry Live in Britain" (ARTV4) – 1982 / Side A ("Stay") is longer on this single release than on the LP.
Stay / Nickels and Dimes – ARIPD464 (Arista) (UK) (7" Picture Disc) / April 1982 / Taken from the Arista album "Barry Live in Britain" (ARTV4) – 1982
Stay / Nickels and Dimes – ARIST-464 (Arista) (Ireland) / April 1982 / Taken from the Arista album "Barry Live in Britain" (ARTV4) - 1982

When I Wanted You / Ships – FLB-113 (Flashback Records) (US)

I Don't Want To Walk Without You / One Voice – FLB-114 (Flashback Records) (US) Reissue of (Arista) AS-0501

Some Kind Of Friend / Oh, Julie / I'm Gonna Sit Right Down And Write Myself A Letter / Heaven – AB-2500 (Arista) (US) (PS) / 12" 33-⅓ RPM EP
Some Kind Of Friend / Oh, Julie / I'm Gonna Sit Right Down And Write Myself A Letter / Heaven – X-14001 (Arista) (Australia) (PS) / 12" 33-⅓ RPM EP
Some Kind Of Friend / Oh, Julie / I'm Gonna Sit Right Down And Write Myself A Letter / Heaven – 6400 720 (Arista) (Brazil) (PS) / 12" 33-⅓ RPM EP
Some Kind Of Friend / Oh, Julie / I'm Gonna Sit Right Down And Write Myself A Letter / Heaven – ATC-2500 (Arista) (US) / (Cassette)
Some Kind Of Friend / Oh, Julie / I'm Gonna Sit Right Down And Write Myself A Letter / Heaven – M-10079 (Arista) (Saudi Arabia) (Cassette)

1983

Read 'Em And Weep / Read 'Em And Weep – AS 1-9101-SAL / SAS (Arista) (US) / Long Version / Short Version / Gold Label – Not For Sale / Mono-Stereo / November 1983
Read 'Em And Weep / One Voice (Live) – AS-1 9101 (Arista) (US) / Side B taken from the Arista album "Barry – Live In Britain" (ARTV-4)
Read 'Em And Weep / One Voice (Live) – AS-1 9101 (Arista) (Canada) / Side B taken from the Arista album "Barry – Live In Britain" (ARTV-4)
Read 'Em And Weep / One Voice (Live) – ARIST-551 (Arista) (UK) (PS) / Side B taken from the Arista album "Barry – Live In Britain" (ARTV-4)
Read 'Em And Weep (Short Version) / One Voice (Live) – ARIDJ-551 (Arista) (UK) (PS) / Side B taken from the Arista album "Barry – Live In Britain" (ARTV-4) / Blue Label / DJ Copy / Not For Sale
Read 'Em And Weep / One Voice (Live) – ARIST-551 (Arista) (Ireland) / Side B taken from the Arista album "Barry – Live In Britain" (ARTV-4)
Leelo En Mis Ojos Y Llora (Read 'Em And Weep) / One Voice (Live) – B-106.036 (Arista) (Spain) (PS) / Marked: Disco Promocional Prohibida Su Venta (Promotional Disc Not For Sale) / Side B taken from the Arista album "Barry – Live In Britain" (ARTV-4)
Read 'Em And Weep / One Voice (Live) – ARI-8359 (Arista) (Europe) (PS) / Side B taken from the Arista album "Barry – Live In Britain" (ARTV-4)
Read 'Em And Weep / One Voice (Live) – ARI-8359 (Arista) (Netherlands) (PS) / Side B taken from the Arista album "Barry – Live In Britain" (ARTV-4)
Read 'Em And Weep / One Voice (Live) – ARS-37111 (Arista) (Italy) / (PS) / Side B taken from the Arista album "Barry – Live In Britain" (ARTV-4)
Read 'Em And Weep / One Voice (Live) – ARISD 551 (Arista) (UK) (Shaped Picture Disc) / December

1983 / Side B taken from the Arista album "Barry – Live In Britain" (ARTV-4)
Read 'Em And Weep / One Voice (Live) – 7RS-88 (Arista) (Japan) (PS) / Side B taken from the Arista album "Barry – Live In Britain" (ARTV-4)
Read 'Em And Weep / One Voice (Live) – ARIST 551 (Arista) (UK) (PS) / Marked: "Includes Free Christmas Card With Message From Barry." Includes a postcard sized Christmas card. / Side B taken from the Arista album "Barry – Live In Britain" (ARTV-4)
Read 'Em And Weep / One Voice (Live) – K-9311 (Arista) (Australia) / Side B taken from the Arista album "Barry – Live In Britain" (ARTV-4)

Read 'Em And Weep (Full Length Version) / Even Now (Live) / We'll Meet Again (Live) / One Voice (Live) / ARIST-12551 – (Arista) (UK) (PS) / 12" 45 RPM EP / Side B taken from the Arista album "Barry – Live In Britain" (ARTV-4)
Read 'Em And Weep (Full Length Version) / Even Now (Live) / We'll Meet Again (Live) / One Voice (Live) / 601 131 – (Arista) (Germany) (PS) / 12" 45 RPM EP / Side B taken from the Arista album "Barry – Live In Britain" (ARTV-4)

Read 'Em And Weep (Short Version) / One Voice – 106 036 (Arista) (Europe) (PS)
Read 'Em And Weep (Short Version) / One Voice – 106 036 (Arista) (Germany) (PS)

Recuerdo (Memory) / Algunas Chicas (Some Girls) – 9335 (Arista) (Argentina) / Marked: "Difusión / Venta Prohibida." (Distribution / Sale Prohibited)

You're Lookin' Hot Tonight / You're Lookin' Hot Tonight – AS 1-9185 (Arista) (US)

You're Lookin' Hot Tonight / Put A Quarter In The Jukebox (with Ronnie Milsap) – AS 1-9185 (Arista) (US)
You're Lookin' Hot Tonight / Put A Quarter In The Jukebox (with Ronnie Milsap) – AS 1-9185 (Arista) (Canada)

You're Lookin' Hot Tonight / Let's Get On With It – K-9177 (Arista) (Australia) (PS)
You're Lookin' Hot Tonight / Let's Get On With It – K9177 (Arista) (New Zealand)
You're Lookin' Hot Tonight / Let's Get On With It – ARI-8343 (Arista) (Netherlands) (PS)
Estas Caliente Esta Noche (You're Lookin' Hot Tonight) / Sigamos con Eso (Let's Get On With It) – B-105.684 (Arista) (Spain) (PS)
You're Lookin' Hot Tonight / Let's Get On With It – ARIST-542 (Arista) (Ireland)
You're Lookin' Hot Tonight / Let's Get On With It – ARIST-542 (Arista) (UK) (PS)
You're Lookin' Hot Tonight / Let's Get On With It – 05 684 / 105 684-100 (Arista) (Europe) (PS)

You're Lookin' Hot Tonight (Long Version) / You're Lookin' Hot Tonight (Short Version) – F-600983 (Arista) (Spain) (PS) / 12" 45 RPM single

You're Lookin' Hot Tonight / Let's Get On With It – ARIST-12542 (Arista) (Great Britain) / 12" 45 RPM single
You're Lookin' Hot Tonight / Let's Get On With It – ARIST-12542 (Arista) (UK) / 12" 45 RPM single
You're Lookin' Hot Tonight / Let's Get On With It – X-12034 (Arista) (Australia) (PS) / 12" 45 RPM single
You're Lookin' Hot Tonight / Let's Get On With It – 600 983 (Arista) (Germany) (PS) / 12" 45 RPM single

You're Lookin' Hot Tonight (Live) / Let's Get On With It – ARILE-542 (Arista) (UK) / Side A recorded August 27, 1983 at Blenheim Palace in England.

You're Lookin' Hot Tonight / Heaven – 7RS-73 (Arista) (Japan) (PS)

D. シルヴィアン & 坂本龍一 – 禁じられた色彩 (Ryuichi Sakamoto & David Sylvian – Forbidden Colours) / Barry Manilow – Copacabana – YPS-019 (Yuusen Broadcasting) / Japanese Yuusen Broadcasting 7" vinyl radio pressing. Yuusen Broadcasting were a cable radio station and had permission to produce records for distribution to radio stations only. White label states "NOT FOR SALE."

1984

Estás Ardiente Esta Noche (You're Lookin' Hot Tonight) / Continuemos Con Esto (Let's Get On With It) – 9352 (Arista) (Argentina) / Marked: "Difusión / Venta Prohibida." (Distribution / Sale Prohibited)
Estás Ardiente Esta Noche (You're Lookin' Hot Tonight) / Continuemos Con Esto (Let's Get On With It) – 9352 (Arista) (Argentina)

You're Lookin' Hot Tonight / One Voice (Live) – ASPD1 (Arista) (US) / Shaped Picture Disc

You're Lookin' Hot Tonight (European Remix) / You're Lookin' Hot Tonight (US Remix) – ADP-9168 (Arista) (US) / 12" 45 RPM single

When October Goes / Paradise Cafe – 7RS-112 (Arista) (Japan) (PS) / November 1984
When October Goes / Paradise Cafe – ARIST-599 (Arista) (PS) / November 1984

When October Goes / Paradise Cafe / Special Interview – ARIST-10599 (Arista) (PS) / 10" 45 RPM / Side B Interview: "Barry in Conversation with Simon Bates, courtesy of British Airways"

When October Goes / When October Goes – ADP-9295 (Arista) (US) 12" 45 RPM single / Promotional copy
When October Goes / When October Goes – 38234 (Arista) (Australia) 12" 45 RPM single / Promotional copy / White Labels rubber stamped in red: *Barry Manilow "When October Goes" From the Album 2.00 am Paradise Café*

Paradise Cafe / Where Have You Gone / Blue (with Sarah Vaughan) / Big City Blues (With Mel Tormé) – ADP-9301 (Arista) 12" 33-⅓ RPM single / Promotional only release

1985

Run To Me / Run To Me (Dionne Warwick and Barry Manilow) – AS1-9341 (Arista) (US) DJ Copy / Not For Sale / Mono-Stereo / April 1985
Run To Me (Dionne Warwick and Barry Manilow) / Bedroom Eyes (Dionne Warwick) – AS1-9341 (Arista) (US) / April 1985
Run To Me (Dionne Warwick and Barry Manilow) / Bedroom Eyes (Dionne Warwick) – AS1-9341 (Arista) (Canada) / April 1985
Run To Me (Dionne Warwick and Barry Manilow) / Bedroom Eyes (Dionne Warwick) – 107 314 (Arista) (Europe) (PS)

Run To Me (Dionne Warwick and Barry Manilow) / It's Love (Dionne Warwick) – K-9617 (Arista) (Australia)

Run To Me (Dionne Warwick And Barry Manilow) / Where Have You Gone (Barry Manilow) – 7RS-118 (Arista) (Japan) (PS)

Run To Me (Dionne Warwick and Barry Manilow) / Heartbreaker (Dionne Warwick) – ARIST-610 (Arista) (UK) (PS) / Side B: ℗ 1982 - Producers: Albhy Galuten / Barry Gibb / Karl Richardson
Run To Me (Dionne Warwick and Barry Manilow) / Heartbreaker (Dionne Warwick) – ARIST-610 (Arista) (Ireland) / Side B: ℗ 1982 - Producers: Albhy Galuten / Barry Gibb / Karl Richardson
Run To Me (Dionne Warwick and Barry Manilow) / Heartbreaker (Dionne Warwick) – 107 314 (Arista) (Germany) (PS) / Side B: ℗ 1982 - Producers: Albhy Galuten / Barry Gibb / Karl Richardson

Run To Me (Dionne Warwick and Barry Manilow) / Heartbreaker (Dionne Warwick) / Paradise Cafe (Barry Manilow) – ARIST 12610 (Arista) (UK) (PS) / 12" 45 RPM 3 track single

In Search Of Love / In Search Of Love – JK-14223 (RCA) (US) / DJ Copy / Not For Sale / Mono-Stereo
In Search Of Love / At The Dance – PB-14223 (RCA) (US) (PS)
In Search Of Love / At The Dance – PB-14223 (RCA) (Canada) (PS)
In Search Of Love / At The Dance – PB-49919 (RCA) (UK) (PS) / November 1985
In Search Of Love / At The Dance – PB-49919 (RCA) (Europe) (PS) / November 1985
En Busca Del amor (In Search Of Love) / At The Dance – PB-4223 (RCA) (Spain) (PS)
In Search Of Love / At The Dance – PB-104482 (PB-14223) (RCA) (Australia) (PS)
In Search Of Love / At The Dance – PD2425 (RCA) (South Africa)
In Search Of Love / At The Dance – RPS-195 (RCA) (Japan) (PS)

In Search Of Love / At The Dance / *Copacabana – PT-49920 (RCA) (UK) / 12" single / * taken from the 1985 television film soundtrack of "Copacabana."
In Search Of Love / At The Dance / *Copacabana – PT-49920 (RCA) (Europe) (PS) / 12" single / *taken from the 1985 television film soundtrack of "Copacabana."

I'm Your Man (Club Mix) / I'm Your Man (Club Mix) – JK-14397 (RCA) (US) / Gold label / DJ Copy / Not For Sale / Stereo-Stereo
I'm Your Man (Club Mix) / I'm Your Man (Dub Mix) – PB14397 (RCA) (US) (PS)
I'm Your Man (Club Mix) / I'm Your Man (Dub Mix) – PB14397 (RCA / Ariola International) (Canada)

I'm Your Man (Extended Club Mix) / I'm Your Man (Extended Dub Mix) – PB14397 (RCA) (US) / 12" 45 RPM Maxi-single / White Label / DJ Copy / Not For Sale / Stereo-Stereo / Additional Production and Remix: Mark Berry / Raul A. Rodriguez
I'm Your Man (Extended Club Mix) / I'm Your Man (Extended Dub Mix) – PB14397 (RCA) (US) / 12" 45 RPM Maxi-single / Additional Production and Remix: Mark Berry / Raul A. Rodriguez
I'm Your Man (Extended Club Mix) / I'm Your Man (Extended Dub Mix) – TDS-348 (RCA) (PS) (Australia & New Zealand) / 12" 45 RPM Maxi-single / Additional Production and Remix: Mark Berry / Raul A. Rodriguez

腕の中へ (In Search Of Love) (Hideki Saijo and Barry Manilow) / 愛の翼 (It's All Behind Us Now) (Hideki Saijo) – RHS-226 / JPBP-0962 (RCA) (Japan) (PS) / November 21, 1985

Copacabana (At The Cop) / Mandy – 103 855 / 103 855-100 (Arista) (UK) (PS) / Original Double Hit Reissue Series / Taken from the Arista LP: "Manilow Magic-The Best Of Barry Manilow" (201 22-320)

Sweet Heaven (I'm In Love Again) / It's All Behind Us Now – 104561 (RCA) (Australia) / Tan RCA labels

It's You (Dionne Warwick & Stevie Wonder) / Run To Me (Dionne Warwick & Barry Manilow) – ESPECIAL 3 (Arista) (Portugal) (PS) / Marked: Só Para Profissionais. Especial Promoção (Only For

Professionals. Special Promotion)

1986

He Doesn't Care (But I Do) / He Doesn't Care (But I Do) – JK-14302 (RCA) (US) / Yellow Label / DJ Copy / Not For Sale / Mono-Stereo
He Doesn't Care (But I Do) / It's All Behind Us Now – PB-14302 (RCA) (US) (PS)
He Doesn't Care (But I Do) / It's All Behind Us Now – PB-14302 (RCA) (Canada) (PS)
この愛とどくまで (He Doesn't Care (But I Do)) / オール・ビハインド・アス (愛の翼) (It's All Behind Us Now) – RPS-206 (RCA) (Japan) (PS)

I'm Your Man (Edited Remix) / He Doesn't Care (But I Do) – PB-49857 (RCA) (UK) (PS) / May 1986

I'm Your Man (Club Mix) / Don't Talk To Me Of Love (Barry Manilow and Mireille Mathieu) – RPS-216 (RCA) (Japan) (PS)

I'm Your Man (Club Mix) / I'm Your Man (Dub Mix) – 104593 (RCA) (Australia)

Mandy / Copacabana (At The Copa) – OG-9650 (Old Gold) (UK) / Reissue

Bermuda Triangle / Lonely Together – OG-9652 (Old Gold) (UK) / Reissue

Don't Talk To Me Of Love (Barry Manilow and Mireille Mathieu) / It's All Behind Us Now– PB49883 (RCA) (Europe) (PS)

Amare Chi Se Manchi Tu (Who Needs To Dream) / In Search Of Love – PB 49885 (RCA) (Italy) (PS)

¡Ay Caramba! (Featuring: Lucía Méndez) / Un Día Feliz (Some Sweet Day) – RX-256 (RCA) (Mexico) (PS)
¡Ay Caramba! (Featuring: Lucía Méndez) / Un Día Feliz (Some Sweet Day) – RX-256 (RCA) (Mexico) (PS) / Marked: Sencillo Promocional. Prohibida Su Venta (Promotional Single Sale Prohibited)

1987

Brooklyn Blues (Featuring Tom Scott) / Brooklyn Blues (Featuring Tom Scott) – ADP-9648 (Arista) (US) (PS) / Translucent blue vinyl / 12" 33-⅓ RPM single / Promotional only release

Swing Street - 4 Song Sampler - Stompin' At The Savoy / Black And Blue (Featuring: Phyllis Hyman / Tom Scott) / Summertime (Featuring: Stan Getz) / Brooklyn Blues (Featuring: Tom Scott) – ADP-9649 (Arista) (US) (PS) / 12" 33-⅓ RPM single / Promotional only release

1988

Swing Street (Radio Version) / Brooklyn Blues (Radio Version) (Featuring Tom Scott) – BMSS-1 (Arista) (UK) / Promotional Only single

Swing Street / Brooklyn Blues (Featuring Tom Scott) / Sweet Heaven / Who Needs To Dream – 209526 (Arista) (UK) (PS) / 10" 33 ⅓ RPM EP / Front cover gives British concert dates / November 1988
Swing Street / Brooklyn Blues (Featuring: Tom Scott) / Sweet Heaven (I'm In Love Again) / Who Needs To Dream – 661 938 (Arista) (UK) / CD EP / Front cover gives British concert dates / December 1988

Swing Street / Brooklyn Blues (Featuring Tom Scott) / Sweet Heaven / Who Needs To Dream – 111 938 (Arista) (Europe / UK) (PS) / 7" 33 ⅓ RPM EP / Front cover gives British concert dates

Hey Mambo (Single Version) (Barry Manilow With Kid Creole And The Coconuts) / Hey Mambo (Caliente Mix / Single Edit) (Barry Manilow With Kid Creole And The Coconuts) – AS-1-9666 (Arista) (US) (PS) / Marked: Promotional Release / Not For Sale
Hey Mambo (Single Version) (Barry Manilow With Kid Creole And The Coconuts) / Hey Mambo (Caliente Mix / Single Edit) (Barry Manilow With Kid Creole And The Coconuts) – AS-1-9666 (Arista) (US) (PS)

Black and Blue (Featuring: Phyllis Hyman / Tom Scott) / Black and Blue (Featuring: Phyllis Hyman / Tom Scott) – AS1-9702 (Arista) (US) / DJ Copy / Not For Sale

Hey Mambo (Barry Manilow With Kid Creole And The Coconuts) / When October Goes – 109 781 (Arista) (UK) (PS) / Side B taken from *2:00AM Paradise Cafe* ℗ 1984 Arista Records, Inc. / March 14, 1988
Hey Mambo (Barry Manilow With Kid Creole And The Coconuts) / When October Goes – 109 781 (Arista) (Europe) (PS) / Side B taken from *2:00AM Paradise Cafe* ℗ 1984 Arista Records, Inc. / March 14, 1988
Hey Mambo (Barry Manilow With Kid Creole And The Coconuts) / When October Goes – A07S-23 (Arista) (Japan) (PS) / Side 2 taken from *2:00AM Paradise Cafe* ℗ 1984 Arista Records, Inc. / April 7, 1988

Hey Mambo (Caliente Mix) (Barry Manilow With Kid Creole And The Coconuts) / Hey Mambo (Album Version) (Barry Manilow With Kid Creole And The Coconuts) / Hey Mambo (Caliente Mix-Single Edit) (Barry Manilow With Kid Creole And The Coconuts) / Hey Mambo (Loco Caliente Mix) (Barry Manilow With Kid Creole And The Coconuts) / Swing Street (Album Version) – 609 902 (Arista / Ariola) (Europe) (PS) / 12" 45 RPM Maxi-Single

Hey Mambo (Caliente Mix) (Barry Manilow With Kid Creole And The Coconuts) / Hey Mambo (Album Version) (Barry Manilow With Kid Creole And The Coconuts) / Hey Mambo (Caliente Mix-Single Edit) (Barry Manilow With Kid Creole And The Coconuts) / Hey Mambo (Loco Caliente Mix) (Barry Manilow With Kid Creole And The Coconuts) / Swing Street (Album Version) – 7855 (Arista / Ariola) (Venezuela) (PS) / 12" 45 RPM Maxi-Single

Hey Mambo (Caliente Mix) (Barry Manilow With Kid Creole And The Coconuts) / Hey Mambo (Album Version) (Barry Manilow With Kid Creole And The Coconuts) / Hey Mambo (Caliente Mix-Single Edit) (Barry Manilow With Kid Creole And The Coconuts) / Hey Mambo (Loco Caliente Mix) (Barry Manilow With Kid Creole And The Coconuts) / Swing Street (Album Version) – AD-1-9665 (Arista / Ariola) (Canada) (PS) / 12" 33-⅓ RPM EP

Hey Mambo (Caliente Mix) (Barry Manilow With Kid Creole And The Coconuts) / Hey Mambo (Album Version) (Barry Manilow With Kid Creole And The Coconuts) / Hey Mambo (Caliente Mix-Single Edit) (Barry Manilow With Kid Creole And The Coconuts) / Hey Mambo (Loco Caliente Mix) (Barry Manilow With Kid Creole And The Coconuts) / Swing Street (Album Version) – ADI-9665 (Arista / Ariola) (Canada) / 12" 33-⅓ RPM EP

Hey Mambo (Caliente Mix) (Barry Manilow With Kid Creole And The Coconuts) / Hey Mambo (Album Version) (Barry Manilow With Kid Creole And The Coconuts) / Hey Mambo (Caliente Mix-Single Edit) (Barry Manilow With Kid Creole And The Coconuts) / Hey Mambo (Loco Caliente Mix) (Barry Manilow With Kid Creole And The Coconuts) / Swing Street (Album Version) – 4605 (Arista / Ariola) (Greece)

(PS) / 12" 45 RPM Maxi-Single
Hey Mambo (Caliente Mix) (Barry Manilow With Kid Creole And The Coconuts) / Hey Mambo (Album Version) (Barry Manilow With Kid Creole And The Coconuts) / When October Goes / Hey Mambo (Loco Caliente Mix) (Barry Manilow With Kid Creole And The Coconuts) / Swing Street (Album Version) – 609 781 (Arista / Ariola) (Europe) (PS) / 12" 45 RPM Maxi-Single

Hey Mambo (Caliente Mix) (Barry Manilow With Kid Creole And The Coconuts) / Hey Mambo (Album Version) (Barry Manilow With Kid Creole And The Coconuts) / Hey Mambo (Caliente Mix-Single Edit) (Barry Manilow With Kid Creole And The Coconuts) / Hey Mambo (Loco Caliente Mix) (Barry Manilow With Kid Creole And The Coconuts) / Swing Street (Album Version) – ASCD-9665 (Arista / Ariola) (US) (PS) CD EP / Promotional Compact Disc

1989

Keep Each Other Warm / Keep Each Other Warm – AS1-9838 (Arista) (US) (PS) / DJ Copy / Not For Sale
Keep Each Other Warm / A Little Travelling Music, Please – AS1-9838 (Arista) (US) (PS)
Keep Each Other Warm / A Little Travelling Music, Please – AS1-9838 (Arista) (Canada) (PS)
Keep Each Other Warm / A Little Travelling Music, Please – CAS-9838 (Arista) (US) (PS) / Cassette Single
Keep Each Other Warm / A Little Travelling Music, Please – A10D-132 (Arista) (Japan) (PS) / CD Single

Keep Each Other Warm / You Begin Again – 112 507 (Arista) (Germany) (PS)

The One That Got Away / The One That Got Away – AS1-9883 (Arista) (US) / DJ Copy / Not For Sale
The One That Got Away / You're My Only Girl, Jenny – AS1-9883 (Arista) (US)
The One That Got Away / You're My Only Girl, Jenny – AS1-9883 (Arista) (Canada)
The One That Got Away / You're My Only Girl, Jenny – 112 652 (Arista) (UK / Europe) (PS) / August 28, 1989 / Photo label

The One That Got Away / You're My Only Girl (Jenny) / Don't Talk To Me Of Love (Barry Manilow and Mireille Mathieu) – 662 652 (Arista) (UK) (PS) / 3 Track CD Single

Eolia / You Begin Again – PRTD-3088 (Arista) (Japan) / White Label Promotional Single
Eolia / You Begin Again – A10D-143 (Arista) (Japan) (PS) / CD Single

Please Don't Be Scared / A Little Travellin' Music, Please – 105045 (Arista) (Australia) (PS)
Please Don't Be Scared / A Little Travellin' Music, Please – 112 186 (Arista) (Europe) (PS)
Please Don't Be Scared / A Little Travellin' Music, Please – 112 186 (Arista) (UK) (PS)
Please Don't Be Scared / A Little Travellin' Music, Please – 112 245 (Arista) (UK) (PS) / Sleeve folds out to poster print
Please Don't Be Scared / A Little Travellin' Music, Please – 112 283 (Arista) (Germany) (PS) / Picture sleeve has a sticker reading: Gekurzte Rundfunk-Version - richtige Spieldauer (Short Broadcast Version - correct playing time 4:14). Label has incorrect longer time.

Please Don't Be Scared / A Little Travellin' Music, Please – A10D-120 (Arista) (Japan) (PS) / CD Single

Please Don't Be Scared / A Little Travelin' Music, Please / Dirt Cheap – 612 186 (Arista) (Germany) (PS) / 12" 45 RPM Maxi-Single

Please Don't Be Scared / A Little Travelin' Music, Please / Dirt Cheap – 612 246 (Arista) (UK) (Picture Disc) / 12" 45 RPM Maxi-Single

Please Don't Be Scared / A Little Travelin' Music, Please / Dirt Cheap – 612 186 (Arista) (UK) (PS) / 12" 45 RPM Maxi-Single

Please Don't Be Scared / A Little Travelin' Music, Please / Dirt Cheap – 662 186 (Arista) (UK) (PS) / CD Single

Forever Your Girl (Paula Abdul) / Please Don't Be Scared (Barry Manilow) – YPS-046 (Virgin / Arista) (Japan) / Dual Artist Promotional Single / Made by / for: Yuusen Broadcasting Corporation Music Service / Non-broadcast – used in direct radio music service only

Please Don't Be Scared / Ready To Take A Chance Again – 990.4013 (RCA) (Brazil) / 12" Single / Marked: Especial Para Promoção Invendavel Anostra Gratis Tributada (Special For Unsaleable Promotion Taxed Free Sample) / December 6, 1989

Mandy / Something's Comin' Up / I Write The Songs / A Nice Boy Like Me – 162051 (Arista) (Austria) (PS) / Original "A" & "B" Series release. CD re-release of 2 singles.

1990

If I Can Dream (Recorded Live) / Even Now – 113 025 (Arista / BMG) (UK) / Side A taken from the album Barry Manilow Live on Broadway / Side B: ℗ 1978 Arista Records / Promotional Only
If I Can Dream (Recorded Live) / Even Now – 113 025 (Arista / BMG) (UK) (PS) / Side A taken from the album Barry Manilow Live on Broadway / Side B: ℗ 1978 Arista Records

If I Can Dream* / Keep Each Other Warm / Sweet Life - It's A Long Way Up* / Even Now+ – 663 025 (Arista / BMG) (UK) (PS) *Taken from the Arista album "Barry Manilow Live On Broadway" / January – February 1990 UK concert dates printed on the back tray insert / +℗ 1978 Arista Records

Some Good Things Never Last (with Debra Byrd – featuring Dana Robbins) / Hangin' On A Nail – 113 202 (Arista) (UK) (PS)

Some Good Things Never Last (with Debra Byrd – featuring Dana Robbins) / Hangin' On A Nail / I'm Your Man – 663 202 (Arista) (Europe) / CD single

Some Good Things Never Last / I'm Your Man* – 613 202 (Arista) (UK) (PS) / 12" 45 RPM Maxi-Single / *℗ 1985 BMG Music

If You Remember Me – ASCD-9948 (Arista) (US) (PS) / Special Promotional CD Single

Jingle Bells (with Exposé) / Jingle Bells (with Exposé) AS-2094 (Arista) (US) / DJ Copy / Not For Sale
Jingle Bells (with Exposé) / Because It's Christmas (For All The Children) – AS-2094 (Arista) (US)
Jingle Bells (with Exposé) / Because It's Christmas (For All The Children) – AS-2094 (Arista) (Canada)
Jingle Bells (with Exposé) / Because It's Christmas (For All The Children) – 115 018 (Arista) (UK)
Jingle Bells (with Exposé) / Because It's Christmas (For All The Children) – 105 184 (Arista) (Australia) (PS)
Jingle Bells (with Exposé) / Because It's Christmas (For All The Children) – 113 938 (Arista) (Europe) (PS) / Marked: Unverkäufliches Muster (Not for Sale)
Jingle Bells (with Exposé) / Because It's Christmas (For All The Children) – 665 018 (Arista) (UK) / CD Single

Jingle Bells (with Exposé) / Because It's Christmas (For All The Children) – 115 024 (Arista) (UK) (Picture Disc)

Jingle Bells (with Exposé) / Because It's Christmas (For All The Children) (Excerpt From Handel's Messiah "For Unto Us A Child Is Born") – BVDA-12 (Arista) (Japan) / 3" Mini CD Single / November 21, 1990

Jingle Bells (with Exposé) / The Christmas Song – BMAN1(Arista) (UK) / Promotional Single

Four Song Christmas Sampler – Jingle Bells (with Exposé) / Because It's Christmas (For All The Children) / Joy To The World – Have Yourself A Merry Little Christmas / Baby, It's Cold Outside (duet with K.T. Oslin) – ASCD-2096 (Arista) (US)

1991

Epilogue (Nancy Wilson and Barry Manilow) / I Can't Teach My Old Heart New Tricks (Nancy Wilson) – ESDB-3265 (Epic / Sony) (Japan) / 3" Mini CD Single / November 1, 1991

Copacabana (At The Copa) / I Made It Through The Rain – 07822 12299-4 (Arista) (US) (PC) / Arista Flashback Series / Cassette single with same two songs on both sides.

Where Or When – ASCD-2386 (Arista) (US) / promotional only single from the forth-coming album "Barry Manilow Show Stoppers"

World In Union (Anna Maria Kaufmann duet With Barry Manilow) / Rhythm Of Love / Somewhere (From "West Side Story") – COL 658316 (Columbia) (Germany) / 3 track promotional CD EP / August 13, 1992 / Also available on Cassette

Jingle Bells (with Exposé) / Jingle Bells (with Exposé) – 115 018DJ (Arista) (UK) / Double A sided promo / White Label / Not For Sale

1992

Another Life – ASCD-2473 (Arista) (US) / Taken from: The Complete Collection and Then Some...

1993

Copacabana (At The Copa) (1993 Remix) / Let Freedom Ring – 74321 13691 7 (Arista) (UK) (PS) / Jukebox promotional single
Copacabana (At The Copa) (1993 Remix) / Let Freedom Ring – 74321 13691 7 (Arista) (UK) (PS)
Copacabana (At The Copa) (1993 Remix) / Let Freedom Ring – 74321 13691 4 (Arista) (UK) (PC) / Cassette single

Copacabana (At The Copa) (1993 Remix) – COPA-1 (Arista) (UK) / 12" 45 RPM single / Single sided white Label promo

Copacabana (At The Copa) (1993 Remix) 7" version / Copacabana (At The Copa) (1993 Remix) 12" Version – 99 091 92 (Arista) (Germany) (PS) / CD Maxi-Single

Copacabana (At The Copa) (The 1993 Remix) (12" Version - Remix – Dave Ford) / Copacabana (At The Copa) (The 1993 Remix) (7" Version - Remix – Dave Ford) / Copacabana (Home Cassette Demo 1977) / Copacabana (At The Copa) (Originally Released On "Even Now" - January 13, 1978) – 74321

13691 1 (Arista) (UK) (PS) / 12" 33 ⅓ RPM

Copacabana (At The Copa) (The 1993 Remix) (12" Version - Remix – Dave Ford) / Copacabana (At The Copa) (The 1993 Remix) (7" Version - Remix – Dave Ford) / Copacabana (Home Cassette Demo 1977) / Copacabana (At The Copa) (Originally Released On "Even Now" - January 13, 1978) – 74321 13691 2 (Arista) (UK) / CD Maxi-Single

Copacabana (At The Copa) (The 1993 Remix) (12" Version - Remix – Dave Ford) / Copacabana (At The Copa) (The 1993 Remix) (7" Version - Remix – Dave Ford) / Copacabana (Home Cassette Demo 1977) / Copacabana (At The Copa) (Originally Released On "Even Now" - January 13, 1978) – 74321 13691 2 (Arista) (Australia) (PS) / CD Maxi-Single

Could It Be Magic 1993 / Could It be Magic (Instrumental) – 74321 174887 (Arista) (UK) (PS) / Re-recording based on the original production.

Could It Be Magic (12" 1993 Remix Version - Remixed by George De Angelis) / Could It Be Magic 1993 / Could It Be Magic (Instrumental) / 3 track 12" 45 RPM Maxi-Single

Could It Be Magic (12" 1993 Remix) / Could It Be Magic (Trevor Horn 1993) / Could It Be Magic (Instrumental) – COULD 1993 / 12" white Label promotional single

Could It Be Magic 1993 / Could It Be Magic (12" 1993 Remix Version - Remixed by George De Angelis) / Could It Be Magic (Instrumental) – 74321 17488 2 (Arista) (UK) (PS) / CD Maxi-Single

You'll Never Walk Alone (Cilla Black and Barry Manilow) / Through The Years (Cilla Black) – 660013 7 (Columbia) (UK / Europe) (PS)

You'll Never Walk Alone (Cilla Black and Barry Manilow) / You'll Never Walk Alone (Hope In Your Heart Mix)(Cilla Black and Barry Manilow) / Through The Years (Cilla Black) – 660013 2 / Three track CD single

If Tomorrow Never Comes – ASCD-2531 (Arista) (US) / Promotional only CD single

1994

Let Me Be Your Wings (duet with Debra Byrd) / Finale: Let Me Be Your Wings / Finale: Follow Your Heart – CDEM-336 / 7243 8 81575 2 0 (EMI) (UK)

Let Me Be Your Wings (duet with Debra Byrd) – CD-P519390 / (Dutch) 1-TRACK PROMO
Let Me Be Your Wings (duet with Debra Byrd) – (Germany) / Promo CD single
Let Me Be Your Wings (duet with Debra Byrd) – CDEM 336 / (EMI UK)
Let Me Be Your Wings (duet with Debra Byrd) – SBK 4KM-58153 (cassette single)

Let Me Be Your Wings (duet with Debra Byrd) / Follow Your Heart (Gino Conforti) – S7-17906 (SBK / ERG) (US) / White Label promo / Marked: For Jukeboxes Only!

Let Me Be Your Wings (End Tide Duet) (duet with Debra Byrd) / Let Me Be Your Wings (Gary Imhoff and Jodi Benson) (Philippines) / promotional only single

I Can't Get Started – ASCD-2783 (Arista) (US) / Promotional only CD single

1996

I'd Really Love To See You Tonight (Tony Moran Extended Club Mix) / I'd Really Love To See You Tonight (Premier Club Mix) / I'd Really Love To See You Tonight (Tony Moran Circuit Mix) – BARRY1 (UK) 12" White Label 33 ⅓ RPM Promotional Single / Marked: Not For Sale

1997

I'd Really Love To See You Tonight (Up-Tempo Radio Mix - Remix: Bob Rosa, Tony Moran) / I'd Really Love To See You Tonight (Tony Moran Extended Dance Mix - Remix: Bob Rosa, Tony Moran) / I'd Really Love To See You Tonight (Circuit Mix - Remix: Bob Rosa, Tony Moran) / I'd Really Love To See You Tonight (Premier Club Mix - Remix: Premier [Credited To]: Gino Olivieri & Ivan Pavlin / I'd Really Love To See You Tonight (Album Version) Co-producer – Michael Omartian - Mixed By – Terry Christian – 74321 45911 2 (Arista) (UK) CD Maxi-Single / June 3, 1997

I'd Really Love To See You Tonight (Tony Moran Extended Dance Mix) / Could It Be Magic (Unreleased Extended Dance Mix) Remix: George D'Angelis / I'd Really Love To See You Tonight (Circuit Mix) Remix – Bob Rosa, Tony Moran – 07822-13379-1 (Arista) (US) 12" 33 ⅓ RPM Single / June 3, 1997

I'd Really Love To See You Tonight (Tony Moran Extended Dance Mix) / Could It Be Magic (Premier Club Mix) / I'd Really Love To See You Tonight (Circuit Mix) – ADP-3291 (Arista) (US) / 12" White Label 33 ⅓ RPM Promotional Single / Marked: Promo Only / June 3, 1997

I'd Really Love To See You Tonight (Tony Moran Extended Dance Mix) / I'd Really Love To See You Tonight (Circuit Mix) / Could It Be Magic (Dance Mix) (Based On The Original Production By: Barry Manilow / Ron Dante) / Could It Be Magic (Unreleased Extended Dance Mix) (Based On The Original Production By: Barry Manilow / Ron Dante) – 07822-13379-2 (Arista) (US) / CD Maxi-Single / Tracks 1 and 2 produced and arranged for Tony Moran Ent. Inc. Engineered at Infinity Studios / June 3, 1997

I'd Really Love To See You Tonight (Up-Tempo Mix - Remix: Bob Rosa / Tony Moran) / Could It Be Magic (Dance Mix - Remix – Gregg Jackman / Trevor Horn) – 07822-13378-2 (Arista) (US) / CD single / Track 1 produced by Michael Omartian and Barry Manilow / Track 2 produced by Ron Dante and Barry Manilow / Comes in a CD card envelope / June 3, 1997

I'd Really Love To See You Tonight (Up-Tempo Radio Mix) / I'd Really Love To See You Tonight (Album Version) – ASCD-3314 (Arista) (US) / Marked: *From his new album: Summer of '78* / Promo Only - Not For Sale / June 3, 1997

I'd Really Love To See You Tonight (Up-Tempo Mix - Remix – Bob Rosa - Tony Moran) / Could It Be Magic (Dance Mix - Remix – Gregg Jackman - Trevor Horn) – 07822-13378-4 (Arista) (US) Track 1 produced by Michael Omartian and Barry Manilow / Track 2 produced by Ron Dante and Barry Manilow. Usual cass-single cardboard sleeve and includes a paper insert for other Barry Manilow music.

只願今晚見來到妳 (I'd Really Love To See You Tonight) (Up-Tempo Radio Mix - Remix: Bob Rosa - Tony Moran) / 只願今晚見來到妳 (I'd Really Love To See You Tonight) (Tony Moran Extended Dance Mix - Remix: Bob Rosa - Tony Moran) / 只願今晚見來到妳 (I'd Really Love To See You Tonight) (Circuit Mix - Remix – Bob Rosa - Tony Moran) / 只願今晚見來到妳 (I'd Really Love To See You Tonight) (Premier Club Mix - Remix: Premier [Credited To]: Gino Olivieri & Ivan Pavlin) / 只願今晚見來到妳 (I'd Really Love To See You Tonight (Album Version) Mixed By – Terry Christian – 74321 45911 2

(Arista) (Taiwan) / Comes with OBI Strip
Sometimes When We Touch (Radio Mix) / Sometimes When We Touch (Album Version) – ASCD-3426
(Arista) (US) / Promotional only CD single

1998

Come Dance With Me / Come Fly With Me / You Make Feel So Young / Saturday Night (Is The
Loneliest Night Of The Week) / Manilow Swings Sinatra Medley – ASCD-3588 (Arista) (US) /
Promotional CD EP / Taken from "Manilow Swings Sinatra"

2001

I Don't Wanna Know / The Walking Wounded / They Dance (extended version) – CCD-2148-2
(Concord) (US) / Taken from "Here At The Mayflower" / Exclusive 2002 Tour Bonus Disc

Turn The Radio Up / They Dance – PRO-CJ-0009 (Concord) (US) / Promotional only CD single

2002

Turn The Radio Up / They Dance – PRO-CJ-0015 (Concord) (US) / Promotional only CD single

Turn The Radio Up / They Dance (Radio Edit) – CCD-2165-2 (Concord) (Europe) / From the New
Compact Disc *Here At The Mayflower* / Marked: For promotional use only. Sale is unlawful.

Turn The Radio Up / They Dance (Radio Edit) – CCD-2165-2 (Concord) (Europe) / From the New
Compact Disc *Here At The Mayflower*

2003

I Won't Be The One To Let Go (Barbra Streisand and Barry Manilow) (Radio Version Edit) / I Won't Be
The One To Let Go (Barbra Streisand and Barry Manilow) Barbra Streisand and Barry Manilow (Radio
Version) – CSK 59450 (Columbia) (US) / For Promotion Only - Not For Sale / From the 2002 *Duets*
album by Barbra Streisand

2004

Copacabana (Ralphi Rosario's Club Vocal Mix) / Copacabana (L.E.X. Latin/Tribal Dub) / Copacabana
(Pete Lorimer Vocal House Excursion) / Copacabana (Ralphi Rosario's Cuban Underground Dub) –
PRO-CJ-0073-1 (Concord) (US) / Two 12" vinyl set / Promotional Only

Copacabana (Ralphi Rosario's Club Vocal Mix) / Copacabana (L.E.X. Latin/Tribal Dub) / Copacabana
(Pete Lorimer Vocal House Excursion) / Copacabana (Ralphi Rosario's Cuban Underground Dub) –
PRO-CJ-0073-2 (Concord) (US) / Two 12" vinyl set

Copacabana (Ralphi Rosario's Club Vocal Radio Edit - Remix – Ralphi Rosario) / Copacabana
(Scores Radio Edit) / Copacabana (L.E.X. Radio Edit - Remix – L.E.X.) / Copacabana (Ralphi
Rosario's Club Vocal Mix - Remix – Ralphi Rosario) / Copacabana (Ralphi Rosario's Big Room Dub 2
- Remix – Ralphi Rosario) / Copacabana (Ralphi Rosario's Cuban Underground Dub - Remix – Ralphi
Rosario) / Copacabana (L.E.X. Main Vocal Mix - Remix – L.E.X.) / Copacabana (L.E.X. Latin/Tribal
Dub - Remix – L.E.X.) / Copacabana (Peter Lorimer Vocal House Excursion - Remix – Peter Lorimer) /
Copacabana (Peter Lorimer House Excursion Dub - Remix – Peter Lorimer) – PRO-CJ-0075-2

(Concord) (US) / CD / Marked: For Promotional Only – Not For Sale

Barry Manilow – Songs From Manilow: Music And Passion: Here's To Las Vegas / Sweet Heaven (I'm In Love Again) (2005 Remix) / Every Single Day (2005 Remix) / Copacabana Remix 1 (Peter Lorimer Vocal House Excursion - Remix – Peter Lorimer) / Copacabana Remix 2 (L.E.X. Latin/Tribal Dub - Remix – L.E.X.) / Copacabana Remix 3 (Ralphi Rosario's Cuban Underground Dub - Remix – Ralphi Rosario) / Copacabana Remix 4 (2005 Extended Dance Mix - Remix – Jez Colin) / Dancin' In The Aisles – PBS (US) / PBS only exclusive release CD (Barcode: 8 74402 00901 1)

Dancin' In The Aisles – Universal Music – Digital Download

2005

Unchained Melody - Album Version – 82876 77950 2 (Arista) (US) / AAC File (Advanced Audio Coding) / Single / Copy Protected File / November 29, 2005

Unchained Melody - Album Version / Unchained Melody - Call Out Hook – 82876 77950 2 (Arista) (US) / CD Single / Promotional Release Only / Taken from The Greatest Songs of The Fifties / In Stores March 2006

2006

Love Is A Many Splendored Thing - Album Version – 82876 83134 2 (Arista) (US) / CD Single / Promotional Release Only / Taken from The Greatest Songs of The Fifties / In Stores March 2006

Can't Take My Eyes Off You / Call Out Hook – 82876-89162-2 (Arista) (US) / CD Single / Promotional Release Only / Taken from The Greatest Songs of The Sixties / October 31, 2006

Barry Manilow – More Manilow: Tryin' To Get The Feeling Again / The Best Seat In The House / I Made It Through The Rain / See The Show Again / One Voice / Studio Tracks: Never My Love - I Swear / My Cherie Amour – A701958 (Arista) (US) / 7 track CD EP

Barry Manilow – More Songs From Manilow: Music And Passion: Here's To Las Vegas / Dancin' In The Aisles / Even Now / It's A Miracle / Copacabana (At The Copa) (1993 Remix) – 82876-78663-2 (Arista) (US) / 5 Track CD EP

Copacabana (At The Copa) [Original Mix] / Copacabana (At The Copa) [Long Version] / Copacabana (At The Copa) [1993 Remix by Dave Ford] / Copacabana (At The Copa) [Spanish Radio Mix] / Copacabana (At The Copa) [Spanish Long Version] (Arista) – FLAC format for download (FLAC is an audio coding format for lossless compression of digital audio) / Track 3 is an edited version of the 1993 6:48 Remix.

Copacabana (Radio) / Copacabana (At The Copa) (Long Version) / Copacabana (At The Copa) (1993 Remix) / Copacabana (At The Copa) (Spanish Radio) / Copacabana (At The Copa) (Spanish Long Version) (Arista) – FLAC format for download (FLAC is an audio coding format for lossless compression of digital audio) / October 31, 2006

2008

Barry Manilow – Songs From The Vault: Nature Boy (Brooklyn, New York - 1948) / Golddigger (Outtake from "Barry" - 1980) / Biggest Part Of Me (featuring Dave Koz) (Outtake from "The Greatest

Songs Of The Eighties" - 2008) / Everybody Wants To Rule The World (Outtake from "The Greatest Songs Of The Eighties" - 2008) / Every Breath You Take (Outtake from "The Greatest Songs Of The Eighties" – 2008) – 88697-64652-2 (Arista) (US) / Limited Edition Release CD EP / Previously Unreleased Material

2012

Copacabana (At The Copa) (Mousse T.'s Radio Edit - Remix – Mousse T.) – 00602527969527 (We Love Music / Universal Music Group) (Germany) / Not For Sale - For Promotion Only (LC: 19045)

Talk To Me – (Stiletto) (UK) / Promotional only single for the album "Live In London" June 25, 2012

  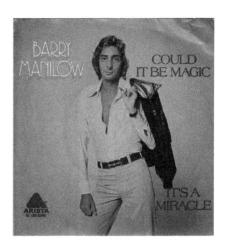

Picture sleeves from the world over...
and some labels too!

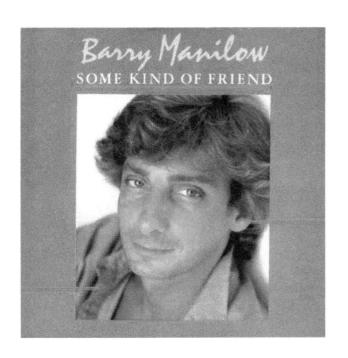

BARRY MANILOW

I wanna do it with you.

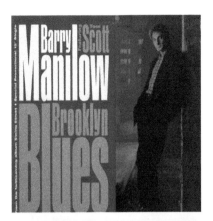
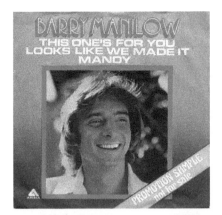

7RS-31 ¥700

ふたりのオールド・ソング

バリー・マニロウ

Side-B 恋は移り気
DON'T FALL IN LOVE WITH ME

ARISTA

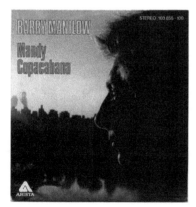

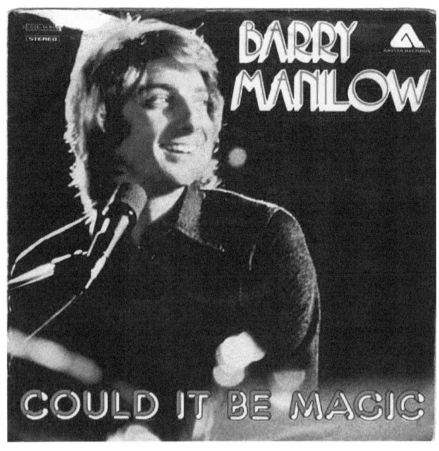

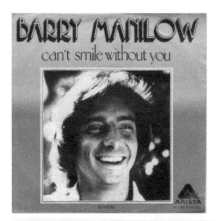

7RS-81
STEREO

●Side 1

メモリー 4'56"
MEMORY

●Side 2「ラッセル・TVCF・イメージソング」

恋はドゥ・イット!! 3'44"
I WANNA DO IT WITH YOU

バリー・マニロウ
BARRY MANILOW

Produced by Barry Manilow
Associate in Production and
Engineer: Bill Drescher

　1983年がとてもすてきな年だったとしていつまでも記憶に残る
であろう理由のひとつに、バリー・マニロウが日本にやってきた
ことが挙げられる。もう7か月が過ぎようとしているが、バリー
のステージに接した時のあの熱い感動は今でもまったく色褪せない。
ところでバリーは"80日間世界一周ツアー"を無事に終えてしば
らく休暇の後にレコーディングに入った。これは12月に発売予定
の「グレイテスト・ヒッツII」に収録される新曲のためのものだ
そうだ。

　さて、この「メモリー」は、アルバム「ヒア・カムズ・ザ・ナ
イト」よりアメリカでのファースト・シングルとして発売され'83
年初めに第39位を記録したナンバー（米ビルボード誌1月15、22
日号HOT 100）だ。バリー以前にはバーブラ・ストライサンドが
ベスト・アルバム「メモリーズ」に収録し、彼女のシングルとし
てもアメリカで'82年3月第52位まで昇ったヒットとなっているが、
元はミュージカル「キャッツ」の主題歌であり、T.S.エリオットの
詩にトレヴァー・ナンが一部を付け加えアンドリュー・ロイド・
ウェーバーが曲を書いた作品である。

　「キャッツ」は'81年5月ロンドンでの初演以来センセーション
を巻き起こし、ブロードウェイでは'82年10月より現在まで続演中。
さらに今年度のトニー賞では7部門を獲得した非常に評価の高い
ミュージカルだ。「メモリー」はそのメイン・テーマということ
で、すでにスタンダードといってもおかしくない名曲であろう。
バリーの歌唱も現代を代表するヴォーカリストにふさわしく、こ
の曲の魅力を十二分に引き出している。なお「メモリー」は「グ
レイテスト・ヒッツII」にも収録される予定。

1983年10月12日　POP-TOWN　矢口清治

MEMORY
A. L. Webber, T. S. Eliot and T. Nunn

Midnight!
Not a sound from the pavement
Has the moon lost her memory
She is smiling alone
In the lamplight the withered leaves collect at my feet
And the wind begins to moan

Memory
All alone in the moonlight
I can smile at the old days
It was beautiful then
I remember the time I knew what happiness was
Let the memory live again

Daylight
I must wait for the sunrise
I must think of a new life
And I mustn't give in
When the dawn comes tonight will be a memory too
And a new day will begin

Burnt out ends of smokey days
The stale cold smell of morning
The streetlamp dies
Another night is over
Another day is dawning

Touch me
It's so easy to leave me
All alone with the memory
Of my days in the sun
If you touch me you'll understand what happiness is
Look a new day has begun

Memory
All alone in the moonlight
I can smile at the old days
It was beautiful then
I remember the time I knew what happiness was
Let the memory live again

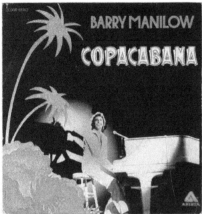

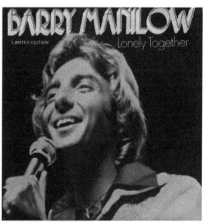

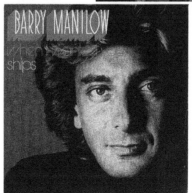

SIDE A

IN SEARCH OF LOVE
Produced by Howie Rice and
Barry Manilow

Music by Barry Manilow and
Howie Rice
Lyric by Allan Rich

©EMI Music Pub Co Ltd
MCA Music Ltd

SIDE B

AT THE DANCE
Produced by Michael Delugg and
Barry Manilow

Music by Barry Manilow and
Charles Fearing
Lyric by Adrienne Anderson

©EMI Music Pub/Angela Music/
Chanzer Music

Barry Manilow International
Fan Club U.K.
P.O. Box 40
Epsom
Surrey
KT19 9EP

Management: STILETTO. Ltd
Los Angeles, California
90069

RCA

From the Album "MANILOW"
PL/PK 87044

PB49919

D: AC F: RC 110 UK: AA

5 012394 991975

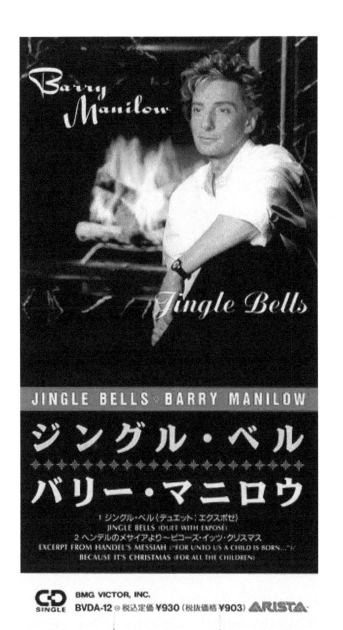

233

LET'S HANG ON!

Let's Hang On

Don't Fall In Love With Me

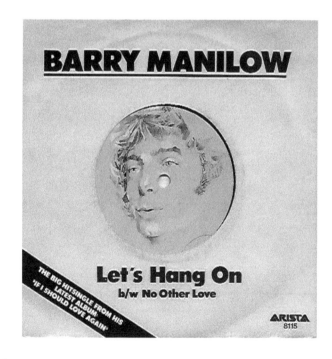

BARRY MANILOW

Let's Hang On
b/w No Other Love

THE BIG HITSINGLE FROM HIS
LATEST ALBUM
"IF I SHOULD LOVE AGAIN"

ARISTA
8115

234

From the 2008 Animated Christmas Special

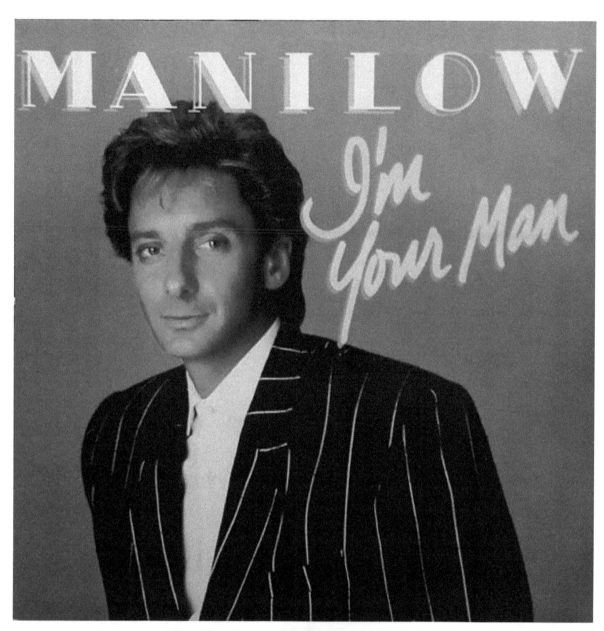

DAYBREAK

SN 006N-60146

BARRY MANILOW
'This one's for you'
This one's for you - Daybreak
- You oughta be home with
me - Jump shout boogie -
Weekend in New England -
Riders to the stars - Let me go
- Looks like we make it - Say
the words - All the time - Why
don't you see the show
again
Arista AL 4090

BARRY MANILOW
'Barry Manilow Live'
PLAAT 1: Riders to the stars -
Why don't we live together -
Looks like we made it - New
York City rhythm - A very
special medley (V.S.M.) -
Jump shout boogie medley:
Jump shout boogie - Avenue C
- Jumpin' at the woodside -
Cloudburst - Bandstand boogie
- This one's for you
PLAAT 2: Beautiful music
(part 1) - Daybreak - Lay me
down - Weekend in New
England - Studio musician -
Beautiful Music (part II) -
Could it be magic/Mandy - It's
a miracle - It's just another
new years eve - I write the
songs - Beautiful music (part
III)
Arista AL 8000

Manufactured under Licensee by NEGRAM b.v. Heemstede, Holland an EMI-HOLLAND Company   Ⓟ 1976

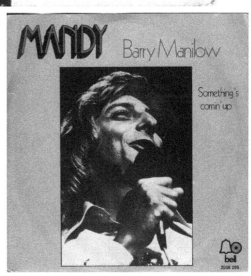

**"Sandra" / "The Two Of Us" single from the Philippines
(BELL-72-096-A / 1974)**

240

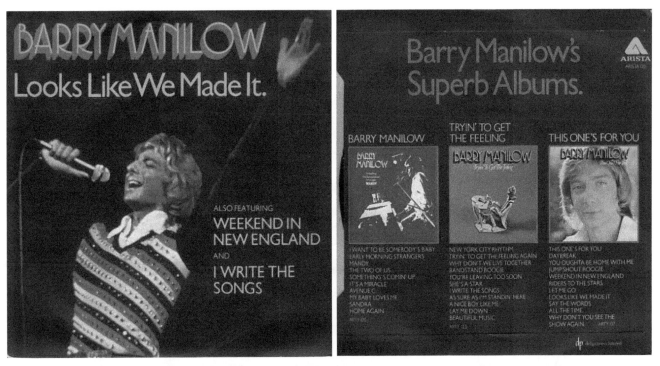

241

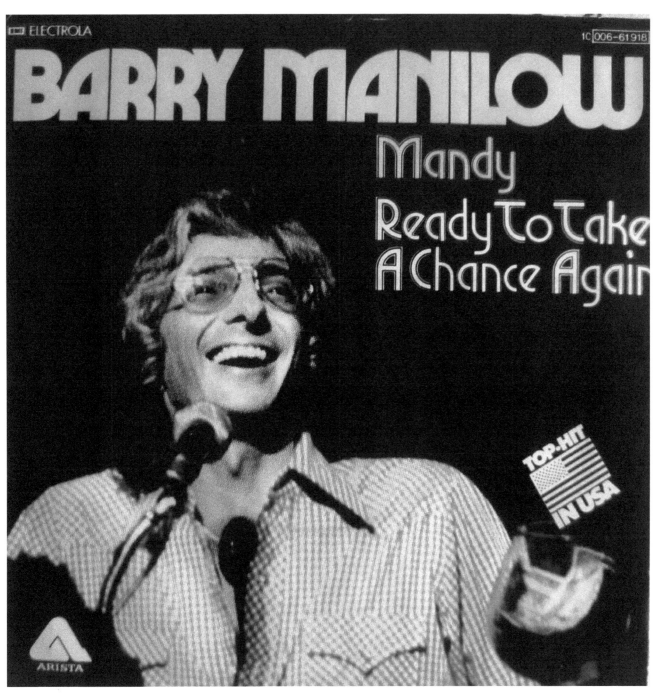

**The shaped picture disc for "Read 'Em and Weep" (ARISD-551 / 1983)
Flip side on next page.**

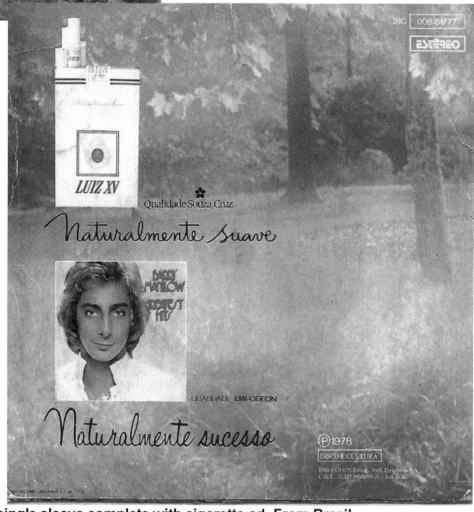

A 1978 single sleeve complete with cigarette ad. From Brazil.

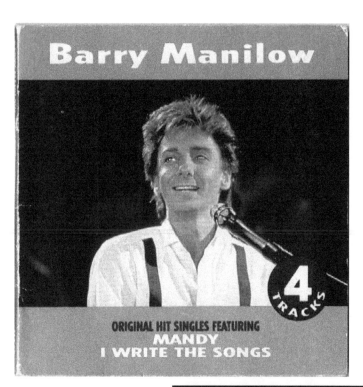

IT'S JUST ANOTHER NEW YEAR'S EVE

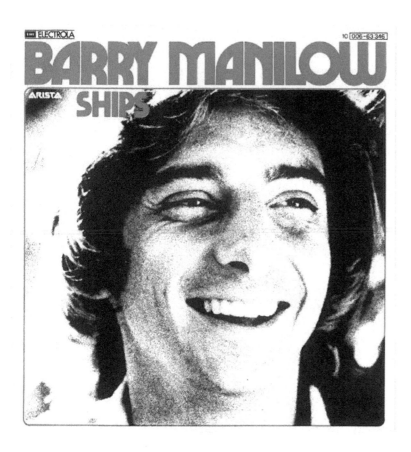

STEREO 1 C 006-63346

(LC) 3484

℗ 1979 Arista Records, Inc.

Coverphoto: Arista

Ships
(Ian Hunter)

They Gave In To The Blues
(Barry Manilow/Marty Panzer)

BARRY MANILOW
Produced by Barry Manilow and Ron Dante

AKTUELLE LP:

💿 1C 064-63292
📼 1C 264-63292

🔲 ELECTROLA

EMI Electrola GmbH, Köln. All rights reserved. Printed in Germany by Druckhaus Maack KG, 5880 Lüdenscheid

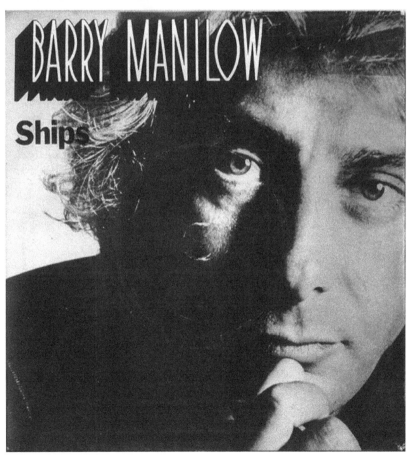

From the 1980 Motion Picture "Tribute." Japanese release.

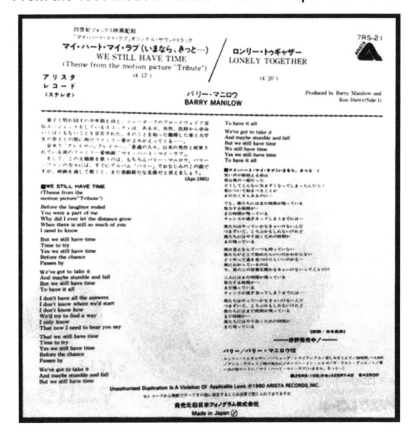

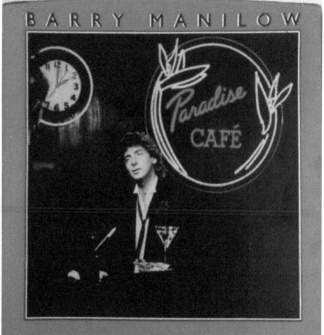

258

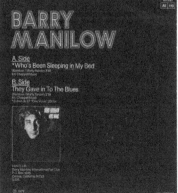

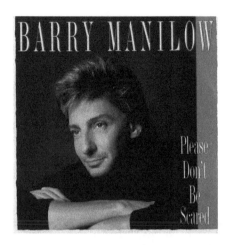

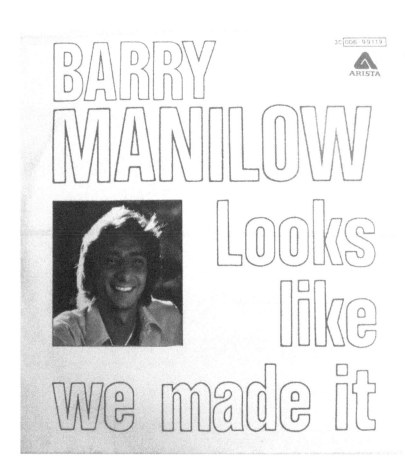

3C 006-99119

ARISTA

BARRY MANILOW
Looks like we made it

ラヴ・ミュージックを華麗に彩どる歌の魔術師、そして現在アメリカのポップ・シーンで
最大の人気を誇るスーパー・エンターテイナー、バリー・マニロウが放つ超強力ヒット！

涙色の微笑
BARRY MANILOW
バリー・マニロウ

SUNRISE サンライズ

Barry
Related
Recordings

This section will concentrate solely on original recordings, either Barry doing a musical guest appearance or a similar type recording such as spoken word, not compiled solo products. Some other appearances can be found in the singles section. It is my hope, that besides the wonderful Barry Manilow tracks on these guest appearances you might not have known about, you'll find you enjoy the entire album and pick up a copy. Some amazing talent showcased here.

A Christmas Miracle (Hospitals Helping Kids)
CM-1005

Track Listing:

Angels We Have Heard On High (Marilyn McCoo) / Joy To The World (Mannheim Steamroller) / O Come All Ye Faithful (Amy Grant) / What Child Is This The Moody Blues / O Tannenbaum (John Tesh) / Jesu, Joy Of Men's Desire (Kurt Bestor) / Deck The Halls (Neil Sedaka) / God Rest Ye Merry Gentlemen (Nancy Sinatra) / Away In The Manger (The Judds) / It Came Up On The Midnight Clear (Tony Orlando) / Jingle Bells (The Jets) / Medley: Deck The Halls / Hark The Herald Angel Sing (Donny Osmond) / The Birth Of A King (Clint Black) / Jennifer Warnes (On A Christmas Day) / Ava Maria (Barry Manilow) / Silent Night (Frank Sinatra)

Notes & Trivia:

* This album was released by Children's Miracle Network on CD and Cassette in October 1998Back of the cover insert

Rosie O'Donnell – Another Rosie Christmas
CK 85102

Track Listing:
Jessica Simpson & Me - Rockin' Around The Christmas Tree / Smash Mouth & Me - Nuttin' For Christmas / Macy Gray & Me - Winter Wonderland / Dixie Chicks & Me - Merry Christmas From The Family / Jewel - Face Of Love / Ricky Martin & Me - Ay, Ay, Ay It's Christmas / Destiny's Child - Spread A Little Love On Christmas Day / Linda Eder - The Bells Of St. Paul / Sugar Ray & Me - Silver Bells / Billy Gilman & Me - I'm Gonna E-Mail Santa / Marc Anthony - Christmas Auld Lang Syne / Trans-Siberian Orchestra Featuring Marlene Danielle (From The Broadway Play "Cats") - The Prince Of Peace Donna Summer - Rosie Christmas / Barry Manilow & Me - Because It's Christmas (For All The Children)

Production Information:
Producers: Cory Rooney / Dan Shea / Ric Wake / Eric Valentine / Andrew Slater / Mark Russell / Arif Mardin / Joe Mardin / Robi Rosa / Beyoncé Knowles / Focus / Jeremy Roberts / Steve Gallagher / Sugar Ray / Blake Chancey / Ray Benson / Robert Kinkel
Recorded at: Sony Music Studios, New York City / Cove City Sound Studios, Glen Cove, NY / Sunset Sound, Los Angeles, CA / The Palace of Auburn Hills, Auburn Hills, MI / Right Track Recording, New York, NY / The Gentlemen's Club, Miami Beach, FL / Murf Dog Studios / Westwood Sound Studio, Nashville, TN / The Dream Factory, New York, NY / Soundtrack Studios, New York, NY / Studio 900, New York, NY / The Hit Factory Criteria, North Miami FL / Crescent Moon Studios, Miami, FL / Sound Kitchen, Nashville, TN
Mixed at: Cove City Sound Studios, Glen Cove, NY / Right Track Recording, New York, NY / Soundtrack Studios, New York, NY / Studio 900, New York, NY
Mastered at: Sony Music Studios, New York City
Mastered by: Vlado Meller
Art Direction: Gail Marowitz
Production Coordinators: Jennifer Patierno / Marc Russell
Design: Maja Blazejewska
Executive Producer: Ric Wake
Cover Illustration: Steve Blevins / Transaction Information Systems*

Notes & Trivia:
- This album released on CD and Cassette in 2000
- Rosie O'Donnell and Guest Artists are contributing their proceeds from the sale of this album to the For All Kids Foundation.

My Favorite Broadway – The Love Songs
HY-20020

Track Listing:
Introduction: Julie Andrews / Tom Wopat: Lullaby Of Broadway (from 42nd Street) / Nathan Lane: Sue Me (from Guys & Dolls) / Heather Headley: He Touched Me (from Drat The Cat) / Ron Raines: Gigi (from Gigi) / Marin Mazzie: When Did I Fall In Love? (from Fiorello) / Robert Goulet: If Ever I Would Leave You (from Camelot) / Linda Eder: Love Song Medley I: Come Rain Or Come Shine (from St. Louis Woman) - I Don't Know How To Love Him (from Jesus Christ Superstar) - What Kind Of Fool Am I? (from Stop The World! I Want To Get Off) / Adam Pascal: Seasons Of Love (from Rent) / Michael Crawford: Music Of The Night (from Phantom Of The Opera) / Barry Manilow: Every Single Day (from Harmony) / Rebecca Luker / Peter Gallagher / Marin Mazzie: Love Song Medley II: Too Late Now (from Royal Wedding) - Sometimes A Day Goes By (from Woman Of The Year) - Not A Day Goes By (from Merrily We Roll Along) / Bebe Neuwirth: I'm A Brass Band (from Sweet Charity) / Chita Rivera: How Lucky Can You Get? (from Funny Lady) / Michael Crawford / Julie Andrews: My Fair Lady Medley: I've Grown Accustomed To Her Face (from My Fair Lady) - The Rain In Spain (from My Fair Lady) / Company: Finally: Lullaby Of Broadway (from 42nd Street)

Production Information:
Conceived and Produced By:Jeff Roland / Allen Newman / Tony Adams
Album Producer: Didier Deutsch
Executive Album Producer: Jeff Roland
Musical Director: Paul Gemignani
A&R Supervisor: Joe Augustine
Directed for the Stage By: Graciela Daniele
Original Concept: Jeff Roland
Recording Engineers: John Harris / Mitch Maketansky for Effanel Music
Mixed and Mastered By: James Nichols
Assistant Mix and Master Engineer: Steven Penny
Photography: Sam Erickson / Joseph Sinott
Art Direction: slow HEARTH studio
Recorded Live At City Center in New York City on Monday, October 16, 2000

Musicians:
The American Theater Orchestra

Notes & Trivia:
- This concert was released on VHS Tape (Cat.#ID0595MO) and DVD (Cat. # ID0595MODVD) on March 13, 2001 by Image Entertainment. In China on DVD (Cat. # RMD018)

Bette Midler – Sings The Peggy Lee Songbook
82876-77509-2

Track Listing:
Fever / Alright, Okay, You Win / I Love Being Here With You (duet with Barry Manilow) / Happiness Is A Thing Called Joe / Is That All There Is? / I'm A Woman / He's A Tramp / The Folks Who Live On The Hill / Big Spender / Mr. Wonderful

Production Information:
Producer: Barry Manilow
Co-producer: David Benson
Associate Producers: Greg Bartheld / Marc Hulett
Executive Producers: Garry C. Kief / Jay Landers
Recorded at: O'Henry Sound Studios, 4200 W Magnolia Blvd / Burbank, CA 91505
Engineered by: Andrew Scheps / David Benson / Greg Bartheld
Assistant Engineers: Darius Fong / Jeremy Miller / Joel Poinsett / Scott Moore
Edited by: Greg Bartheld
Mixed at: Bill Schnee Studios by Bill Schnee
Mastered at: The Mastering Lab by: Doug Sax / Robert Hadley
Photography by: Firooz Zahedi
Illustration: Robert W. Richards
Art Direction: Gail Marowitz
Design: Michelle Holme
Arranged by: Barry Manilow / Don Sebesky / Randy Newman / Ray Ellis / Bill Ross / George Shelby

Musicians:
Piano: Mike Lang / Ron Pedley
Guitar: Jim Fox / Steve Cotter
Drums: Ramon Banda / Russ McKinnon
Percussion: Joseph DeLeon
Bass: Dave Carpenter / Robert Hurst
Hammond B-3 Organ : Joey DeFrancesco
Accordion: Nick Ariondo
Background Vocals: Bob Joyce / Clydene Jackson / Kevin Dorsey / Melanie Taylor / Randy Crenshaw / Yvonne Williams

Notes & Trivia:
- This album released on CD on October 25, 2005 on Columbia Records.
- Released by Barnes & Noble with a bonus track: "He Needs Me"

Dave Koz – At The Movies / CDP 0946 3 11405 2 5

Track Listing:
Over The Rainbow (The Wizard Of Oz) (Vocal Introduction by Judy Garland) / Moon River (Breakfast At Tiffany's) - Featuring Barry Manilow / As Time Goes By Casablanca) / Somewhere (West Side Story) - Featuring Anita Baker / The Shadow Of Your Smile / (Love Theme From The Sandpiper) - Featuring Johnny Mathis And Chris Botti / The Pink Panther (The Pink Panther) / The Way We Were (The Way We Were) - Featuring Vanessa Williams / The Summer Knows (Theme From Summer Of '42) / It Might Be You (Tootsie) - Featuring India.Arie / Cinema Paradiso Suite (Cinema Paradiso) / A Whole New World (Aladdin) - Featuring Donna Summer / Schindler's List (Main Theme From Schindler's List) / It Might Be You (Instrumental Version) - Featuring Peter White / The Shadow Of Your Smile (Instrumental Version) - Featuring Chris Botti And Norman Brown

Production Information:
Producer: Phil Ramone
Recorded at: Capitol Studios, Los Angeles, CA / Right Track Studios, New York City, NY / Sound on Sound, New York City, NY / Avatar Studios, New York City, NY / Bennett Studios, Englewood, New Jersey / Paul Gilman Music, Palm Springs, CA / Schnee Studios, North Hollywood, CA
Engineered by: Al Schmitt / Dave O'Donnell / Frank Filipetti
Additional Engineering by: Bill Schnee / Bruce Feagle / David Benson / Jan Folkson / Michael O'Reilly
Assistant Engineers: Angie Teo / Darius Fong / Justin Shturtz / Tim Whitney
Pro-tools Engineers: Andrew Felluss / Darius Fong
Mixed at: Capitol Studios, Los Angeles, CA.
Mixed by: Al Schmitt
Assistant Mix Engineers: Bill Smith / Steve Genewick
Mastered at: The Mastering Lab, Ojai, CA
Mastered by: Doug Sax / Sangwook "Sunny" Nam
Photography by: Ellen Von Unwerth
Art Direction: Eric Roinestad / Megan Steinman
Design: Eric Roinestad

Musicians:
Piano: Randy Waldman / Rob Mathes / Rob Mounsey
Drums: Gregg Field / Shawn Pelton
Electric Guitar: Michael Thompson
Guitar: Jeffrey Mironov / Rodney Jones
Acoustic Guitar: Dean Parks
Bassoon: Marc Goldberg / Ron Jannelli

Clarinet / Flute: Charlie Pillow / David Mann
Double Bass : Gail Kruvand / Larry Glazener / David Finck / Kevin Axt
English Horn: Bill Meredith
Flute: Pamela Sklar
French Horn: Anne Scharer / Joe Anderer / Julie Landsman / Patrick Milando / Stewart Rose
Clarinet: John Manasse
Harp: Stacy Shames
Keyboards: Jim Cox / Philippe Saisse
Oboe / English Horn: Diane Lesser
Percussion: Jim Saporito
Soprano / Tenor / Alto Saxophone: Dave Koz
Timpani: Joe Passaro
Tuba: Chris Hall
Viola: Adria Benjamin / Craig Mumm / Crystal Garner / Judy Witmer / Maxine Roach / Vincent Lionti
Violin: Abe Appleman / Ann Leathers / Ann Lehman / Avril Brown / Cenovia Cummins / David Chan /
Jan Mullen / Jean Ingraham / Jonathan Dinklage / Katherine Fong / Laura McGinniss / Marti Sweet /
Ricky Sortomme / Yuri Vodovoz
Cello: Diane Barere / Ellen Westerman / Eugene Moye / Jeanne LeBlanc / Richard Locker
Concertmaster: Elena Barere
Arranged by: Randy Waldman / Rob Mathes / Rob Mounsey / Victor Vanacore
Conductors: Rob Mathes / Rob Mounsey

Notes & Trivia:

- This album was released on CD and CD with DVD (Cat.# 509995 17392 25) on January30, 2007.This album was released on Cassette in Indonesia (Cat. # Capitol / EMI 00946 3 87025 4 2 / E01207)

The cover for the CD/DVD combination showing full color graphics

Olivia Newton-John – Christmas Wish
ONJ / Compass Productions – 5-09993-09002-2-6

Track Listing:
O Come All Ye Faithful / Angels We Have Heard On High (Interlude) / Every Time It Snows (Featuring Jon Secada) / Away In A Manger (Interlude) / We Three Kings / The First Noël (Interlude) / A Mother's Christmas Wish (Featuring Jim Brickman) / Jesu, Joy Of Man's Desiring (Interlude) / Angels In The Snow / What Child Is This? (Interlude) (Featuring Pavlo) / Silent Night (Featuring Jann Arden) / O Come, O Come Emmanuel (Interlude) / All Through The Night (Featuring Michael McDonald) / Little Drummer Boy (Interlude) / Underneath The Same Sky / O Christmas Tree (Interlude) / Little Star Of Bethlehem / Deck The Halls (Interlude) / Instrument Of Peace (Featuring Marc Jordan) / We Wish You A Merry Christmas (Interlude) / Christmas On My Radio / A Gift Of Love (Featuring Barry Manilow)

Production Information:
Producers: Amy Sky / Barry Manilow / Robbie Buchanan
Recorded At: Concrete Jungle, Toronto, Ontario, Canada / Phase One Studios, Toronto, Ontario, Canada / Lenz Entertainment, Toronto, Ontario, Canada / Silverbirch Productions, Toronto, Ontario, Canada / Chartmaker Studios, Malibu, CA / The Cat's Room / The Document Room, Malibu, CA / Gari Entertainment / Shelter Island Sound, New York, NY / Ocean Way, Nashville, Tenn / Wild Sound, Minneapolis, MN / Capitol Studios, Studio A, Hollywood, CA / The Nucleus, Toronto, Ontario, Canada
Engineered by: Bill Schnee / Brian Friedman / Brian Wohlgemuth / David Bryant / Dustin Su / Humberto Gatica / Jared Kvitka / Jim Beeman / Matt Zimmerman / Michael Jack / Michael Medina / Steve Addabo / Ted Onyszczak / Vic Florence / Zack Fagan
Assistant Engineers: Greg Kolchinsky / Rocky Grisez / Scott Erickson / Steve Crowder
Additional Engineering: Azra Ross / Greg Johnston / Mark Kelso / Steven MacKinnon
Mixed at: Concrete Jungle, Toronto, Ontario, Canada
Mixed by: Bill Schnee (tracks: 22) / Vic Florencia (tracks: 1 to 21)
Additional Mixing: Vic Florencia (tracks: 22)
Mastered at: Joao Carvalho Mastering, Toronto, Ontario, Canada
Mastered by: Joao Carvalho
Photography by: J. Michael Lafond
Art Direction: Megan Schaefer
Cover Design: Michael Caprio
Graphic Design: Jennifer Bergstrom

Notes & Trivia:
- This album released on CD on October 18, 2007
- "A Gift of Love" was written by Barry Manilow and Bruce Sussman

Elaine Paige – Elaine Paige And Friends
Rhino Records – 5249828742

Track Listing:
Mi Morena (duet with Jon Secada) / Take A Bow (duet with Idina Menzel) / The Prayer (duet with Barry Manilow) / Just The Way You Are (duet with Paul Anka) / Closest Thing To Crazy (duet with LeAnn Rimes) Where Is The Love? (duet with John Barrowman) / It's Only Life (duet with Sinéad O'Connor) / You Are Everything (duet with Billy Ocean) / It Might Be You (duet with Johnny Mathis) / Amoreuse (duet with Olivia Newton-John) / Make It With You (duet with Neil Sedaka) / All The Way (duet with Michael Bolton) / Thank You For Being A Friend (duet with Dionne Warwick)

Production Information:
Main Producer: Phil Ramone / "The Prayer" co-produced by Barry Manilow
Mastered by: Rob Ludwig at Gateway Mastering, Portland, Maine

Notes & Trivia:
- This CD was released on November 16, 2010
- This is a UK only release. An early 2011 US release was planned, but not sure it was released.

Melissa Manchester – The Fellas
Long Run Entertainment – 2614569

Track Listing:
Ain't That A Kick In The Head / Chances Are / They Say It's Wonderful / For Me And My Gal (Featuring: Barry Manilow) / Love Is Just Around The Corner / Smile / Night And Day / How Do You Keep The Music Playing

Production Information:
Produced by: Melissa Manchester, Robert Slack
Recorded and Mixed at: Glendora College Studios, Glendora CA
Engineered and Mixed by: Tim Jaquette
Mastered by: Bernie Grundman
Graphic Design / Art Direction: Lena Ringstad

Notes & Trivia:
- This album was released on CD on September 8, 2017
- This album was recorded in two weeks time with Dean Bob Slack of Citrus College and their Blue Note Orchestra.

Gary Barlow – Music Played By Humans
Polydor – 352 146-7

Notes & Trivia:

- There are various issues of this album both on CD and vinyl and Barry appears on one track with the catalog number above for the CD and Polydor – 351 693-9 for the two LP vinyl release. The song title is "You Make The Sun Shine."
- This is a UK and European only release. Released in November 2020.

It Takes 2 – 80 Timeless Duets
Reader's Digest (Australia) Pty Limited – 0352676-1/2/3

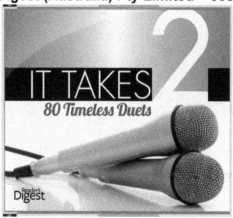

Notes & Trivia:

- This is an Australian four CD set with 80 duets. Barry has one track on it with the late Rosemary Clooney titled "How About You?"

Dionne Warwick – Hits & Rarities 1974-1999
Arista Records LLC / Sony Music / TJL Ventures, LLC – 19075872782

Track Listing:
Then Came You With The Spinners / I'll Never Love This Way Again / Déjà Vu / No Night So Long / Friends In Love (duet with Johnny Mathis) / Heartbreaker / How Many Times Can We Say Goodbye duet with Luther Vandross) / That's What Friends Are For (With Elton John, Gladys Knight & Stevie Wonder) / Love Power (duet with Jeffrey Osborne) / Love Will Find A Way (duet with Whitney Houston) / Sail Away / The Last One To Be Loved / Never Gonna Let You Get Away (duet with Barry Manilow) / Let It Be Me (duet with Barry Gibb) / In Love Alone (duet with Richard Carpenter) / You'd Be So Nice To Come Home To / What Becomes Of Love (From The Television Miniseries "Jacqueline Susann's Valley Of The Dolls") / On My Way (From The Motion Picture "Isn't She Great") / Welcome To My World (Live) / Touch Me In The Morning (Live) / The Love Boat Theme (From The Television Series "The Love Boat" Complete Version)

Notes & Trivia:
- This PBS only promotion was released in 2018.
- The track with Barry Manilow (Never Gonna Let You Get Away) is a previously unreleased outtake from the 1979 "Dionne" album which was produced by Barry for Arista Records.
- CD / Compilation / Special Edition

Claptone - Closer
DIF-490LP/CD/DA

Track Listing:

Claptone & Two Another– Golden / Claptone– Feel This Way Featuring – Mayer Hawthorne / Claptone & Apre– My Night / Claptone– Fade Away Featuring – Spelles / Claptone & Seal– Just A Ghost / Claptone– Queen Of Ice / Claptone, Like Mike & Mansionair– Right Into You / Claptone– Make Love Not War Featuring – Nathan Nicholson / Claptone & James Vincent McMorrow– Wake Up / Claptone– Zero / Claptone– Is This Love Featuring – Nathan Nicholson / Claptone– Beautiful / Claptone– Satellite Featuring – Peter Bjorn And John / Claptone– Nobody Featuring – Barry Manilow

Production Information:

Producer: Claptone / Stuart Price

Notes & Trivia:

- This album was released on LP / CD and 14 file FLAC formats on November 12, 2021
- 2LP limited deluxe edition of 500 pictured above
- Pressed on neon black vinyl with hand numbered spot UV cover
- Joining Claptone on the album, *Closer* will be a plethora of global collaborators including Peter Bjorn and John on "Satellite," Seal on "Just A Ghost," and Barry Manilow featured on the standout album track, "Nobody."

National UNICEF Day PSAs
DWP-4966 / DWP-4977

1

National UNICEF Day PSAs

PLEASE PLAY DURING SEPTEMBER AND OCTOBER

1977

1. Dennis Weaver :30
2. Barry Manilow :30
3. Lily Tomlin :30
4. George Segal :30
5. Henry Fonda :30
6. Penny Marshall :30
7. Saturday Night Live :30
8. Captain Kangaroo :30
9. Chicago :30
10. Dionne Warwicke :60

DWP 4966

2

UNICEF Greeting Card PSAs

PLEASE PLAY DURING NOVEMBER AND DECEMBER

1977

1. Ed Asner :60
2. Dustin Hoffman :30
3. Faye Dunaway :30
4. Gregory Peck :30
5. Danny Kaye :10
6. Pearl Bailey :30
7. Dolly Parton :30
8. Johnny Carson :30
9. Arthur Miller :60
10. Marlon Brando :60

DWP 4977

Barry and many other personalities gave their time to help others in various spoken recordings. Here is the Christmas Season UNICEF PSAs.

UNICEF Public Service Radio Spots: 1981-82
DWP-929-A/B

UNICEF
PUBLIC SERVICE
RADIO SPOTS
SIDE ONE

NATIONAL UNICEF DAY
1. Kermit the Frog :30
2. Paul Simon :30
3. Kenny Rogers :30
4. Ted Nugent :30
5. Barry Manilow :30
6. Gladys Knight :30

COMBINED CAMPAIGN
7. Marlon Brando :30
8. Leontyne Price :30
9. Michael Landon :10
10. Dick Cavett :10

1981-82

DWP929A

UNICEF
PUBLIC SERVICE
RADIO SPOTS
SIDE TWO

YEAR-ROUND
1. Danny Kaye :30
2. Dolly Parton :30
3. Dustin Hoffman :10
4. Katharine Hepburn :10

UNICEF GREETING CARDS
5. Roger Moore :30
6. Johnny Carson :30
7. Olivia Newton-John :30
8. Michael Landon :30
9. Liv Ullmann :30
10. Dick Cavett :30

1981-82

DWP929B

**Barry and all the performers seen here were always willing to give time to help others.
You never get anywhere alone usually.**

The
Videos

This section concentrates on videos released by or featuring Barry Manilow. Of Note: Several of these videos have been reissued and are not presented here, nor are all compilation videos.

The First Barry Manilow Special
March 2, 1977 / ABC-TV

Song Include:

It's A Miracle / This One's For You / Could It Be Magic / Mandy / Jump Shout Boogie / Avenue C / Jumpin' At The Woodside / Cloudburst / Bandstand Boogie / A Very Strange Medley / New York City Rhythm / Sandra / Early Morning Stranger / I Write The Songs.

Notes & Trivia:

- Recorded on-stage at Ravinia Music Festival in Chicago, "live" on the streets of New York City and in Hollywood at ABC-TV. This Emmy-Award winning special was broadcast to record-breaking ratings on ABC in 1977 when more than 34 million people tuned in to see Barry's first national special. Nominated for three Emmy awards, it won one for "Outstanding Special" in the "Comedy-Variety or Music" category.
- This television special was first released on CED, Laserdisc and VHS formats. Later on DVD.

With the late Penny Marshall as she appeared on Barry's first special.

Barry Manilow in Concert At The Greek Theater
August 27, 1978

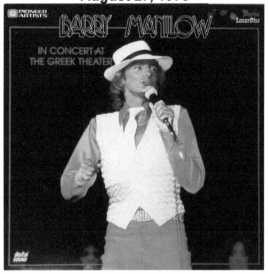

Songs Include:

Here We Go Again / New York City Rhythm / Daybreak / Even Now / Medley: Jump Shout Boogie - Avenue C - Jumpin' at the Woodside - Cloudburst - Bandstand Boogie / Ready to Take a Chance Again / Weekend in New England / Looks Like We Made It / Beautiful Music / I Was A Fool (To Let You Go) / All the Time / Copacabana / Beautiful Music / Hits Medley: Trying to Get the Feeling - This One's For You - Mandy - Could It Be Magic / It's a Miracle / Can't Smile Without You / I Write the Songs

Notes & Trivia:

- This program was released on Beta (PAL) videotape in the UK in January 1984 (Cat.# 6127) and LaserDisc in March 1985 by Guild Home Video, LaserDisc in the US by Pioneer Artists (Cat.# PA-84-065) in 1984, on VHS in the UK by The Video Collection on November 4, 1985 (Cat.# VC4005), on VHS tape in the UK by Futurevision Ltd on November 3, 1986 and on DVD by Stiletto / New Media (Cat.# Rhino R2 517642) on September 15, 2009. The Beta videotape cover insert from the UK

Barry Manilow in Concert – Live At The Pittsburgh Civic Center
November 24, 1981

Set List:
I Write the Songs / Can't Smile Without You / Medley: The Old Songs - I Don't Want to Walk Without You - Let's Hang On / Tryin' to Get the Feeling Again / Even Now / Nickels and Dimes / I Was a Fool (to Let You Go) / Beautiful Music / I Made It Through the Rain / A Weekend in New England / Break Down the Door - Who's Been Sleeping in My Bed / Commercial Jingles / If I Should Love Again / It's a Miracle / Bandstand Boogie / Daybreak / This One's for You / Looks Like We Made It / Mandy - Could It Be Magic / Let's Take All Night (To Say Goodbye) / One Voice

Notes & Trivia:
- This program was released on VHS and Beta (PAL) videotape by Peppermint Video Music (Cat.# 6142) in May 1985. This program was also released on VHS tape in Japan by Townsway Entertainment (Cat.# PVM-9)
- Barry gave two concerts in Pittsburgh over two days; November 23 and 24, 1981.
- The show was performed in the round on a rotating stage and was videotaped for cablecasting on the Showtime network (it began running on March 8, 1982). At one point in the concert, Barry took off his vest and shirt with puffy silver sleeves to show a Terry Bradshaw jersey underneath, much to the delight of the crowd.
- Barry performed at the Pittsburgh Civic Center several more times: October 26, 1984, March 3, 1988, October 8, 2004 and July 6, 2009.
- Do you know who the first performer was PCC? Judy Garland on October 19, 1961. There was a sold out crown of 12,365 people. The last performers were James Taylor and Carole King on July 26, 2010. The arena was demolished on September 26, 2010.

Goldie (Hawn) & Kids – Listen to Us
May 8, 1982 / ABC-TV

Show Information:

This 40 year old Goldie Hawn TV Special focuses it's time and energy on something Goldie loves and continues helping today in 2022 and that is children! In this special children are asked questions about their feelings and life and are allowed to be heard. Barry Manilow is the special guest and he sings and does some acting with Goldie in some touching sketches.

Notes & Trivia:

- This special has been released on VHS tape in the US in 1986 by Prism Entertainment (Cat. # 9506V) and in 1991 by StarMaker (Cat.# 2010). Both companies now defunct.
- Won a Primetime Emmy Award in 1982 in the category - "Outstanding Directing in a Variety or Music Program" (Director; Dwight Hemion)
- Barry sings "Sunday Father," "I Am Your Child" and "One Voice."

The two US VHS videotape slip cases for the TV special

283

Barry Manilow – Live at Blenheim Palace
August 27, 1983

Set List:
Act 1:
You're Lookin' Hot Tonight / It's a Miracle / Here Comes the Night / Medley: The Old Songs - I Don't Want to Walk Without You - Let's Hang On / New York City Rhythm / Memory / Some Girls / Bandstand Boogie / No Other Love / Mandy / Beautiful Music / I Made It Through the Rain / Beautiful Music (reprise) / Intermission
Act 2:
The Lion Sleeps Tonight / This One's for You / Even Now / Lay Me Down / Some Kind of Friend / Can't Smile Without You / Medley: Something Like This - Copacabana - Daybreak - Lonely Together - Looks Like We Made It / Could It Be Magic / I Write the Songs
Encore:
We'll Meet Again - One Voice - You're Lookin' Hot Tonight (reprise)
Encore 2:
I Want to Do It With You

Notes & Trivia:
- The concert was attended by over 40,000 fans.
- The concert was videotaped and released initially in the us on VHS tape (Cat.# 60637) by RCA, LaserDisc by Pioneer Artists (Cat.# PA-87-181) and DVD by Stiletto Entertainment (Cat.# 874402 009370) The Stiletto release is the only one that has the complete concert.
- This concert is available on video from shopmanilow.com

The US VHS videotape slip case from 1985

The Making Of 2:00AM Paradise Cafe

Songs on tape:
Paradise Café / When Love Is Gone / What Am I Doin' Here / Blue (duet with Sarah Vaughan) / When October Goes / Say No More / Big City Blues (duet with Mel Tormé) / Night Song

Production Information:
Producer – Les Joyce
Directed By – Don Clark
Executive-Producer – Garry C. Kief

Musicians:
Piano: Barry Manilow
Bass: George Duvivier
Drums: Shelly Manne
Guitar: Mundell Lowe
Rhodes Piano: Bill Mays
Baritone Saxophone: Gerry Mulligan

Notes & Trivia:
- A "Music Vision" series release featuring the rehearsal and recording phases of Barry Manilow's first jazz inspired album *2:00 AM Paradise Cafe.* Special Appearances by Sarah Vaughn and Mel Tormé.
- This program was released in the US on VHS tape by RCA / Columbia Home Video (Cat.# 60417) in 1985. This program was also released in the UK on VHS (PAL) tape by Peppermint Video Music (Cat.# 6125) in January 1985. Other versions may have been released.
- © Stiletto Ltd. 1984.
- Program Length: 55 minutes

Barry Manilow – Magic - Live At The N.E.C.
November 22, 1984

Set List:
That's Why They Call Her Sugar / The Old Songs / It's a Miracle / Let's Hang On! / Even Now / Can't Smile Without You / Some Kind of Friend / No Other Love / Mandy / Copacabana (at the Copa) / I Write the Songs / I Made It Through the Rain / One Voice / Come With Me / Merry Christmas / Have Yourself a Merry Little Christmas / Paradise Café / Big City Blues / When Love Is Gone / Encore: Paradise Café – When October Goes – Stay

Notes & Trivia:
- This concert was recorded at the NEC Arena in Birmingham, England. The songs listed above is the shows set list, the released video contained fewer songs: That's Why They Call Her Sugar / The Old Songs / It's A Miracle / Let's Hang On / Even Now / Can't Smile Without You / Some Kind Of Friend / No Other Love / Mandy / Copacabana (At The Copa) / I Write The Songs / I Made It Through The Rain / One Voice / Come With Me.
- This program was released in the UK on VHS (PAL) tape by Pickwick Video (Cat.# PGP-2127) in 1989.
- Released on DVD in Mexico as "Barry Manilow En Concierto" with fewer songs by On Screen Films (Cat.# DVDA-3487).

The back side of the UK VHS snap case

Barry Manilow – Live In Japan

Set List:

Overture - Come With Me / At The Dance / Can't Smile Without You / Memory / Some Kind Of Friend - In Search Of Love / No Other Love / Mandy / Copacabana / ¡Aye Carumba! / Sweet Heaven / Paradise Café / Blue / Read 'Em And Weep / Medley: It's A Miracle - Daybreak - Somewhere In The Night - Ready To Take A Chance Again - Could It Be Magic - I Write The Songs / Sakura, Sakura / You're Lookin' Hot Tonight / Paradise Cafe (Reprise)

Notes & Trivia:

- Recorded live at Osaka-Jo Hall in Osaka, Japan on June 6, 1985
- This program was released in Japan on VHS tape and LaserDisc by Lobster Kikaku Ltd (Cat.# LVD-509) in 1985.
- Program Length: 85 minutes.

The back jacket of the Japanese LaserDisc

287

Barry Manilow – Live On Broadway
December 2 and December 3, 1989

Set List:
Sweet Life / It's A Long Way Up / Brooklyn Blues / I Am Your Child / Ships / Dirt Cheap (Barry, Debra Byrd and Company) / God Bless The Other 99 (Barry and Company) / Mandy / Please Don't Be Scared / The One That Got Away / Some Good Things Never Last (duet with Debra Byrd) / Keep Each Other Warm / Hey Mambo (Billy Kidd, Barry and Company) / The Gonzo Hits Medley: One Voice - I Write The Songs - The Old Songs - Bandstand Boogie - I Don't Want To Walk Without You - Weekend In New England - Even Now - Some Kind Of Friend - New York City Rhythm - Copacabana - Read 'Em And Weep - When I Wanted You - Somewhere Down The Road - This One's For You - Tryin' To Get The Feeling - Ready To Take A Change Again - It's A Miracle - Let's Hang On - Somewhere In The Night - Could It Be Magic - I Made It Through The Rain - Daybreak - I Write The Songs) / When The Good Times Come Again

Production Information:
Producers: James M. Nederlander / Kevin Carlisle / Michael DeLugg / Barry Manilow
Director: Kevin Carlisle
Lighting Director J. T. McDonald
Lighting Director Kieran Healy
Production Manager Jeremy Railton
Created by: Joe Gannon
Written-By Barry Manilow / Ken Welch / Mitzie Welch / Roberta Kent
Management: Garry C. Kief / Steve Wax / Eric Borenstein

Notes & Trivia:
- This program was released in the US on VHS tape by 6 West Home Video (Cat.# SW 5708) and LaserDisc by Pioneer Artists (Cat.# PA-90-022) / 1990 release.
- This concert was released on LP / CD / Cassette. Please see the "Live Albums" section.
- Program Length: 90 minutes

Barry Manilow – Live in Britain

Set List:
It's A Miracle / London / Can't Smile Without You / The Old Songs Medley: The Old Songs - I Don't Wanna Walk Without You - Let's Hang On / This One's For You / Even Now / Nickels & Dimes / I Was A Fool (To Let You Go) / Somewhere Down The Road / Beautiful Music / I Made It Through The Rain / Break Down The Door / Who's Been Sleeping In My Bed / Sunday Father / Ships / If I Should Love Again / Copacabana (At The Copa) / Could It Be Magic? / Mandy / We'll meet Again / One Voice / I Write The Songs

Notes & Trivia:
- This video is footage of the concert given at The Royal Albert Hall on January 11 and 12, 1982.
- This program was released in the US on VHS tape by Pickwick / Stiletto Entertainment (Cat.# PGP-2137) in 1991.
- This concert was released on LP / CD / Cassette. Please see the "Live Albums" section.
- Program Length: 115 Minutes

VHS insert from the UK

Barry Manilow – Because It's Christmas

Songs:
The Christmas Song / Jingle Bells / White Christmas / Because Its Christmas / Its Just Another New Years Eve

Production Information:
Producer [Music]: Barry Manilow / Garry C. Kief
Backing Vocals: Sinoa Loren (tracks: 3)
Engineer: Don Murray
Executive Producer: Garry C. Kief
Producer: Joel Hinman
Director: Kathy Dougherty
Lighting Director: Patrick Melly

Notes & Trivia:
- This program was released in the US on VHS tape by Arista Records (Cat.# 15716-3) and in Japan on a single sided Laserdisc by BMG Video (Cat.# BVLP-82 / November 1, 1992).
- Material from this program appears on the 1991 Christmas album of the same name.
- Program content © 1991 Stiletto
- Program Length: 25 Minutes

Barry Manilow - The Greatest Hits...And Then Some

Set List:
The Best Of Me (Intro) / Ready To Take A Chance Again / Daybreak / Medley: The Old Songs - This One's For You - Tryin' To Get The Feeling / I Don't Want To Walk Without You / Medley: Send In The Clowns - Looks Like We Made It / Travelin' Medley: A Little Travelin' Music Please - New York City Rhythm - Avenue C - Jumpin' At The Woodside / Bandstand Boogie / Weekend In New England / Can't Smile Without You / Copacabana (At The Copa) / Stay / If Tomorrow Never Comes / Could It Be Magic / Medley: Mandy - Could It Be Magic / I Write The Songs / I'm Your Man / The Best Of Me

Production Information:
Produced by: Kim Tuberville
Directed by: Gavin Taylor
Front Cover Photography: Wendy Wright
Artist Management: Garry Kief / Stiletto Management

Notes & Trivia:
- This Concert was taped at Wembley Arena, London, on Saturday, 17 April 1993, during Barry Manilow's "Greatest Hits Tour."
- This program was released in the US on VHS tape by BMG Video (Cat. # 14766-3), on DVD (Cat.# BMG 14766DVD) and on Laserdisc (Cat.# 14766-6)
- Remastered in 5.1 Surround Sound
- Program Length: 95 minutes

Manilow Fund For Health & Hope

Program Content:
Please Don't Be Scared (Video)
A Personal Message from Barry Manilow
One Voice (Live)

Notes & Trivia:
- This program was a limited release promotional video released on VHS tape by Stiletto Entertainment to those who had a "Manilow Fund for Health and Hope" Visa Credit Card.
- Program Length: 20 minutes
- ©1998 Stiletto Entertainment

The back side of the VHS slip case

Barry Manilow – Close Up!
UK Tour '98

Set List:
I'd Really Love to See You Tonight / Reminiscing / I Wanna Do It With You / One Voice / Don't Get Around Much Anymore / As Time Goes By / No Other Love / If I Should Love Again / I'm Your Man / Sweet Heaven / Could It Be Magic? / Mandy / Bermuda Triangle / Even Now / I Write the Songs / It's A Miracle / You're There / We Live On Borrowed Time

Notes & Trivia:
- This video was complied from footage taken during the series of 13 concerts Barry gave in the UK in 1998. It takes you on stage with Barry in an intimately close and personal way.
- This program was released in the US by Stiletto Entertainment on DVD and VHS tape. In the UK it was released by Stiletto Entertainment on DVD and VHS (PAL) tape.

The back side of the VHS slip case

Barry Manilow – Live

Set List:

Could It Be Magic / Somewhere In The Night / Tryin' To Get The Feeling Again / Can't Smile Without You / Bandstand Boogie / Mandy / Even Now / Daybreak / Flight Of The Bumblebee / All The Time / New York City Rhythm / Every Single Day / I Am Your Child / This One's For You / My Kind Of Town (Chicago Is) / That's Life / When October Goes / Weekend In New England / Copacabana (At The Copa) / I Made It Through The Rain / One Voice / I Write The Songs / Stars In The Night / Could It Be Magic (reprise)

Production Information:

Produced by: Mark Angotti
Directed by: Lawrence Jordan
Written by: Mitzie and Ken Welch / Barry Manilow / Larry Amoros
Concert Produced by: Garry Kief / Barry Manilow
Executive Producers: Mark Angotti / Garry Kief / Tony Shepherd

Notes & Trivia:

- This concert was taped during Barry's two night concert engagement on February 15-16, 2000 at the Tennessee PAC in Nashville, TN.
- This video was made available on DirecTV.
- This program was released in the US by Image Entertainment on VHS tape (Cat.# ID9530SJ), on DVD (Cat.# ID9531SJDVD), on Hi-Def DVD (Cat.# ID3801SJHD) on Blu-ray (Cat.# ID5084SJBD). In Europe it was released on Blu-ray (Cat.# 88697418609). In the Netherlands it was released on DVD (PAL) (Cat.# IX9531SJBXD). In Mexico it was released on DVD (Cat.# DVDA-7305). In Hong Kong it was released on Blu-ray (Cat.# EVOB072).
- Special Features Include: Audio Commentary by Barry Manilow / Barry Manilow Biography / Barry Manilow Discography. It also includes approximately 30 minutes of extra footage, not part of the DirecTV broadcast; DVD includes an additional audio track of Barry's comments on the program, the songs, and the concerts.
- Video Copyright © Stiletto Entertainment, Inc.
- Original Video Release Date: August 29, 2000.

Big Fun on Swing Street

Songs on tape:
Brooklyn Blues / Swing Street / Big Fun / Right This Way / Copacabana / If You Want To Be Happy For The Rest Of Your Life / Hey Mambo / Stardust / Not Another Night Of This / Summertime / It Don't Mean A Thing / When October Goes / Black & Blue / Paradise Café / Evie / Blue / Dancin' Fool / Stompin' At The Savoy / One More Time

Production Info:
Directed by: Steve Binder
Producers: Steve Binder / Jack Feldman / Barry Manilow / Bruce Sussman
Executive producer Garry C. Kief
Co-producer: Howard G. Malley
Written by: Jack Feldman / Barry Manilow / Bruce Sussman
Production Designer: Charles Lisanby
Editor: William Flicker
Make-Up: Brian McManus
Art Department: Chris Tashima

Notes & Trivia:
- This special was originally aired on CBS-TV on March 7, 1988.
- Includes Exclusive Music Video of Hey Mambo!
- Released on VHS tape by Stiletto Entertainment in 2000. Later released as part of the 5 DVD set: *Barry Manilow The First Television Specials* (Cat.# R2-334908) by Rhino / Stiletto New Media in 2007.

Ultimate Manilow

Set List:
Disc 1: Broadcast Version (As Originally Aired):
The Gonzo Opening / Weekend In New England / Even Now / Turn The Radio Up / They Dance! / Looks Like We Made It / Mandy / Can't Smile Without You / Copacabana (At The Copa) / I Write The Song / End Credits
Disc 2: Extended Uncut Version (As Recorded)
Producer's Warm Up / The Gonzo Opening / Weekend In New England (Take One) / Even Now / Turn The Radio Up / Weekend In New England (Take Two) / They Dance! / Looks Like We Made It (Take One) / Looks Like We Made It (Take Two) / Somewhere Down The Road / Mandy / Can't Smile Without You / Copacabana (At The Copa) / I Write The Song

Production Information:
Produced by Ken Ehrlich
Directed by Bruce Gowers
Written by Barry Manilow and Mitzie & Ken Welch
Concert Produced by Garry Kief, Barry Manilow
Executive Producers: Garry Kief, Rob Kief

Notes & Trivia:
- Taped Wednesday, April 24, 2002, at the Kodak Theatre in Hollywood, California.
- This program aired on CBS-TV on Saturday, May 18, 2002.
- This program was released in the US on DVD by BMG/Stiletto Entertainment (Cat.# 75517 483349) in November 2003 (for the BMIFC) and on April 6, 2004 (Commercial release).
- This set contains both the edited CBS-TV broadcast version and the un-edited version with never-before-seen footage. The set includes exclusive photos from the taping, commentary from Barry, bloopers and outtakes, show rundowns, song lyrics and more.
- Ultimate Features: Audio Commentary by Barry Manilow; Biography; Discography; Photo Gallery; Concert Rundowns; Song Lyrics.

Clay Aiken – A Clay Aiken Christmas

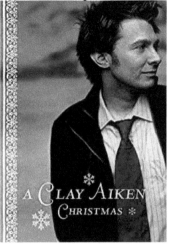

<u>Set List:</u>
Clay Aiken: Have Yourself A Merry Little Christmas / Barry Manilow: Happy Holidays / White Christmas / Clay Aiken: Christmas Waltz / Yolanda Adams: O, Holy Night / Clay Aiken: Merry Christmas With Love / Clay Aiken - Barry Manilow - Yolanda Adams: Santa Claus Is Coming To Town / Clay Aiken - Quiana Parler: Silver Bells / Clay Aiken: Mary, Did You Know / Clay Aiken - Barry Manilow - Yolanda Adams: Because It's Christmas (For All The Children)

<u>Production Information:</u>
Executive Producers: Clay Aiken / Richard Frank / Louis J. Horvitz
Associate Producer: Nick Leisey
Directed by: Louis J. Horvitz
Assistant Director: Deborah Read
Assistant to Director: Joanie Michele
Music by: Glen Roven
Production Design by: Dean Tschetter
Art Direction by: Marcia Hinda
Effects Costume / Hair Stylist / Makeup Artist: John Dahlstrom   ...
Key Makeup Artist: Robyn Fisher
Set Dressers: Kami Laprade / Jared MacLane
Art Coordinator: Michele Starbuck
Camera Operator: Kris Wilson
Assistant Editor: Ben Folts
Composer - Additional Music: Ray Colcord
Production Assistant: James Cheeks III / Andrea Rennard
Production Coordinator: Aaron B. Cooke
Audio Mixer: Ed Greene
Taped at CenterStaging, Burbank, CA

<u>Notes & Trivia:</u>
- This special was originally aired on NBC-TV on December 8, 2004
- This program was released in the US on DVD by RCA / 19 Recordings / S Records (Cat.# 82876 66261-9) on December 14, 2004
- Includes: Behind-The-Scenes Footage Special Feature

Manilow: Music & Passion

Set List:

Disc 1:

Opening It's A Miracle / Opening Medley: Daybreak - Somewhere In The Night - This One's For You / Mandy/Could It Be Magic? / I Made It Through The Rain / Here's To Las Vegas (Intro) / See The Show Again / Can't Smile Without You / Fifties Medley: Bandstand Boogie / Venus / Love Is A Many Splendored Thing / Unchained Melody / Mayflower Medley: Brooklyn Blues - Do You Know Who's Livin' Next Door? - Come Monday / They Dance! - Boogie Wonderland - Hot Stuff - Signed, Sealed, Delivered, I'm Yours - Brooklyn Blues (Reprise) / Weekend In New England / If I Can Dream / Somewhere Down The Road / Here's To Las Vegas / I Write The Songs / Copacabana (At The Copa) / It's A Miracle (Reprise)

Encore: One Voice

Disc 2:

"Inside Manilow: Music & Passion" A documentary-style, behind-the-scenes look at the rehearsals, the build out of the stage, the costume design and the lighting and choreography for Barry's Las Vegas show. Barry shares his feelings about his music and his passion in an exclusive interview. "Making the PBS Special" -- This video diary puts you at the Las Vegas Hilton during the television shoot on December 12, 2005, and features Barry's narration of what goes into making a television special. It also has the bonus song, "The Best Seat In The House," as well as never-before-seen bloopers and outtakes.

Tryin' To Get The Feeling Again

Even Now - Performed on December 17, 2005

Unchained Melody - Music Video

Photo Gallery

Production Information:

Produced by: Paul Morphos / Dione Orrom / Rob Kief

Executive Producers: Garry C. Kief / Mark C. Grove / Troy P. Queen

Directed by: David Mallet

Written by: Barry Manilow / Mitzie & Ken Welch

Notes & Trivia:

- This concert was taped December 12, 2005 at the Hilton in Las Vegas, Nevada
- This concert aired on PBS on March 9, 2006
- This two disc program was released in the US on DVD by Rhino/WEA (Cat.#R2 971624) on March 28, 2006.

Barry Manilow – First and Farewell

Set List:
Disc 1:
The First Rehearsal at Carroll's Studio, New York City, November 1974 / Introduction / It's A Miracle / Cloudburst / One Of These Days / Oh My Lady / The Shadow of Your Smile - Hello Dolly / Commercials Medley: Dr. Pepper - State Farm Insurance - Stri-Dex - Vitalis - Franco American - Bowlene - Schaefer Beer - Pepsi - McDonald's / Seven More Years / Could It Be Magic? / Easy Evil (The Harlettes) / Armed and Extremely Dangerous (The Harlettes) / Sweet Life / Make Our Garden Grow / Let's Take Some Time To Say Goodbye / Sweet Life (Reprise)

Disc 2:
One Night Live! One Last Time! / The Farewell Tour / Anaheim, CA, November 2004 / Act 1: It's A Miracle / Opening Medley: Daybreak - Somewhere In The Night - This One's For You / Why Don't We Live Together / Mandy / Even Now / They Dance! / Somewhere Down The Road / Brooklyn Blues (with Dave Koz and George Shelby) / Could It Be Magic? / Act 2: Can't Simile Without You / Jump, Shout, Boogie / I Made It Through The Rain / Weekend In New England / River / Dancin' Fool / Copacabana (At The Copa) / I Write The Songs / Closing Medley: Why Don't We Live Together - One Voice - My Country 'Tis Of Thee - Dancin' In The Aisles - Dancin' In The Street / It's A Miracle (Reprise)
Bonus Features / Disc 2:
One Night Live! - Las Vegas - June 5, 2004
Harmony (with the Cast of Harmony)
Every Single Day (with Brian d'Arcy James)
One Night Live! One Last Time! - Chicago - October 21, 2004
Chicago (My Kind Of Town)

Production Information:
Executive Producers: Garry C. Kief / Mark C. Grove / Troy P. Queen
Produced by: Rob Kief
Audio Mix and Mastering: Tom Davis
Editors: Dinh Long Thai / Jim Yukich
Art Director - Photography: Sara Zickuhr
DVD Design: Rupesh Pattni
DVD Authoring: Ignacio Monge

Notes & Trivia:
- This two disc program was released in the US on DVD by Stiletto-New Media / Rhino (Cat.#R2 R2 971488) on October 31, 2006.

Barry Manilow – The First Television Specials

Disc One:
The First Barry Manilow Special / March 2, 1977
It's a Miracle / This One's for You / Could It Be Magic? / Mandy / Jump, Shout Boogie Medley / Bandstand Boogie (with Penny Marshall) / A Very Strange Medley / New York City Rhythm / Sandra / Early Morning Strangers / I Write the Songs. 50 minutes.

Disc Two:
The Second Barry Manilow Special / February 24,1978
Beautiful Music / Daybreak / I Was A Fool (To Let You Go) / Copacabana (At The Copa) / One Of These Days (Ray Charles) / It's A Miracle (with Ray Charles) / Tryin' To Get The Feeling Again / All The Time / Can't Smile Without You / Looks Like We Made It. 50 minutes.

Disc Three:
The Third Barry Manilow Special / May 23, 1979
Ready To Take A Chance Again / Weekend In New England / (Why Don't We Try) A Slow Dance / I Write The Songs / What's On Your Mind (John Denver) / Everly Brothers Medley (with John Denver) / Copacabana (At The Copa) / Even Now / Somewhere In The Night. 50 minutes.

Disc Four:
One Voice / May 19, 1980
You Could Show Me / Who's Been Sleeping In My Bed / Rain / When I Wanted You / I Don't Wanna Walk Without You / We'll Meet Again / After You (Dionne Warwick) / Deja Vu (with Dionne Warwick) / I'll Never Love This Way Again (with Dionne Warwick) / Sunday Father / Ships / One Voice. 50 minutes.

Disc Five:
Barry Manilow: Big Fun on Swing Street / March 7, 1988
Swing Street / Big Fun / Right This Way / Hey Mambo (with Kid Creole and The Coconuts) / Stardust / Not Another Night Of This (Phyllis Hyman) / It Don't Mean A Thing (If It Ain't Got That Swing) (with Diane Schuur) / When October Goes / Black & Blue (with Phyllis Hyman) / Paradise Café / Evie / Blue (with Carmen McRae) / Dancin' Fool / Stompin' At The Savoy / One More Time. 50 Minutes.

Notes & Trivia:
- This five disc program was released in the US on DVD by Stiletto-New Media / Rhino (Cat.# R2 334908) on November 6, 2007.

Barry Manilow – Happy Holiday!
Special Guests: Cyndi Lauper and Jose Feliciano

Set List:
Happy Holiday/White Christmas / My Favorite Things / Jingle Bells / The Christmas Waltz / Have Yourself A Merry Little Christmas / Feliz Navidad (Jose Feliciano) / Rudolph The Red-Nosed Reindeer (with Jose Feliciano) / I've Got My Love To Keep Me Warm / At Last (Cyndi Lauper) / Santa Claus Is Coming To Town (with Cyndi Lauper) / Copacabana (At The Copa) / (There's No Place Like) Home For The Holidays / I'll Be Home For Christmas/It's Just Another New Year's Eve / Christmas Medley: Deck The Halls / Jingle Bell Rock / The Christmas Song (Chestnuts Roasting On An Open Fire) / Because It's Christmas (For All The Children)

Production Information:
Executive Producers: Garry C. Kief, Mark C. Grove, Troy P. Queen
Producer: Rob Kief
Music Director: Steve Welch
Art Direction: Sara Zickuhr
For A&E Live by Request: Executive Producers: Danny Bennett, Paul Rappaport, Andy Kadison; Producer: Jodi Hurwitz; Directed by Lawrence Jordan

Musicians:
Piano: Steve Welch
Keyboards: Ron Pedley
Bass: Larry Antonino
Guitar: Mike Lent
Drums: Russ McKinnon
Percussion: Bashiri Johnson / David Rozenblatt
Background Vocals: Debra Byrd / Cindy Mizelle / Monica Page

Notes & Trivia:
- Barry took phone in requests during this live A&E special broadcast from New York City on a cold, snowy night on December 5, 2003. This show is still one of the highest rated "A&E Live By Request" broadcasts ever.
- This program was released in the US on DVD by Stiletto-New Media / Rhino (Cat.# R2 327164) / OPDV-8217 in November 2007. Released in Germany in 2008.

Barry Manilow – Songs from The Seventies

Set List:
Disc 1:
Mandy / New York City Rhythm / I Am Your Child / The Commercials (Again!): a. Band-Aids - b. State Farm Insurance - c. McDonald's - d. Vicks / Could It Be Magic? / Copacabana (At The Copa) / My Eyes Adored You / Looks Like We Made It / He Ain't Heavy, He's My Brother / The Way We Were / It Never Rains In Southern California / The Old Songs (Intro) / Seventies Hits Medley: a. Can't Smile Without You - b. Even Now - c. It's A Miracle - d. I Made It Through The Rain - e. Daybreak - f. This One's For You - g. I Write The Songs / One Voice

Disc 2: Extra Special Outtakes:
Who's Been Sleeping In My Bed? / The Way We Were Medley: a. The Way We Were - b. It Never Rains In Southern California - c. You've Got A Friend - d. The Way We Were / All The Time

Production Information:
Executive Producers: Garry C. Kief / Mark C. Grove / Troy P. Queen
Directed by: David Mallet
Written by: Barry Manilow
Produced by: Barry Manilow / Paul Morphos / Rob Kief

Notes & Trivia:
- This two disc set was released in the US on DVD by Rhino/Stiletto Television (Cat.#R2 415292) on January 29, 2008.
- Features Dolby Digital 5.1 Surround Sound & PCM Stereo for pure immersion of Manilow music!
- This special was taped at the old Navy Yard in Brooklyn, New York, near Williamsburg where Barry grew up, in September 2007. Disc 2 features behind the scenes footage and more.

The Yule Log
Featuring the Classic Holiday Album:
Barry Manilow - A Christmas Gift Of Love

Track Listing:
Winter Wonderland / Happy Holiday - White Christmas / Santa Claus Is Coming To Town / (There's No Place Like) Home For The Holidays / I'll Be Home For Christmas / My Favorite Things / The Christmas Waltz / I've Got My Love To Keep Me Warm / River / What Are You Doing New Year's Eve? / A Gift Of Love

Notes & Trivia:
- This disc was released October 19, 2010
- Nothing better than a warm fire and Barry Manilow's 2002 Christmas album: "A Christmas Gift Of Love," with three scenes to choose from: Yule Log / Snowy Cabin / Cozy Christmas Cottage
- Barry does not appear on this DVD. This DVD has Christmas scenes set to Barry's album.

A MusiCares Tribute to Barbra Streisand

Set List:
Diana Krall: Down With Love / Seal: Guilty / Leona Lewis: Somewhere / Herbie Hancock - Nikki Yanofsky: On A Clear Day (You Can See Forever) - Lazy Afternoon / Lea Michele: My Man / Jeff Beck - LeAnn Rimes - BeBe Winans: Come Rain Or Come Shine / Faith Hill: Send In The Clowns / Kristin Chenoweth - Matthew Morrison: One Less Bell To Answer - A House Is Not A Home / Barry Manilow: Memory / Tony Bennett: Smile / Stevie Wonder Featuring Arturo Sandoval: People / Barbra Streisand: Windmills Of Your Mind / Barbra Streisand: The Promise (I'll Never Say Goodbye)

Notes & Trivia:
- Taped on February 11, 2011 at a gala event in Los Angeles.
- This program was released in the US on DVD and Blu-ray on November 13, 2012.
- Released in Brazil in 2013.
- Copyright ©MusiCares Foundation
- Program Length: 65 minutes

Sheet Music
&
Songbooks

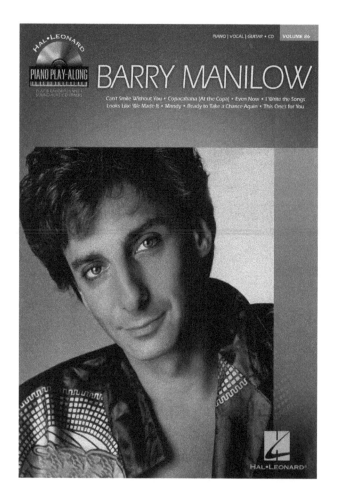

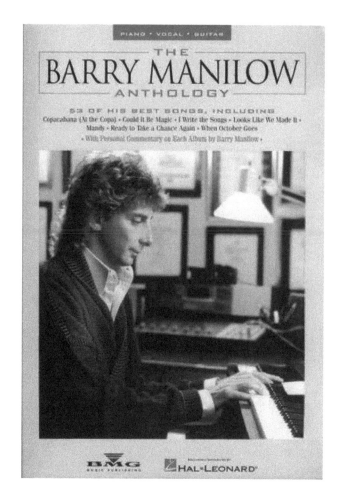

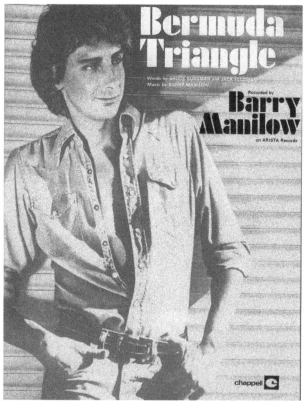

Daybreak

Lyrics by ADRIENNE ANDERSON Music by BARRY MANILOW
Recorded by BARRY MANILOW on ARISTA Records

$2.95

KAMAKAZI MUSIC CORP. and ANGELA MUSIC CO.
New York, New York

Distributed by
big3

SIMPLIFIED PIANO

EVEN NOW

BIG NOTES • WORDS • CHORDS

Arranged by
JOHN LANE

big3
KAMAKAZI MUSIC CORP.

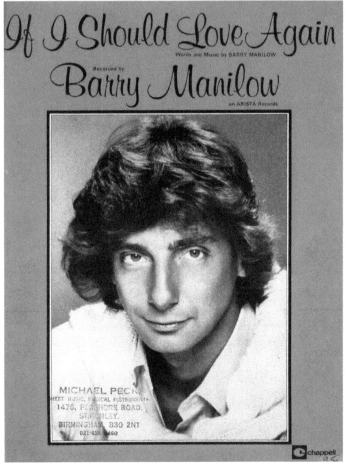

If I Should Love Again

Words and Music by BARRY MANILOW

Recorded by

Barry Manilow

on ARISTA Records

MICHAEL PECK
SHEET MUSIC, MUSICAL INSTRUMENTS
1476, PERSHORE ROAD,
STIRCHLEY,
BIRMINGHAM, B30 2NT
021-458 0460

chappell

307

I Don't Want To Walk Without You

Words by FRANK LOESSER Music by JULE STYNE

Recorded by Barry Manilow on ARISTA Records

FAMOUS CHAPPELL

 chappell 60/70 Roden Street Ilford Essex

Recorded by **BARRY MANILOW**
on Arista Records

PIANO/VOCAL EDITION

I MADE IT THROUGH THE RAIN

Music by GERARD KENNY • Lyrics by DREY SHEPPERD,
BARRY MANILOW, JACK FELDMAN and BRUCE SUSSMAN

COPACABANA

AT THE COPA

Words by BRUCE SUSSMAN and JACK FELDMAN Music by BARRY MANILOW

Recorded by

BARRY MANILOW

on ARISTA Records

 chappell 60/70 Roden Street Ilford Essex

Music by Barry Manilow
and Howie Rice
Lyric by Allan Rich

As recorded by *Barry Manilow* on RCA/Ariola
International Records and Tapes

BARRY ⌐ MANILOW

I WANNA DO IT WITH YOU

Words & Music by LAYNG MARTINE JNR

Recorded by BARRY MANILOW on ARISTA RECORDS

CHAPPELL MUSIC LTD

DISTRIBUTED BY IMP

SHIPS

Words and Music by IAN HUNTER

RECORDED BY

BARRY MANILOW

ON **ARISTA** RECORDS

APRIL MUSIC LTD./MUSIC SALES LTD.

78 Newman Street • London W.1.

60p

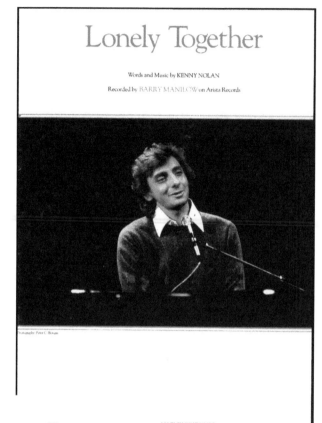

Weekend In New England

Words and Music by RANDY EDELMAN
Recorded by BARRY MANILOW on ARISTA Records

(Why Don't We Try)
A Slow Dance

Lyrics by BRUCE SUSSMAN and JACK FELDMAN   Music by BARRY MANILOW

Recorded by BARRY MANILOW on ARISTA Records

KAMAKAZI MUSIC CORP., APPOGGIATURA MUSIC, and CAMP SONGS MUSIC
New York, New York

95

Recorded by

Words by MARTY PANZER Music by BARRY MANILOW

BARRY MANILOW

on ARISTA Records

chappell 60/70 Roden Street Ilford Essex

Read 'Em and Weep
Barry Manilow

Words and Music by
JIM STEINMAN
Recorded on Arista Records

© 1983 HTC, Inc.

$2.5
in U.S.

Ships

As Recorded by
BARRY MANILOW
on Arista Records

Words and Music by IAN HUNTER

When I Wanted You

Words and Music by
Gino Cunico

As Recorded
and Arranged by Barry Manilow
on Arista Records

Exclusive Distributor:
BRADLEY PUBLICATIONS
a division of R&R Communications, Inc.
43 West 61 Street
New York, N.Y. 10023

$1.95
in U.S.A.

april-blackwood
publications

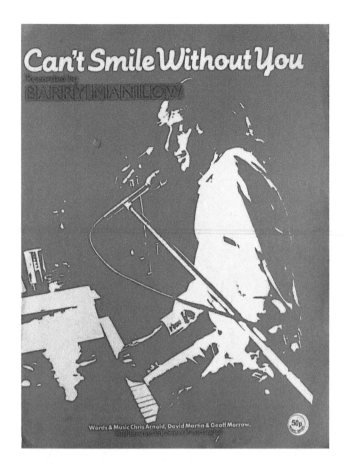

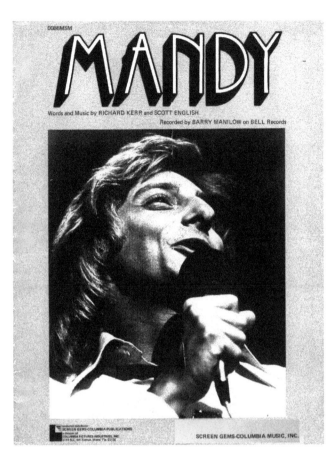

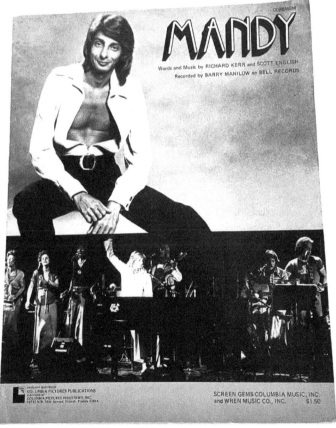

Magazine Covers

**In his career Barry has appeared on hundreds of magazine covers....
here are just a few!**

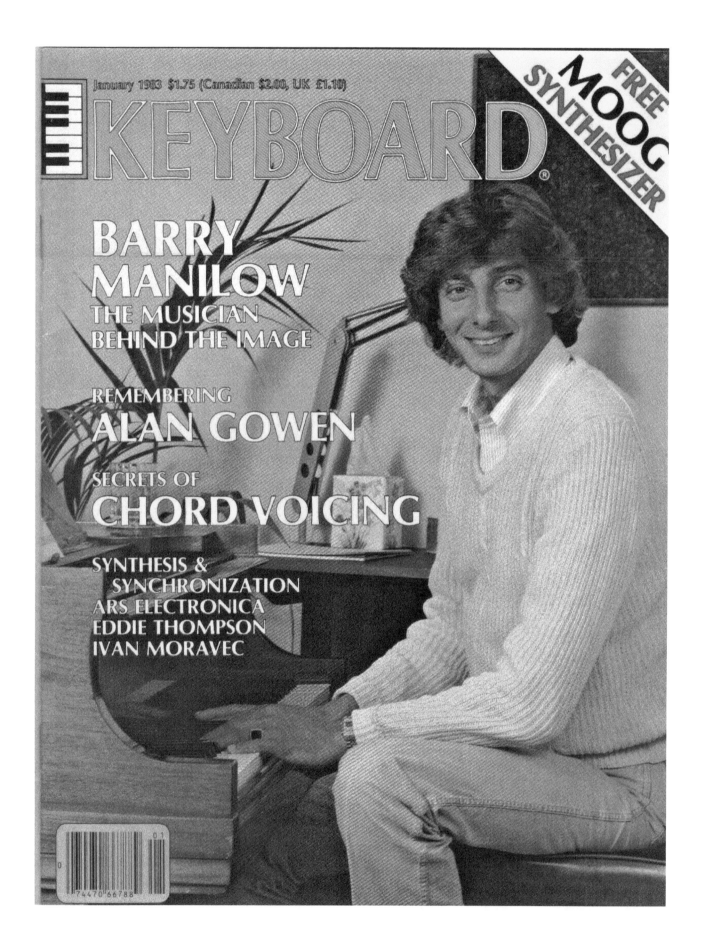

January 1983 $1.75 (Canadian $2.00, UK £1.10)

KEYBOARD.

BARRY MANILOW
THE MUSICIAN BEHIND THE IMAGE

REMEMBERING
ALAN GOWEN

SECRETS OF
CHORD VOICING

SYNTHESIS &
  SYNCHRONIZATION
ARS ELECTRONICA
EDDIE THOMPSON
IVAN MORAVEC

0   74470 66788   01

THE NATIONAL MAGAZINE OF ENTERTAINMENT JUNE 1976

AFTER DARK

COLLEEN
DEWHURST

TENNESSEE
WILLIAMS

"STAY
HUNGRY"
AND
JEFF
BRIDGES

BARRY
MANILOW

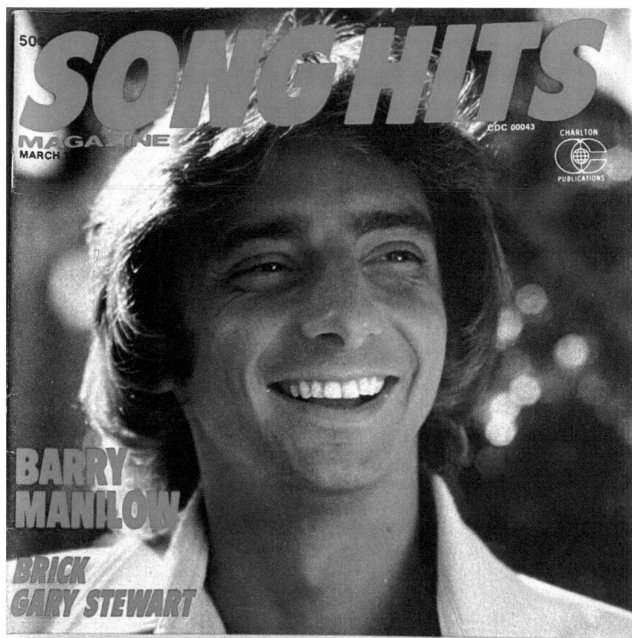

50¢

SONG HITS

MAGAZINE

MARCH

CDC 00043

CHARLTON PUBLICATIONS

BARRY MANILOW

BRICK
GARY STEWART

WORDS TO OVER 60 HIT SONGS

POP

WE ARE THE CHAMPIONS ● POINT OF KNOW RETURN ● GILRS' SCHOOL/MULL OF KINTYRE ● YOU'RE IN MY HEART (The Final Acclaim) ● MY WAY ● SLIP SLIDIN' AWAY ● TURN TO STONE ● (Love Is) THICKER THAN WATER

SOUL

AS ● LOVELY DAY ● RUNNIN' FOR YOUR LOVIN' ● GETTIN' READY FOR LOVE ● BELLE ● SORRY DOESN'T ALWAYS MAKE IT RIGHT ● GALAXY ● OOH BOY

COUNTRY

SAVIN' THIS LOVE SONG ● ABILENE ● QUITS ● ONE OF A KIND ● EVERY DAY I HAVE TO CRY ● HERE YOU COME AGAIN ● DON'T LET ME TOUCH YOU ● SHE JUST LOVED THE CHEATIN' OUT OF ME

The Philadelphia Inquirer

TV WEEK

Barry Manilow
Terrific at the Top
See Page 4

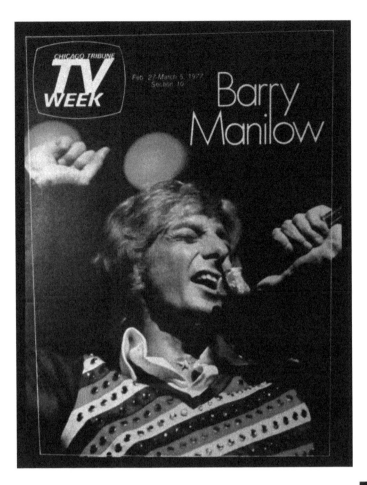

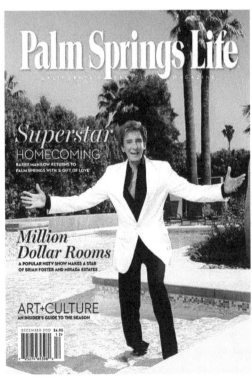

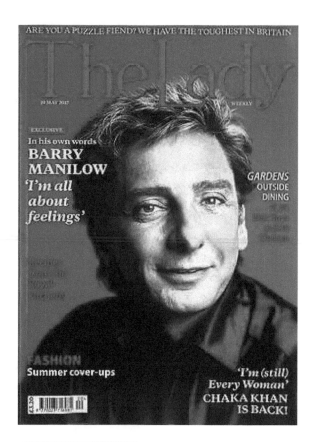

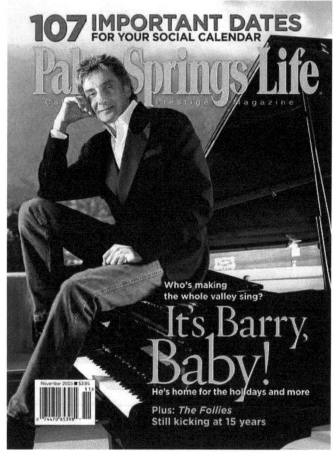

336

1970's
Tour
Dates

Barry brought a lot of people happiness starting with his 1970's tours
and many I have spoken with hold on to that happiness to this day!
He continues to bring people pure joy to this day in 2022!
Not every tour date may be represented here, such as private shows.

Barry Manilow Concert Tours 1971-1979

1971

September 4-5, 1971 Continental Baths, New York City, NY (Music director for Bette Midler)
September 7-11, 1971 The Duplex, New York City, NY (Music director for Bette Midler)
September 20-October 16, 1971 Downstairs At The Upstairs, New York City, NY (Music director for Bette Midler)
November 26-27, 1971 Continental Baths, New York City, NY (Music director for Bette Midler)
December 3-4, 1971 Continental Baths, New York City, NY (Music director for Bette Midler)
December 13-31, 1971 Downstairs At The Upstairs, New York City, NY (Music director for Bette Midler)

1972

January 1-8, 1972 Downstairs At The Upstairs, New York City, NY (Music director for Bette Midler)
January 14-15, 1972 Continental Baths, New York City, NY (Music director for Bette Midler)
January 21-22, 1972 Continental Baths, New York City, NY (Music director for Bette Midler)
February 4-5, 1972 Continental Baths, New York City, NY (Music director for Bette Midler)
February 17-26, 1972 The Frog And Nightgown, Raleigh, NC (3 shows on the 17th & 22nd, music director for Bette Midler)
April 21-28, 1972 Sahara Hotel's Congo Room, Las Vegas, NV (Music director for Bette Midler)
May 1, 1972 Boldly Blue Paradise Ballroom, Los Angeles, CA (Music director for Bette Midler)
May 10-15, 1972 Bitter End, New York City, NY (3 shows each night, music director for Bette Midler)
June 12-18, 1972 Mister Kelly's, Chicago, IL (Music director for Bette Midler)
June 23, 1972 Carnegie Hall, New York City, NY (Music director for Bette Midler)
June 26-July 2, 1972 Lennie's On The Turnpike, Peabody, MA (Music director for Bette Midler)
July 25-30, 1972 Bergen Mall Playhouse, Paramus, NJ (Music director for Bette Midler)
August 16, 1972 Central Park, New York City, NY (Schaefer Music Festival, music director for Bette Midler)
September 18-October 1, 1972 Mister Kelly's, Chicago, IL (Music director for Bette Midler)
October 27, 1972 Symphony Hall, Boston, MA (Music director for Bette Midler)
October 28, 1972 Continental Baths, New York City, NY (Music director for Bette Midler)
November 28-December 3, 1972 Boarding House, San Francisco, CA (Music director for Bette Midler)
December 5-10, 1972 Troubadour, Los Angeles, CA (Music director for Bette Midler)
December 13-16, 1972 Bijou Cafe, Philadelphia, PA (2 shows 13th & 14th 8.00 & 10.30, 15th 9.00 & 11.30, 3 shows 16th 8.30, 10.30 & 12.30, music director for Bette Midler)
December 31, 1972 Philharmonic Hall, New York City, NY (2 shows 8.00 & 11.00, music director for Bette Midler)

1973

January 19, 1973 Rochester War Memorial, Rochester, NY (Music director for Bette Midler)
January 20, 1973 Music Hall, Cleveland, OH (Music director for Bette Midler)
January 21, 1973 Masonic Auditorium, Detroit, MI (Music director for Bette Midler)
February 15, 1973 Uihlein Hall, Milwaukee, WI (Music director for Bette Midler)
February 16-17, 1973 Auditorium Theatre, Chicago, IL (Music director for Bette Midler)
February 19, 1973 Alexander Hall, Princeton, NJ (Music director for Bette Midler)
February 23, 1973 RPI Field House, Troy, NY (Music director for Bette Midler)
February 24, 1973 Music Hall, Boston, MA (Music director for Bette Midler)
February 25, 1973 Kleinhans Music Hall, Buffalo, NY (Music director for Bette Midler)
February 26, 1973 Massey Hall, Toronto, ON (Music director for Bette Midler)

March 1-4, 1973 Frog And Nightgown, Raleigh, NC (2 shows each night, music director for Bette Midler)
March 9, 1973 Syria Mosque, Pittsburgh, PA (Music director for Bette Midler)
March 10, 1973 Capitol Theatre, Passaic, NJ (Music director for Bette Midler)
March 11, 1973 Kennedy Center Concert Hall, Washington, DC (Music director for Bette Midler)
March 17, 1973 Dorothy Chandler Pavilion, Los Angeles, CA (Music director for Bette Midler)
March 18, 1973 Berkeley Community Theatre, Berkeley, CA (Music director for Bette Midler, 2 shows 7.00 & 10.00)
March 22, 1973 Music Hall, Houston, TX (Music director for Bette Midler)
March 23, 1973 Music Hall, Dallas, TX (Music director for Bette Midler)
March 24, 1973 Armadillo World Headquarters, Austin, TX (Music director for Bette Midler)
March 25, 1973 Civic Center Music Hall, Oklahoma City, OK (Music director for Bette Midler)
March 28, 1973 Municipal Theater, Tulsa, OK (Music director for Bette Midler)
March 30, 1973 Municipal Auditorium, Kansas City, MO (Music director for Bette Midler)
March 31, 1973 Hill Auditorium, Ann Arbor, MI (Music director for Bette Midler)
April 7, 1973 Horace Bushness Memorial Hall, Hartford, CT (Music director for Bette Midler)
April 8, 1973 Palace Theatre, Providence, RI (Music director for Bette Midler)
April 11, 1973 Loew's State Theatre, Syracuse, NY (Music director for Bette Midler)
April 13, 1973 Chrysler Hall, Norfolk, VA (Music director for Bette Midler)
April 14, 1973 Veterans Memorial Theatre, Columbus, OH (Music director for Bette Midler)
April 15, 1973 Academy Of Music, Philadelphia, PA (Music director for Bette Midler)
June 1-2, 1973 Continental Baths, New York City, NY
August 24, 1973 Merriweather Post Pavilion, Columbia, MD (Music director for Bette Midler)
August 28, 1973 Edwardsville, IL (Mississippi River Festival, as music director for Bette Midler)
August 30, 1973 Blossom Music Center, Cuyahoga Falls, OH (Music director for Bette Midler)
September 1, 1973 Red Rocks Amphitheatre, Denver, CO (Music director for Bette Midler)
September 6-7, 1973 Honolulu International Center, Honolulu, HI (Music director for Bette Midler)
September 10-16, 1973 Universal Amphitheatre, Los Angeles, CA (Music director for Bette Midler)
September 19, 1973 Sports Arena Amphitheatre, San Diego, CA (Music director for Bette Midler)
September 21, 1973 Hill Auditorium, Portland, OR (Music director for Bette Midler)
September 22, 1973 Queen Elizabeth Theatre, Vancouver, BC (Music director for Bette Midler)
September 23, 1973 Opera House, Seattle, WA (Music director for Bette Midler)
September 27-30, 1973 Berkeley Community Theatre, Berkeley, CA (Music director for Bette Midler)
October 3, 1973 Civic Plaza, Phoenix, AZ (Music director for Bette Midler)
October 4, 1973 Popejoy Hall, Albuquerque, NM (Music director for Bette Midler)
October 7, 1973 Hofheinz Pavillion, Houston, TX (Music director for Bette Midler)
October 8, 1973 Municipal Auditorium, New Orleans, LA]] (Music director for Bette Midler)
October 12-14, 1973 Auditorium Theater, Chicago, IL (Music director for Bette Midler)
October 16, 1973 Dane County Coliseum, Madison, WI (Music director for Bette Midler)
October 18-20, 1973 Masonic Temple, Detroit, MI (Music director for Bette Midler)
October 21, 1973 Kiel Opera House, St. Louis, MO (Music director for Bette Midler)
October 24, 1973 Civic Center Auditorium, Atlanta, GA (Music director for Bette Midler)
October 25, 1973 Civic Auditorium, Jacksonville, FL (Music director for Bette Midler)
October 26, 1973 Miami Beach Auditorium, Miami, FL (Music director for Bette Midler)
October 31, 1973 Curtis Hixton Hall, Tampa, FL (Music director for Bette Midler)
November 1, 1973 War Memorial, Nashville, TN (Music director for Bette Midler)
November 2, 1973 Stokely Athletic Center, Knoxville, TN (Music director for Bette Midler)
November 3, 1973 Ellis Auditorium, Memphis, TN (Music director for Bette Midler)
November 4, 1973 Music Hall, Cincinnati, OH (Music director for Bette Midler)
November 9, 1973 Ithaca College, Ithaca, NY (Music director for Bette Midler)
November 11, 1973 Syria Mosque, Pittsburgh, PA (Music director for Bette Midler)

November 14-15, 1973 Music Hall, Boston, MA (Music director for Bette Midler)
November 16, 1973 Brown University Meehan Auditorium, Providence, RI (Music director for Bette Midler)
November 17, 1973 Veterans Memorial Coliseum, New Haven, CT (Music director for Bette Midler)
November 25-26 & 28, 1973 Academy of Music, Philadelphia, PA (Music director for Bette Midler)
December 3-23, 1973 Palace Theatre, New York City, NY (Music director for Bette Midler.) The 23rd was a special performance for the Actors Fund of America

1974

March 4-10, 1974 Paul's Mall, Boston, MA (supporting Freddie Hubbard)
March 11-16, 1974 Bijou Cafe, Philadelphia, PA
March 18-24, 1974 Mister Kelly's, Chicago, IL
April 9-13, 1974 Lafayette's Music Room, Memphis, TN
April 16-21, 1974 Great Southeast Music Hall And Emporium, Atlanta, GA (with Country Joe and The Fish, Melissa Manchester & The Entire Firesign Theater)
April 22-27, 1974 Cellar Door, Washington, DC
May 7-12, 1974 Bottom Line, New York City, NY (supported by Barnaby Bye)
June 26, 1974 Central Park Wollman Rink, New York City, NY (Schaefer Music Festival, supporting Dionne Warwick, War & Jane Olivor)
October 21-26, 1974 Bijou Cafe, Philadelphia, PA (2 shows each night, supported by Andy Kaufmann)
October 28-November 3, 1974 Paul's Mall, Boston, MA November 5-9, 1974 Exit/In, Nashville, TN
November 13-16, 1974 Lafayette's Music Room, Memphis, TN
November 21, 1974 Carnegie Hall, New York City, NY
December 17-22, 1974 Cellar Door, Washington, DC
December 26-31, 1974 Bottom Line, New York City, NY

1975

January 12, 1975 Academy of Music, Philadelphia, PA
January 18, 1975 Kleinhans Symphony Hall, Buffalo, NY
January 19, 1975 Ford Auditorium, Detroit, MI
January 20-February 1, 1975 Mister Kelly's, Chicago, IL
February 11-16, 1975 Boarding House, San Francisco, CA
February 25-March 2, 1975 Troubadour, Los Angeles, CA
March 7, 1975 Convention Center, Fresno, CA March 11-16, 1975 Ebbets Field, Denver, CO
March 20, 1975 Music Hall, Oklahoma City, OK March 21, 1975 Music Hall, Houston, TX
March 22, 1975 Coliseum, Jackson, MS
March 23, 1975 Ellis Auditorium, Memphis, TN
April 6, 1975 War Memorial Auditorium, Nashville, TN
April 8, 1975 University of Tennessee, Martin, TN
April 9, 1975 University of Mississippi, Oxford, MS
April 10, 1975 Mississippi State University, Starkville, MS
April 11, 1975 Arkansas State University, Jonesboro, AR
April 13, 1975 Veterans Memorial Auditorium, Columbus, OH
April 14, 1975 Electric Lady Studios, New York City, NY
April 19-20, 1975 Westbury Music Fair, Westbury, NY
April 24, 1975 Music Hall, Cincinnati, OH
April 25, 1975 Bethany College, Bethany, WV
April 27, 1975 Masonic Auditorium, Toledo, OH
April 28, 1975 Clam Shop, Detroit, MI

May 1, 1975 Freedom Hall, Louisville, KY (101st Kentucky Derby Concert)
May 2, 1975 Robinson Auditorium, Little Rock, AR
May 3, 1975 Lambuth University Gym, Jackson, TN
May 4, 1975 Six Flags Over Mid-America, Eureka, MO
May 9, 1975 Constitution Hall, Washington, DC
May 18, 1975 Masonic Auditorium, Scranton, PA
May 23, 1975 Brooklyn College Gershwin Theater, Brooklyn, NY
May 30, 1975 U.S. Naval Academy, Annapolis, MD
May 31, 1975 Gusman Hall, Miami, FL
July 28-30, 1975 Soundstage, Chicago, IL
July 31, 1975 Highland Park, IL (Ravinia Festival)
August 1, 1975 Masonic Auditorium, Detroit, MI
August 3, 1975 New Fairfield, CT (Candlewood Festival)
August 4-6, 1975 Monticello Raceway, Monticello, NY
August 26, 1975 Ottawa High School, Ottawa, IL
August 27, 1975 Blossom Music Center, Cuyahoga Falls, OH (supporting Helen Reddy)
August 28, 1975 Municipal Auditorium, Erie, PA (supporting Roberta Flack)
August 29, 1975 Broome County Arena, Binghamton, NY (supporting Roberta Flack)
August 30, 1975 Convention Center, Niagara Falls, NY
August 31, 1975 War Memorial Auditorium, Rochester, NY (supporting Roberta Flack)
September 12, 1975 Central Park Wollman Rink, New York City, NY (Schaefer Music Festival, with Melissa Manchester)
September 13, 1975 Academy of Music, Philadelphia, PA
September 17, 1975 Bushnell Auditorium, Hartford, CT
September 19, 1975 Calderone Theater, Hempstead, NY
September 21, 1975 New York City, NY (Arista Festival)
September 24, 1975 Municipal Auditorium, Charleston, SC
September 26, 1975 Chrysler Hall, Norfolk, VA
September 27, 1975 Mosque, Richmond, VA
September 28, 1975 Heinz Hall, Pittsburgh, PA
October 4, 1975 Constitution Hall, Washington, DC
October 12, 1975 Wilkes College Gym, Wilkes-Barre, PA (Free concert)
October 16, 1975 Century II, Wichita, KS
October 17, 1975 Music Hall, Oklahoma City, OK
October 18, 1975 Fort Hays State College, Hays, KS
October 19, 1975 Kearney State College, Kearney, NB
October 21, 1975 Buddy's Place, New York City, NY
October 24, 1975 Auditorium Theater, Chicago, IL
October 25, 1975 St. Mary's High School McBroom Gymnasium, St. Mary, OH
October 26, 1975 Whiting Auditorium, Flint, MI
October 29, 1975 Orchestra Hall, Minneapolis, MN
October 31, 1975 University of Cincinnati, Cincinnati, OH
November 1, 1975 Masonic Auditorium, Toledo, OH
November 3, 1975 Delta State University, Cleveland, MS
November 6, 1975 Gusman Hall, Miami, FL
November 8, 1975 Irmo High School Activity Arena, Irmo, SC
November 10, 1975 Clowes Memorial Hall, Indianapolis, IN
November 11, 1975 Illinois State University, Normal, IL
November 14, 1975 Coliseum, Jackson, TN
November 16, 1975 Ellis Auditorium, Memphis, TN
November 19, 1975 Eastern Kentucky University, Richmond, KY (supporting The Spinners)

November 21, 1975 Theatre for the Performing Arts, New Orleans, LA
November 23, 1975 Music Hall, Houston, TX
November 28, 1975 Amarillo Auditorium, Amarillo, TX
November 29, 1975 Civic Center, El Paso, TX
November 30, 1975 Convention Center, Albuquerque, NM
December 2, 1975 Golden Hall, San Diego, CA
December 5, 1975 Paramount Theater, Portland, OR
December 6, 1975 Paramount Theater, Seattle, WA
December 7, 1975 Queen Elizabeth Hall, Vancouver, BC
December 8, 1975 Opera House, Spokane, WA
December 12-13, 1975 Circle Star Theater, San Carlos, CA
December 15, 1975 Dorothy Chandler Music Pavilion, Los Angeles, CA
December 18, 1975 Masonic Temple, Davenport, IA
December 19, 1975 Kiel Auditorium, St. Louis, MO
December 20, 1975 Veterans Memorial Auditorium, Columbus, OH
December 21, 1975 Music Hall, Cleveland, OH
December 31, 1975 Beacon Theater, New York City, NY

1976

January 15-28, 1976 MGM Grand Hotel, Las Vegas, NV (supporting Helen Reddy)
July 31, 1976 Robin Hood Dell, Philadelphia, PA
 August 1, 1976 Merriweather Post Pavilion, Columbia, MD
August 5, 1976 Blossom Music Center, Cuyahoga Falls, OH
August 6, 1976 Highland Park, IL (Ravinia Festival)
August 7, 1976 SIU Campus, Edwardsville, IL (Mississippi River Festival)
August 9, 1976 Highland Park, IL (Ravinia Festival)
August 11, 1976 Red Rocks Amphitheatre, Morrison, CO (Canceled due of laryngitis)
August 13-15, 1976 Universal Amphitheatre, Los Angeles, CA
August 18, 1976 Concord Pavilion, Concord, CA
August 20-23, 1976 Masonic Auditorium, Toledo, OH
August 25, 1976 Rochester, MI (Meadow Brook Festival)
August 26, 1976 Indiana State University Hulman Center, Terre Haute, IN
August 27, 1976 Rochester, MI (Meadow Brook Festival)
August 29, 1976 Saratoga Performing Arts Center, Saratoga Springs, NY
September 25, 1976 Paramount Theater, Seattle, WA
September 26, 1976 Paramount Theater, Portland, OR (supported by Lady Flash)
September 28, 1976 Spokane Coliseum, Spokane, WA
October 8-9, 1976 Illinois State University, Normal, IL
October 10, 1976 Roberts Stadium, Evansville, IL
October 12, 1976 Eastern Illinois University, Charleston, IL (supported by Melissa Manchester)
October 14, 1976 Kiel Auditorium, St. Louis, MO
October 15, 1976 Municipal Auditorium, Kansas City, MO
October 16, 1976 Assembly Center, Tulsa, OK
October 18-19, 1976 Robinson Auditorium, Little Rock, AR
October 22, 1976 McFarlin Auditorium, Dallas, TX
October 23, 1976 Jones Hall, Houston, TX
October 27, 1976 University of Texas, Austin, TX
October 29, 1976 Louisiana State University, Baton Rouge, LA
October 30, 1976 Municipal Auditorium, Birmingham, AL
November 10, 1976 Civic Center, Lakeland, FL

November 12, 1976 Civic Center, Atlanta, GA
November 13, 1976 Von Braun Civic Center, Huntsville, AL
November 14, 1976 Grand Ole Opry, Nashville, TN
November 15, 1976 Western Kentucky University E.A. Diddle Arena, Bowling Green, KY
November 19, 1976 Civic Center, Springfield, MA
November 20-21, 1976 Music Hall, Boston, MA
November 26, 1976 Scope, Norfolk, VA
November 27, 1976 Richmond Coliseum, Richmond, VA
November 28, 1976 Kennedy Cente, Washington, DC
December 3, 1976 Arena, Tucson, AZ
December 4, 1976 Symphony Hall, Phoenix, AZ
December 5, 1976 Convention Center, Anaheim, CA
December 7, 1976 Selland Arena, Fresno, CA
December 9, 1976 Memorial Auditorium, Sacramento, CA
December 10, 1976 Civic Center, San Francisco, CA
December 11, 1976 Civic Center, San Diego, CA
December 19, 1976 Astor Theater, Reading, PA
December 21, 1976-January 2, 1977 Uris Theatre, New York City, NY

1977

January 12-15, 1977 Auditorium Theater, Chicago, IL
January 19, 1977 Milwaukee Auditorium, Milwaukee, WI
January 20-21, 1977 Veterans Memorial Auditorium, Columbus, OH
January 22, 1977 Convention Center, Indianapolis, IN
January 29-30, 1977 Music Hall, Cleveland, OH
January 31-February 1, 1977 Music Hall, Cincinnati, OH
February 4, 1977 Broome County Arena, Binghamton, NY
February 6-9, 1977 Academy of Music, Philadelphia, PA
February 11, 1977 Civic Center Theater, Syracuse, NY
February 12, 1977 Kings College, Wilkes-Barre, PA
February 13, 1977 Erie County Fieldhouse, Erie, PA
February 23, 1977 Heinz Hall, Pittsburgh, PA
February 25-27, 1977 Ellis Auditorium, Memphis, TN
March 25-27, 1977 Sahara Tahoe Hotel, Lake Tahoe, NV (2 shows each night, supported by Billy Crystal)
March 31-April 13, 1977 MGM Grand Hotel, Las Vegas, NV

1978

May 7, 1978 Dorothy Chandler Pavilion, Los Angeles, CA
June 23-25, 1978 Civic Center, Providence, RI
June 28-July 1, 1978 Merriweather Post Pavilion, Columbia, MD
July 3-8, 1978 Garden State Arts Center, Holmdel, NJ
July 9, 1978 Saratoga Performing Arts Center, Saratoga Springs, NY
July 12-13, 1978 Robin Hood Dell, Philadelphia, PA
July 16-18, 1978 Blossom Music Center, Cuyahoga Falls, OH
July 20-23, 1978 Pine Knob Music Theater, Clarkston, MI
July 25-26, 1978 Highland Park, IL (Ravinia Festival)
July 28-29, 1978 Forest Hills Tennis Stadium, Queens, NY
July 31, 1978 Harvard Stadium, Cambridge, MA

August 3-5 & 8-16, 1978 Riviera Hotel, Las Vegas, NV
August 19-20, 1978 Red Rocks Amphitheater, Morrison, CO
August 22, 1978 Hyatt Regency Hotel, Chicago, IL
August 23-24, 1978 Concord Pavilion, Concord, CA
August 27-September 3, 1978 Greek Theater, Los Angeles, CA
September 12-18, 1978 Greek Theater, Los Angeles, CA
September 22, 1978 Riverfront Coliseum, Cincinnati, OH
September 24, 1978 Nassau Veterans Memorial Coliseum, Uniondale, NY
September 25-26, 1978 Spectrum, Philadelphia, PA
September 29-30, 1978 Chicago Stadium, Chicago, IL
October 9-14, 1978 London Palladium, London, ENG
October 16, 1978 Concertgebouw, Amsterdam, NED
October 23, 1978 Royal Albert Hall, England, London, ENG
October 25, 1978 Olympia Theatre, Paris, FRA
October 31, 1978 Jahrhunderthalle, Frankfurt, GER
November 3, 1978 Deutsches Museum, Munich, GER

1979

December 1979 Roxy, Los Angeles, CA (Preview of new material)

Headlining

II Tour (1974-75)
Barry Manilow in Person (1975-76)
This One's for You Tour (1976-77)
Even Now Tour (1978)
1980 World Tour (1980)
In the Round World Tour (1981-82)
Around the World in 80 Dates (1982)
Hot Tonight Tour (1983)
Paradise Tour (1984-85)
Big Fun Tour de Force (1987-89)
Barry Manilow in Concert (1989-90)
Showstoppers Tour (1991-92)
Greatest Hits...and Then Some Tour (1992-95)
World Tour '96 (1996)
Reminiscing Tour (1997-98)
Manilow Live! (1999-2000)
Live 2002 (2002)
One Night Live! One Last Time! Tour (2004)
An Evening of Music and Passion (2006, 2008)
The Hits...and Then Some Tour (2009)
2012 Tour (2012)
Manilow in Concert: Direct from Broadway (2013)
2014 Tour (2014)
One Last Time! Tour (2015-16)
A Very Barry Christmas (2017, 2018)
This is My Town Tour (2017-18)
2022 UK Tour (2022)

Opening Act

Freddie Hubbard in Concert (for Freddie Hubbard) (1974)
No Way to Treat a Lady Tour (for Helen Reddy) (1975)
An Evening with Roberta Flack (for Roberta Flack) (1975)

Residency shows

Showcase at the Continental Baths (1973)
On Broadway...in Manhattan (1976-77)
Barry at the Gershwin (1989)
Barry Manilow on Broadway (1989)
Music and Passion (2005-08)
Ultimate Manilow: The Hits (2008-09)
A Gift of Love (2009, 2012, 2015, 2017, 2021)
Manilow (2010-11)
Live at the St. James (2013)
The Hits Come Home (2018-Present)
Live at the Lunt-Fontanne Theatre (2019)

Some TV & Radio Appearances

(This list is not complete)

The Tonight Show with Johnny Carson– November 17, 1972 (with Bette Midler)

The Tonight Show with Johnny Carson – September 12, 1973 (with Bette Midler)

The Dick Cavett Show – September 19, 1974 (with Bette Davis, Barry accompanies Bette in a song)

The Mike Douglas Show (1974 – 1978 / 5 Appearances

The Smothers Brothers Show – February 24, 1975

Saturday Night Live with Howard Cosell – October 11, 1975

ABC Special: The First Barry Manilow Special – March 2, 1977

The Donny & Marie Show October 1977 (Barry presented Marie with a puppy which was named Biscuit and the dog lived a very happy life on the Osmond's ranch in Utah).

ABC Special: The Second Barry Manilow Special – February 24, 1978

ABC Special: The Stars Salute Israel At 30 – May 8, 1978

ABC Special: The Third Barry Manilow Special – May 23, 1979

ABC Special: Barry Manilow: One Voice – May 19, 1980

Goldie & Kids Listen too Us with Goldie Hawn. Barry acted in skits and sang "One Voice", "Sunday Father", and "I Am Your Child" – May 8, 1982

Copacabana – December 3, 1985. Barry wrote and starred in this television movie–musical which was inspired by his 1978 hit song "Copacabana."

Tonight Show – November 29, 1985 – Singing his new hit "In Search of Love."

CBS special We The People 200: The Constitutional Gala taped at the Philadelphia Civic Center in Philadelphia, Pennsylvania to debut his song "Let Freedom Ring." – September 17, 1987

CBS special: Barry Manilow: Big Fun on Swing Street – March 7, 1988

The Arsenio Hall Show – May 17, 1989, he made the first of eight appearances as a guest on over five years.

CBS sitcom *Murphy Brown* – May 17, 1993. On the show, Candice Bergen's title character had frequently made reference to her hatred of Barry's music, but after she became a mother, Barry appeared to sing her a sweet version of his tune "I Am Your Child," winning her over with the song about a parent's bond with a child.

Dark comedy film *Unconditional Love* starring Kathy Bates and Rupert Everett. Barry appeared as himself in a cameo. – 2002

NBC sitcom Will & Grace – December 11, 2003. Barry appeared on the as himself backstage between tour stops. The name of the episode is "Fanilow" as in "a fan of Manilow."

American Idol – April 20–21, 2004. Barry reunited with Debra Byrd, his former backup singer, who is now the vocal coach when he appeared as a guest judge and worked with the top seven finalists for the show where the season three contestants sang his songs as the theme for the week.

A Clay Aiken Christmas – December 8, 2004, Barry appeared on the NBC special, hosted by the former Idol runner-up.

Jacob and Joshua: Nemesis Rising – November 2006, Barry appeared on Logo's reality show as himself in Las Vegas for a recording session with the twins.

The X Factor – December 2, 2006. Barry was the celebrity guest and theme for the week on series three of where he assisted the top four acts with their performances.

Royal Variety Performance – December 12, 2006, Barry appeared live and performed a selection from his latest album.

The Tonight Show with Jay Leno on October 31, 2007, on November 17, 2008, and on July 12, 2011.

The Family Guy in "Back to the Woods" – February 17, 2008

The Graham Norton Show – December 4, 2008 (UK)

Strictly Come Dancing – December 7, 2008

Cranberry Christmas – December 8, 2008, Barry narrated and wrote original music for the Ocean Spray Christmas special.

Friday Night with Jonathan Ross – September 11, 2009 (UK)

BBC Radio 4's Desert Island Discs – October 2, 2009 (UK)

The Jay Leno Show – December 10, 2009

The Tonight Show with Conan O'Brien – January 21, 2010

Jimmy Kimmel Live! – February 6, 2010

Nobel Peace Prize Concert – December 11, 2010, Barry ended the show in Oslo, Norway singing four of his most known and popular songs. The Nobel Peace Prize was awarded to the Chinese dissident Liu Xiaobo.

Good Morning America – June 15, 2011, Barry appeared and performed songs from his new album, "Fifteen Minutes."

Piers Morgan Tonight – June 23, 2011

Paul O'Grady Live – June 24, 2011 (UK)

An Audience With... Barry Manilow – October 28, 2011 (UK)

Text Santa: The Launch – December 11, 2011 (UK).

The Royal Variety Show – December 14, 2011 (UK)

Katie – January 23, 2013, Barry sang a medley of songs for host Katie Couric and promoted his "Manilow on Broadway" show at the St. James Theatre scheduled to run January through February 2013.

The Diane Rehm Show – July 3, 2013 Barry discussed his career for the NPR listeners.

A Capitol Fourth – July 4, 2015, Barry sang on the program and fireworks were set off from Washington, D.C.

Tonight at the London Palladium – May 10, 2017 (UK)

Dionne Warwick - Then Came You – August 1, 2018

The Late Late Show with James Corden – May 5, 2020

The Kelly Clarkson Show – October 6, 2021

Awards

1977 Emmy for Outstanding Special – Comedy, Variety or Music – The Barry Manilow Special

1977 Special Tony Award – Barry Manilow on Broadway

1978 American Music Awards – Favorite Pop/Rock Male Artist

1978 Grammy – Copacabana Best Pop Male Vocal Performance

1979 American Music Awards – Favorite Pop/Rock Male Artist

1980 American Music Awards – Favorite Pop/Rock Male Artist

1980 Star on the Hollywood Walk of Fame

2002 Songwriter's Hall of Fame

2003 Society of Singers Lifetime Achievement Award

2006 Emmy for Outstanding Individual Performance in a Variety or Music Program – Barry Manilow: Music And Passion

2007 RIAA – Plaque commemorating worldwide record sales of 75 million

2009 Clio Awards – Honorary Clio Award for 1960s work as a jingle writer and singer at the 50th

Anniversary CLIO Awards in Las Vegas.

Printed in the USA
CPSIA information can be obtained
at www.ICGtesting.com
LVHW070203271023
762086LV00008B/22